The Road to El-Aguzein

This book is dedicated to the memories of
Jessie Webb
Margaret A. Murray
Tessa Verney Wheeler

The Road to El-Aguzein

M. V. Seton-Williams

Routledge
Taylor & Francis Group

LONDON AND NEW YORK

First published 1998 by Kegan Paul International

2 Park Square, Milton Park, Abingdon, Oxon OX14 4RN
711 Third Avenue, New York, NY 10017, USA

Routledge is an imprint of the Taylor & Francis Group, an informa business

First issued in paperback 2016

Copyright © 1998 M. V. Seton-Williams

All rights reserved. No part of this book may be reprinted or reproduced or utilised in any form or by any electronic, mechanical, or other means, now known or hereafter invented, including photocopying and recording, or in any information storage or retrieval system, without permission in writing from the publishers.

Notice:
Product or corporate names may be trademarks or registered trademarks, and are used only for identification and explanation without intent to infringe.

British Library Cataloguing in Publication Data
A catalogue record for this book is available from the British Library

ISBN 978-1-138-98549-0 (pbk)
ISBN 978-0-7103-0286-1 (hbk)

Publisher's Note
The publisher has gone to great lengths to ensure the quality of this reprint but points out that some imperfections in the original copies may be apparent. The publisher has made every effort to contact original copyright holders and would welcome correspondence from those they have been unable to trace.

Contents

Introduction	*1*
1 Forbears	*2*
2 Childhood and Youth – 1910–1934	*7*
3 England – 1934–1935	*19*
4 Sinai – 1935–1936	*34*
5 Palestine, Turkey and England – 1936	*49*
6 Turkey – 1936–1937	*57*
7 England, Ireland and Greece – 1937	*69*
8 Palestine, Trans-Jordan and the United States – 1937–1938	*74*
9 Syria, Cyprus, England and the War – 1939–1947	*86*
10 Round the World, Australia and Turkey – 1948–1957	*99*
11 Syria, Egypt, Syria – 1956–1964	*114*
12 Balsham and Egypt – 1957–1968	*126*
13 Swan Song	*133*
Other publications	*145*
Select bibliography	*146*
Glossary	*147*
Index	*149*

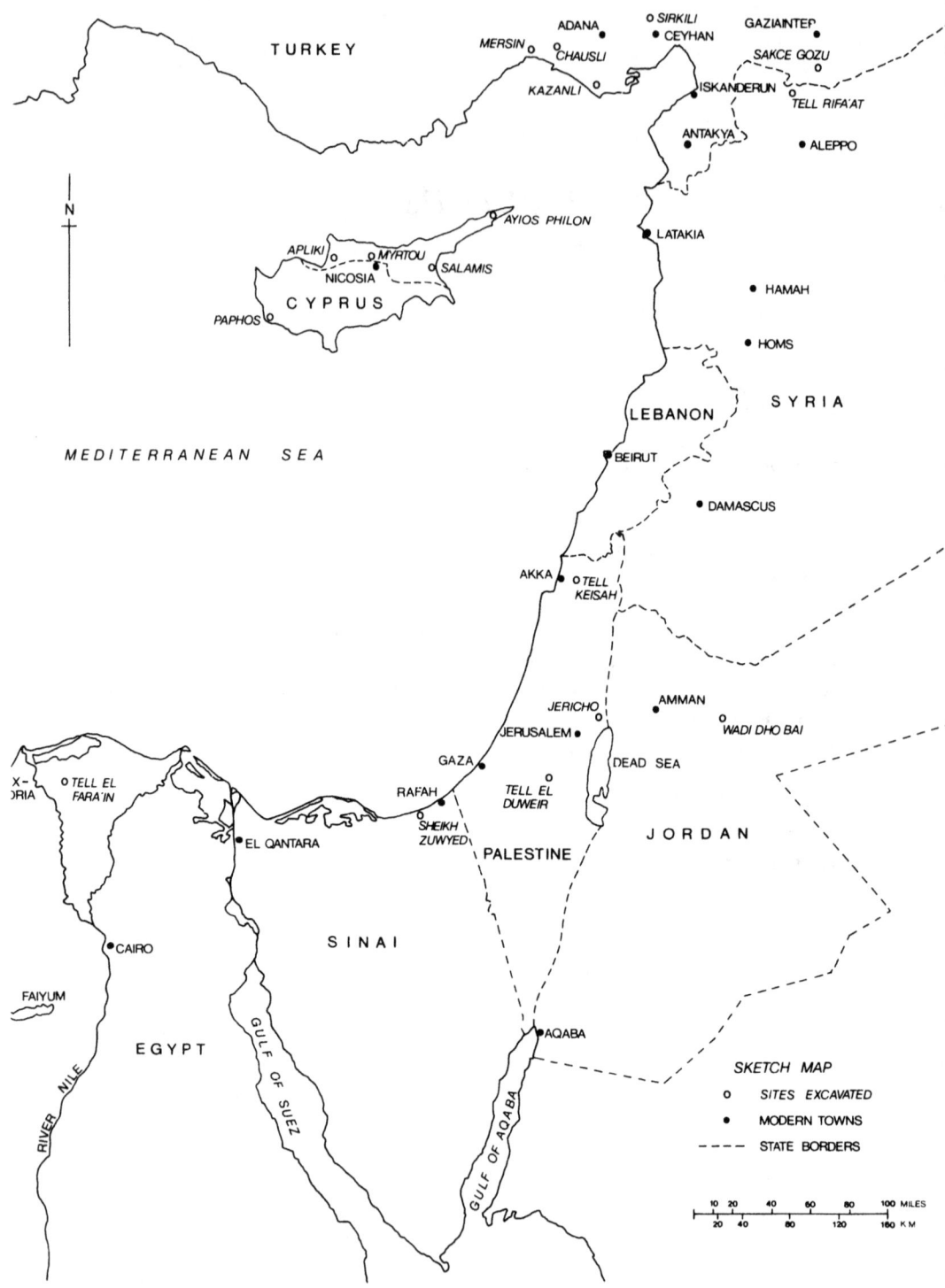

Acknowledgements

I would like to thank the following people: the family of Harry Riley for permission to reproduce one of his first water colours on the jacket – it was painted during the First World War on the coast of Palestine, while he was in the Sharpshooters; the National Gallery of Victoria for permission to reproduce 'The Synnot Children' by Joseph Wright, painted in 1781, portraying my great-grandfather Walter Synnot; Barbara Falk for supplying information from the archives of Melbourne University; my cousin, Christopher Staughton, who researched the Staughton family tree; Dr Young who put the family trees on her word processor; my cousins Patsy Hawker and Helen Harris for information about the Synnot family; Stephanie Gee for typing the first draft of my manuscript, Penny Rhodes who typed the second draft with Angela Godfrey who also drew the map and rendered invaluable assistance in collating all the material for publication; Brian Stinton who drew the map; Barbara Sharp and Anne Pemberton who helped to get it published; Penny Clarke and Kim Worts for their work on editing and Peter Hopkins of Routledge and Kegan Paul Ltd. Finally to the passengers on Swan's Nile Cruises who were always asking me to write my autobiography and without whose encouragement it would never have been done.

Balsham 1988

Family Tree
Father's side

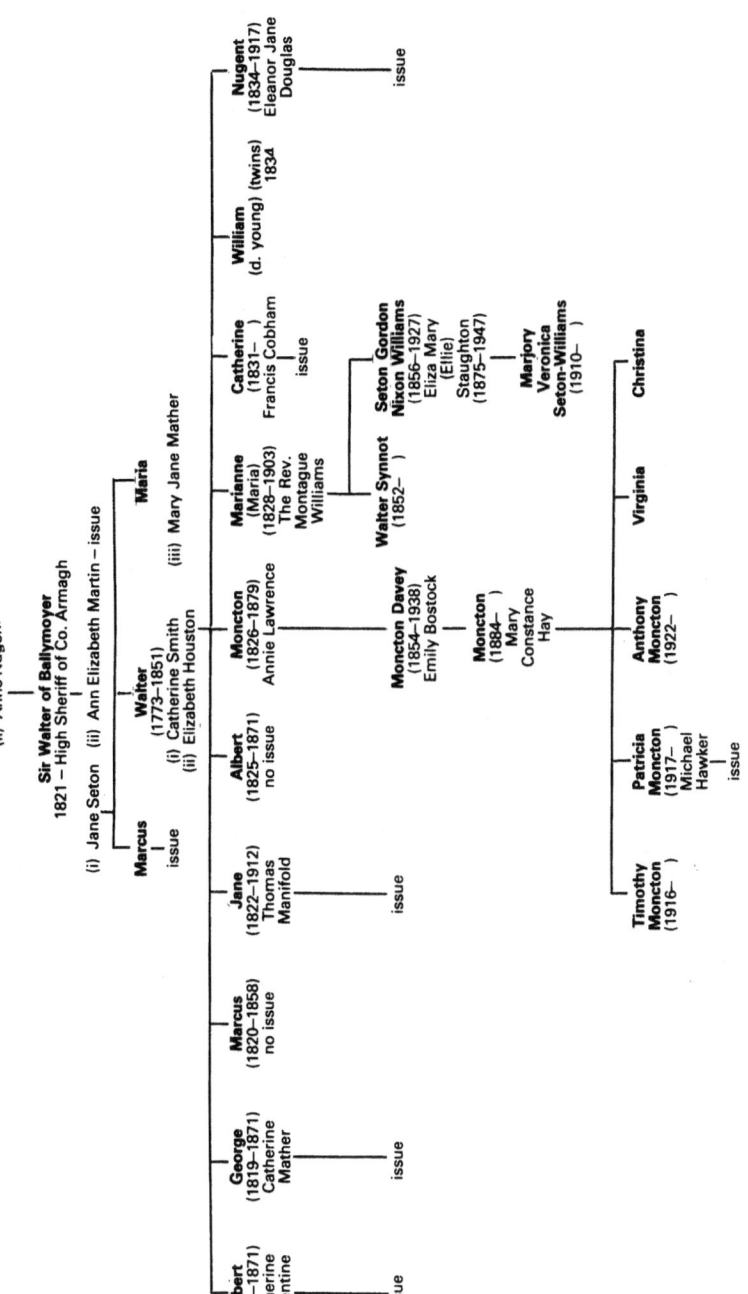

Family Tree
Mother's side

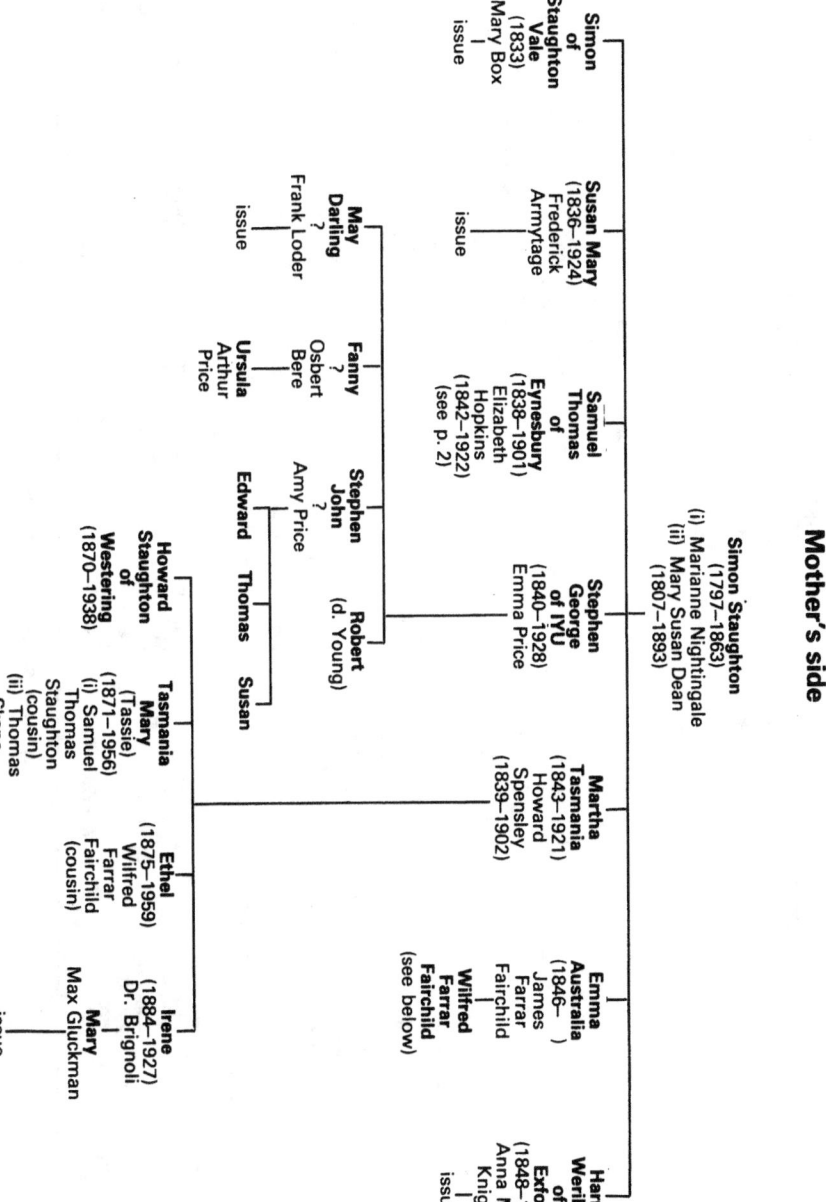

1.

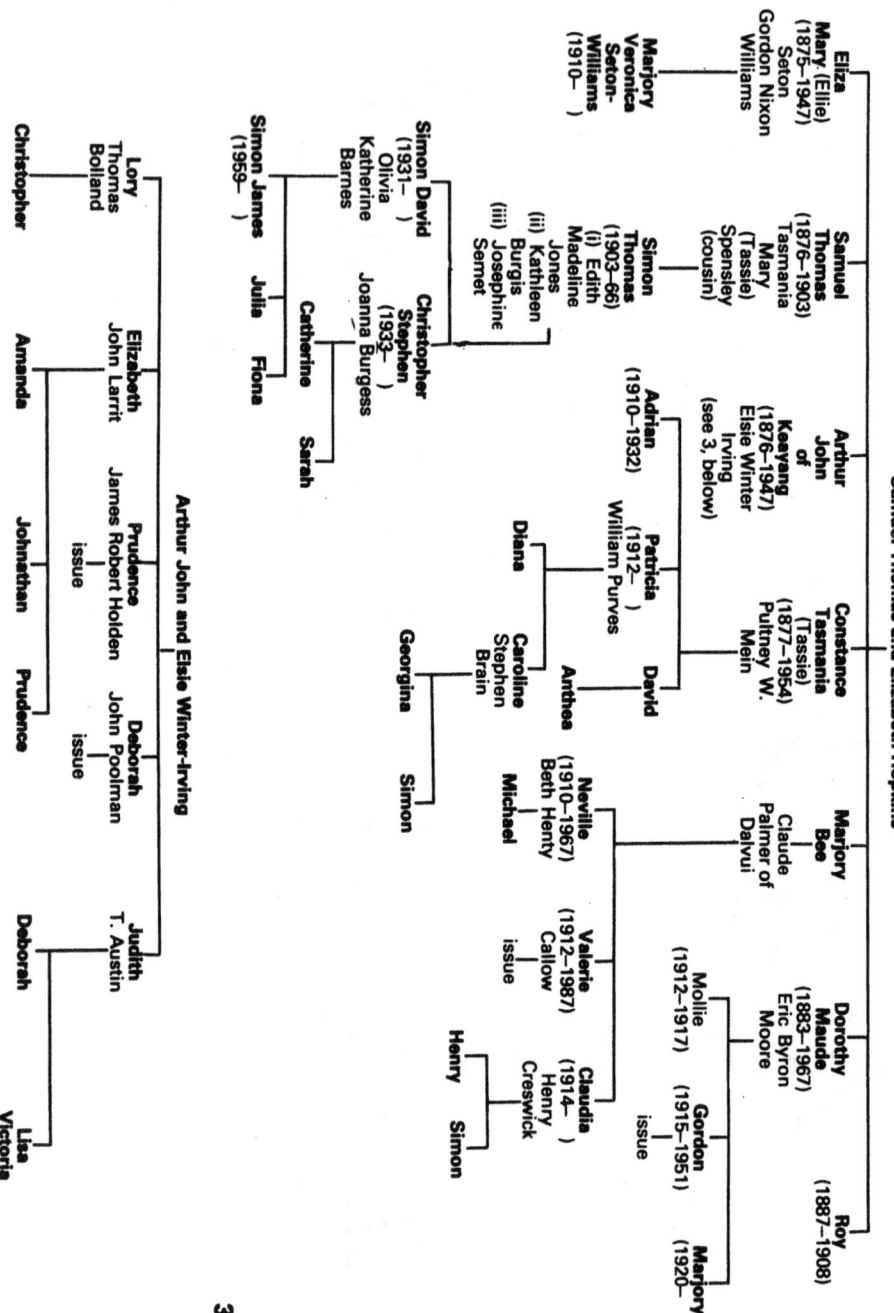

Introduction

My adult life has been spent to a large extent in and around the Middle East. From the spring of 1934, when I first set eyes on the spectacular backdrop of the hills behind Aden and passed through the Suez Canal with the dun-coloured desert stretching out on either hand, I have been committed to this region, its people and its places – an area which has been the scene of wars, rebellions, riots, civil wars, floods and earthquakes. As an archaeologist my main interest was in getting on with my job, to finish whatever I was doing, to record it and, if possible, to publish the results. However, Middle Eastern archaeologists are not always masters of their fate and this is particularly true for Egyptologists. Internal and external events beyond their control often prevent well laid plans and carefully thought out arrangements coming to pass. It has therefore been necessary in the following pages to add some historical comments as background to the events recorded to make them more intelligible, or to explain why it was sometimes impossible to return to finish work already begun. In addition, our expeditions were constantly plagued by lack of funds to carry out our work.

I owe much to my teachers and colleagues, the men and women whose vision led me to pursue the course I did, although I came to Egyptology by choice, not by accident as so many of my colleagues and contemporaries did. But more than to my teachers do I owe a debt to the people in whose lands I had the privilege and pleasure of working – the Arabs, the Egyptians, the Greeks, the Turks – without whom the work would have been impossible and with whom it was both a pleasure and a joy.

Aleppo 1979–Cairo 1986

Chapter One
Forbears

I believe far more in heredity than in environment. Both help but one is predominant. I would not be what I am if I had not had the parents and grandparents that I had and through whom I have inherited whatever skills I possess.

I was born on 20 April 1910, in Melbourne, Australia, early on a Wednesday morning to very disparate parents. My father, a lawyer, was a short, black-haired, blue-eyed Celt, my mother was a tall, fair, grey-eyed East Anglian. My father was fond of horses and hunting though he had given up the latter by the time I knew him. He had come to the Australian Bar late, having spent his early youth as a kangaroo hunter in the bush and only taken up law in middle age. Even so he must have been extremely fit as he won the high jump at Melbourne University when he was nearly forty. He was not really suited to city life and was, I think, only too glad when we moved out into the country when I was small. He used to take me to the horse sales at Kirk's Bazaar, long since demolished, and on Saturday afternoons down to the Melbourne Docks to see the tall sailing ships at anchor – this was long before the days of the grain races were over.

When I was about eight or nine I was taken by my mother to an exhibition about the clipper ships in a Melbourne gallery, where I met an old sea captain who was surprised to find a little girl taking such an interest in the history of the clippers. After talking to me for some time he invited us to his home in Williamstown for tea. I was delighted when my mother accepted as I was doubtful that she would. The following week we went to his little cottage which was entirely filled with pictures of sailing ships – I was enthralled, and so was my mother, a keen gardener, because in his garden was a blue poppy, brought by one of his relations from the Himalayas.

I know nothing of the early history of my paternal grandfather, Montague

Williams, save that he was brought up somewhere in Wales by two maiden aunts, his parents apparently having died. There was sufficient money for him to be educated at Oxford and to take Holy Orders; he must have been ordained before he left England and had a parish of his own, as there is a record in the family that his parishioners presented him with an inscribed silver tray on his 'leaving for another sphere'. He was sent out to Australia as one of six Church of England clergymen to minister to the garrison and convicts. In fact he went to Van Diemen's Land, now Tasmania. On 5 March 1846 he was ordained Deacon in St David's Cathedral, Hobart, by Bishop Nixon, the first Bishop of Tasmania. Five days later he was appointed Minister and Chaplain of Deloraine, in the parish of Calstock, Tasmania. While he was minister there he married, on 11 February 1851, Marianne (known as Maria) Synnots, the second daughter and seventh child of Walter Synnots, Captain of the 66th Regiment of Foot (later the Berkshire Regiment).

The Synnots family must have had a wandering life as all Walter's children seem to have been born in different countries; some in South Africa at the Cape where Captain Synnots was appointed assistant Landdrost (magistrate) in 1821. However, the family, who were Old English, must have returned to Ireland some time before my grandmother, Maria, was born on 4 December 1828, at Ballywater (now Balliate). Six years later, on 12 June 1834 my great-grandmother had twins, William and Nugent, brothers to Maria. Apparently Captain Synnots had served an earlier period in Van Diemen's Land as his eldest daughter, Jane, was married when only sixteen to Thomas Manifold at Invermay, Launceston, on 4 June 1838. The Synnots family, the name is spelt in various ways, seem mainly to have been soldiers. My father, Seton Gordon Nixon Williams, was born on 26 December 1856, the second of two sons, his elder brother, Walter Synnots Williams, having been born four years earlier.

My grandmother, Maria, was a keen correspondent and collected a huge amount of data about the family which unfortunately was dispersed after her death. She wrote regularly to Monsignor Seton, a kinsman then a cardinal in Rome, and to the rest of the Setons and Synots. It is pleasant to think that in the year 1975, when I began writing my life, Mother Seton of New York was beatified as the first American saint, and that I can regard her as a distant kinswoman. But I prefer to look farther back at the long line of Border Setons and to those who rode with Bruce to overthrow the English king at Bannockburn and who gained their three crescents on an azure field as a coat of arms for fighting with Richard Coeur de Lion in the Holy Land.

The Synots family in Ireland, spelt either as Synot or Synagh, were members of the Old English group or Sean-Ghail, a term used to denote the descendants of those Normans and English who had been sent to colonise Ireland under the Angevin kings in the twelfth century. These families were concentrated mainly in the five counties of the Pale – Dublin, Meath, Louth, Kildare and

Kilkenny. A few had penetrated West Meath, Wexford and Galway; there were comparatively few in Ulster. They were large landowners, Catholics originally, and dominated the ports and to a large extent the inland Irish towns. In the medieval period in Ireland there were three divisions, the Pale (the five counties governed directly from England), the Irish (Ireland beyond the Pale) and the dissident English trying to carve a place for themselves in the kind of no-man's land between the two.

The question of religious strife did not arise until the Tudor period as previously all the people were of one faith. When James Fitzmaurice Fitzgerald, who was a member of the Old English, rebelled against Elizabeth I in 1598 he based his case upon papal dominion which thus for the first time became an issue in Ireland. Also in the Tudor period many Protestant English and Scots families were settled there. They caused difficulties with the Old English who held their estates according to traditional Irish custom which was not always regarded as valid in the eyes of English lawyers. Many of the Old English had close bonds with England, spending most of their time in England, and educating their sons in English schools and universities. Their younger sons had previously been trained in English law schools and had held many of the Irish administrative posts. However, the English Act of Uniformity in 1563 was held to apply to Ireland. The Old English refused to accept this. They were thus debarred from the English universities and so tended to go abroad to France for their education. This kept them within the main body of Catholic opinion but tended to alienate them from England.

The 2nd Earl of Essex began the system of colonising Ulster with Protestants which was to lead to such difficulties afterwards. In the years that followed 1608, many of the Old English were dispossessed of their lands, but, on the whole, their loyalty to the crown and to the old religion remained unaffected. At the time of the Civil War Ireland remained largely Royalist and caused Cromwell a certain amount of trouble, so much so that he finally decided to make an example of the country. By 1649 the Commonwealth government in England faced the almost complete recovery of the Royalist ascendency in Ireland, and the Royalists occupied nearly all the country except Derry and Dublin. By August Cromwell himself had arrived to take command, determined to conquer and, if necessary, exterminate the Irish and Catholicism. On 11 September he took Drogheda and massacred the whole garrison, most of whom were English Royalists, and many of the unarmed townsfolk.

He then turned his attention to Wexford in the south. The town was commanded by my kinsman Colonel David Synots, and the garrison were largely Irish Catholics. The commander of the castle treacherously surrendered to Cromwell and the garrison and many of the inhabitants, including Colonel Synots, were massacred. The Synots had been in Wexford since 1290 when a David Synagh was a tenant-in-chief of the crown under Edward I. His grandson, Nicholas Synagh, was made chief sergeant of the

Forbears

County Palatine of Wexford under Edward III by a patent of 25 June 1375.

Under the Protector Cromwell's Commission for the County of Wexford in 1656, eight Synots are listed as owning freehold properties. Many others lost their estates at this time. Colonel Synots' young son Timothy was somehow saved by a friend and brought up as a Protestant. The family moved to Londonderry where they remained staunchly Protestant, as they have been ever since. Many of the Synots retained their Norman first names, such as Walter, Jasper, Pierce, Stephen, Marcus and Richard, and have done to to the present day.

My grandmother, Maria Synots, was the granddaughter of Sir Walter Synots of Ballymoya, County Armagh, who married in 1770 Jane Seton, daughter of John Seton of New York. He belonged to yet another branch of the Seton family, the Polwarth branch, who had migrated to America after his father, James Seton, a West India merchant, was murdered by slaves on a voyage to Jamaica. John Seton married his cousin Elizabeth Seton, born at Belsois near Ormiston on 19 February 1719. John Seton had seven children of whom my great-great grandmother, Jane, was the fourth child. Sir Walter Synots' son Walter became a captain in the 66th Regiment of Foot and went to Van Diemen's Land among other places and was my great-grandfather.

My mother was a third-generation Australian on her father's side. Her paternal grandfather, Simon Staughton, had come from Eynesbury, near St Neots in Huntingdonshire. He, his wife and four eldest children sailed from Plymouth in the *Himalaya* arriving in Port Phillip, Melbourne, in 1842. He took up a selection (a grant of land) in St Kilda which he gave up because the grass was not of good quality. Had he kept it we would have become millionaires as it is now a suburb of Melbourne. He is reputed to have built the first stone house in Melbourne in Little Bourke Street. Subsequently he became the owner of 60 000 acres on the Weribee River in Victoria which he divided into the stations of Staughton Vale, Eynesbury and Exford; this was good sheep country. None of these properties are now in Staughton hands. He also owned property in Melbourne which included the Royal Arcade and the Eastern Arcade.

Simon married twice, his first wife dying with their children in a fire before he left England. His second wife, Mary, did not like Australia or anything about it and left him in due course and returned to England. My grandfather, Samuel Thomas Staughton, was sent home to be educated at Mill Hill, an English public school, as there was then little opportunity for education in Australia. He and his brother Steven then went on to Cambridge where he read law.

Samuel returned to Australia to live at Eynesbury and married Elizabeth Hopkins in 1874. He eventually became a member of the Legislative Council of Victoria, and took rather more interest in politics than the rest of the family, whose interests were exclusively in the land. After their marriage

Elizabeth and Samuel were shipwrecked in the Pacific on their way to England for their honeymoon, and lived on an island for some months. I never really heard much about this episode, but only know that the house was full of things that they had collected when in England at that time.

My mother Eliza Mary, called Ellie, their eldest child, was born near Grosvenor Square, London, in March 1875. She was brought up at Eynesbury, in the bluestone house her grandfather had built out of quarries on his land. She married my father, Gordon Seton-Williams in 1896 when she was twenty-one. My grandfather gave her Rameta, where I was born, as a wedding portion. My mixed Irish–Scots ancestry from my father was an advantage as he was always pressing forward with no thought for the consequences. I think he must have inherited the Seton motto 'Hazard zet Forward', rather than his own father's more cautious one of 'Dread God'.

Chapter Two
Childhood and Youth 1910–1934

The earliest thing that I remember was the clip-clop of the milkman's horse as it went down Thomas Street in the early morning. We lived at Rameta, a large square red-brick Victorian house on the corner of Commercial Road and Thomas Street, Melbourne. It looked like a doctor's house, which it later became, though it has now been pulled down and a filling station put in its place; but I remember comparatively little about the place where I was born as we moved from there when I was five years of age and went to live in the country. However, I do recall the German bands playing in the King's Domain (a park) on Sundays. This must have been before 1914, as with the advent of the First World War the bands disappeared from our lives.

It is always the minutiae of life that one remembers when one looks back. Thus I have a clear picture of my third birthday, even of the cake with three candles which I was allowed to blow out, the dapple grey rocking-horse, Dobbin, that was my pride and joy, and the garden striped with autumn sunlight falling across the lawn.

Curiously enough it is not always of Rameta that I think when I remember my early and secure childhood, but my cousins' house, Milliara, in Wallace Avenue, Toorak. This was, like so many other Australian houses of the period, a long low house, single storeyed and with a large garden. I often stayed there as a child and, perhaps because they had a nursery where we had tea in front of a fire with a vast brass fire-guard, I am more conscious of it than where I ate or slept in my own home. My cousin Adrian was one day younger than I was and Patricia, his younger sister, was eighteen months our junior. These were the cousins with whom I was to have the closest links. They were the children of my mother's sister, Tasmania, known to the family as Aunt Tassie, who was the nearest in age to my mother and her favourite sister. She was tall, slim and elegant and married to my Uncle

The Road to El-Aguzein

Pultney Walford Mein, a gentleman of leisure with a small neat moustache. My cousins were very patriotic and prayed at length, and by name, for each member of the royal family. I listened entranced: no-one had ever required me to perform such an exercise. I was ignorant of the other names of the royal family, as I still am, but I felt that these prayers must for some reason establish a special relationship from which I was excluded. I can still hear my cousin Adrian intoning their names, as he knelt by his bed: perhaps their devotion to the royal family was occasioned by their name of Mein, which we all maintained was German in origin and which they stoutly averred was Scots. As England turned its back on the Old Commonwealth in 1948, it would be as well to remember the thousands who, like myself, were brought up to consider themselves as hundred per cent British, to look on England as Home to which they would all return some day, and to look upon the King and Queen as the natural heads of that family.

Although I was an only child, I had a very large number of first cousins on my mother's side. Her brother Arthur and his wife Elsie lived at Keayang, an old low station house near Terang in the Western District of Victoria. It was a sheep station and I greatly enjoyed staying there as a child. There were five girls in the family, two older and three younger than I. Elizabeth, the second daughter, served my uncle as his right hand on the place; the eldest, Lory, had already left home. We used to have energetic rat hunts in the stables and have splendid picnic lunches with rabbits shot by my uncle and cooked in a billy over a camp fire with lots of onions. I think I enjoyed all this much more than my mother who always complained the rabbits were tough and inedible, a fact that never worried my young appetite. I always remember Keyang as a comfortable house to stay in with deep easy chairs and plenty to read. When I wish to send myself to sleep it is always of the Keyang woolshed that I think and the sheep going down one by one into the sheep dip.

It was very different when we went to stay at Dalvui with my Aunt Marjory, my godmother, who was married to Claude Palmer. My Aunt Marjory was a small energetic woman who tyrannized her family as she had previously tyrannized her brothers and sisters. She and her husband also had a sheep station the house of which had been built by a man who went down on the ss *Waratah* just before the First World War. It was a large house with a porte-cochère, a huge hall and hideous stained glass in the dining-room windows, but it was not comfortable to stay in. The gardens had been laid out by the same man, William Guilfoyle who had laid out the Melbourne Botanic Gardens, and on much the same scale, with rare plants and shrubs, lakes and trees. It was really a town house set in the midst of the country with few attempts at compromise. As a small child I hated it because the children were never allowed up the front stairs which were for grown-ups only, and I was relegated to the nursery with my cousins, Neville, about three years my senior, Valerie, known as Bobbie, about eighteen months my junior, and Claudia, who was younger still. Children, said my aunt, should be seen but not heard. She was also very like my maternal grandmother – always finding something useful for us to do.

This reminds me of the only true ghost story that I know. My Aunt Tassie and Uncle Pultney had lived at a sheep station called IYU for a short time when Adrian was still quite a small boy. He must have been about three years of age and he asked his mother one day who was the bearded man who used to come into his room. There was no bearded man in the house, but soon afterwards one of the maids saw the same figure on the stairs. After some enquiries my aunt discovered that about forty years before a bushranger had been shot in the house and that he had died in the room she was using as a night nursery. Neither Adrian nor the maid had been afraid as they had not realised that they were seeing a ghostly visitation. Shortly afterwards my aunt and uncle gave up the place, but I am sure that this story had nothing to do with their actions.

There was always a lot of sympathy in Australia for the bushranger element, the lone figure set against the forces of law and order. This sympathy derived largely from the Irish element transported for political offences in the nineteenth century and found expression in such ballads as 'Bold Jack Donahoe', 'The Wild Colonial Boy' and the less well-known 'Dan Gilbert' and 'Ben Hall'. This admiration has culminated now in what is almost a Ned Kelly cult. But my parents, who lived through the wilder days of the colonial bushrangers, saw in them nothing to admire or respect. The Kellys were a criminal family; the father had been transported for theft and the three sons, Ned, James and Dan, were all expert cattle duffers (rustlers) and horse thieves. In 1876 the second son, James, was imprisoned by the New South Wales police for highway robbery. The Kellys disrupted the north-eastern part of Victoria, around the Warby and Strathbogie Ranges, for several years from 1878. They held up banks and sheep stations, murdered policemen and terrorised the countryside for nearly two years, until Ned Kelly's capture at Glenrowan and the death of the rest of the gang. I often heard my mother speak with disgust of Kate Kelly's behaviour at the execution of her brother in November to which she rode on horseback splendidly dressed. My father was a friend of Superintendent Hare who was instrumental in the Kelly's capture, during which he was wounded. It is this Irish-Australian element which has always been anti-British, and from which much of the Labour Party in Australia gets its strength. As in America, it was also the Irish who largely manned the police forces, so it was rather a case of cops and robbers both being Irish and enjoying a fight, like the troopers that were shot down by the Kelly gang at a place called Stringybark who were nearly all Irish. It is not perhaps accidental that one of the tunes to which 'Bold Jack Donahoe' can be sung is 'The Wearing of the Green'.

When I was five we moved to a house called Highmoor at Bayswater near the foothills of the Dandenongs, the mountains that were to dominate my life for the next fifteen years. We did not own Highmoor but rented it from Judge Box. It was a long low single-storey building with deep verandahs surrounded by paddocks with many trees. It had splendid views of the hills but we seemed to leave here rather suddenly after the dining-room ceiling fell in, smashing the table and doing other damage. The ceilings in the house were all very heavy and ornamental, with elaborate central decorations. The other thing about Highmoor were the snakes, they used to come into the house from the garden through the French windows. I remember our dog, Lufra, who was a kind of kelpie (sheepdog), attacking one in the sitting-room.

From Highmoor we moved to a house called The Uplands set on a hill about three-quarters of a mile from the small township of Vermont, and fourteen miles from Melbourne. This was to be my home for the rest of my childhood and youth. It, too, was a long, low single-storeyed wooden house painted red, again with splendid views over the neighbouring countryside. It was set among pines in the middle of twenty-two acres of land and was a mixed farm with horses, Jersey cows, pigs and poultry. We had peacocks, which were kept partly as watch animals and partly for decoration. My mother had intended that they should spend their time on the lawns in ornamental fashion, but they preferred the stable yard where they fought unending battles with the guinea-fowl and finally died of heart failure, falling out of the pines one night. This attack, the vet assured us, was brought on by rage with their feathered rivals. However, they were excellent watch-dogs and screamed loudly whenever strangers came near the place.

Here for the next six years I led a rather solitary existence, save for the constant stream of governesses with whom I was always at war, and the dogs of whom we had four. There were two Australian terriers – Ratatosk, called after the squirrel in the tree of life in Norse mythology, whose name was, I regret to say, usually shortened to Ratty, and her son, Souris (the result of a misalliance), a fawn terrier with grey eyes and an engaging disposition to whom I was entirely devoted. A spaniel called Scamp and the sheepdog Lufra completed the quartet. The two terriers slept in the house and the others outside. Every morning the two big dogs called for the others to go hunting. The terriers could get out through the wire mesh mosquito doors which opened outwards but the big dogs could not get in. They made a splendid pack, the large ones hunting the rabbits round to where the terriers could go in for the kill. They then divided the results with perfect harmony.

During the First World War I saw little of my parents. My father was at his office every day and my mother was engaged in various patriotic duties for the French Red Cross for several days a week and some voluntary cooking service on another two. The Great War, as it was then called, filled our horizon. How were we to know that the Napoleonic War had been known as the Great War to those who lived through it at the beginning of the nineteenth century: thus each war eclipses its predecessor.

It is difficult now to convey the effect that the Great War had on all of us. It is true that we were not rationed save for brown sugar instead of white and a reduced quantity of flour, and that we heard no guns fired in anger. But even in this remote corner of the Empire it dominated our lives: the weeklies with their war pictures, Bruce Bainsfather's drawings in the *Bystander*, the long articles in the *Observer*, and the *War in Pictures* which arrived every week. The first event that I remember in the Great War was the retreat from Mons in the autumn of 1914, followed by the Anzac attack at Gallipoli in April 1915. The long columns of men marching off to the war through the Melbourne streets, the returning wounded and the endless hospital ships all left an indelible impression. My grandmother's house, St Neots in Domain Road, was full of Red Cross sewing parties, endless bandages and people making poilu nightshirts. When did they wear them, I wondered.

My father was too old for military service, but my Uncle Arthur was engaged in collecting remounts for the AIF (Australian Imperial Forces) and for the Indian Army. But I think it was the constant scene of troops leaving and ships returning with men in hospital blue that made the deepest impression on me.

I have never seen Bruce Bainsfather's drawings since but I still remember Old Bill at the bottom of a shell hole, saying to the other chap, 'If you know a better 'ole, go to it', or the love-lorn girl looking at the moon and saying 'Just think – the same moon is shining on my beloved in France', while he curses the same moon for the light it sheds on his activities in No-Man's Land. We may have been a long way away but we felt involved and it was our war too. The thought was well expressed by J. D. Burns of Scotch College who enlisted in 1914 when he left school and who was killed at Gallipoli in 1915.

> *O England, I heard the cry of those that died for thee,*
> *Sounding like an organ-voice across the winter sea;*
> *They lived and died for England, and gladly went their way –*
> *England, O England – how could I stay.*
>   An Austral Garden of Verse, 102

In 1915 the Chinese community in Melbourne, which was quite large, put on a show to raise money for the Red Cross and I can still visualise the dragon floats, the acrobats and jugglers as seen from the window of my father's office at 230 Collins Street. In the country the Chinese were mainly market gardeners: there were a lot of them on the rich Weribee Flats, for instance. But in town there were quite a number of Chinese traders. We always bought our tea from a Chinese tea merchant in Little Bourke Street. He was a very dignified old gentleman with wonderful robes, a pigtail and immensely long little finger nails. He, like the Chinese show, belonged to the old China that would soon be swept away.

We had three driving horses, for it was before the days when cars were common. Two roans, Rebellion and Cheeky, and Belle, a vast black pacer who stood about $17\frac{1}{2}$ hands and had either been too large or the wrong shape for pacing. She had a wonderful action and could outpace the train as she had to on several occasions when my father was late, and had to catch it at the next station. We lived about one and a half miles from the station, Mitcham, where there was also a butcher and a pub. I did not realise at the time that all the names on our little suburban lines were English, like Tunstall, Ringwood and Boxhill. It was not until the line got up into the Dandenongs at Sassafras that the names went native, ending with Paradise.

As well as our driving horses there were the three ponies – Blackie and her son Peter, and Beaumont, who had a nasty habit of rearing up and falling back on her rider to get rid of them. Later I got a big rangy bay called Killarney for my own. I had to do a lot of riding as a child as it was the only way of getting about; the mail had to be fetched daily from the local store about a mile away and there were always other things to be got from there, but I never shared my father's fondness for horses. Fortunately most of our supplies came once a month and were stored in vast wooden bins in my mother's storeroom. We made all our own jam, bottled all our own fruit, grew oats as feeding stuff for the animals and maize which we fed to the hens. We put down our own eggs in four-gallon kerosene tins. We kept Jersey cows and scalded the milk so that I grew up on clotted cream which I was allowed to suck off the skimmer as a great treat in the cool dairy under the cherry-plum tree.

In 1916 Mademoiselle Benoit arrived to deal with my education. She was a Bordelaise who had come to Australia after delivering her wounded cousin home to Noumea, because she had to find a job in order to obtain enough money to return to France. She was a musician and from her I obtained a certain fluency in the French language as well as an unfortunate knowledge of French swear words. She had not a word of English so that all communication had, perforce, to be held in her language and after less than two years she left us to return home, to our great regret. However, my education did not proceed apace. During the next two years there seemed to be a procession of people who tried without much success to teach me the rudiments of learning. The next one was a mad Englishwoman who was horrified to discover the depths of my ignorance. 'The child', she said, 'cannot supply me with the definition of geography.' This lapse might have been made good had she been prepared to stick to this subject. However, she was later found prowling through the house muttering 'I am the British bulldog, I am the British bulldog! Dirty little Australian terriers.' My father was away at this time; my mother felt she could not cope alone with her so she sent her away.

Childhood and Youth 1910–1934

Looking back, it always seems to have been sunny. On the long hot summer afternoons I remember lying on the cool linoleum or the floors of polished jarrah (a hardwood from *Eucalyptus marginata*) reading – I was always reading after I learnt how to in a small English history book with a picture of the Houses of Parliament. This habit of mine was not well thought of as it was considered that I should have been doing something useful outside such as weeding the garden, dead-heading the flowers, collecting snails or picking mushrooms. I was sorry for the snails of which we had an inordinate number and where possible I saved them to train as racers. As for the mushrooms, it was always a cold autumn day with rain or a strong wind when they had to be picked and I did not like them anyway. It was as I worked through the books in the house that I came on the one that was to influence the course of my life. It was a small green history of ancient Egypt. As I gazed wide-eyed at the pictures of the Sphinx and the Pyramids, I decided then and there to become an Egyptologist although, at the age of seven, I can have had no conception of what this really meant. I realised that to do this I must go to Egypt and do some study and find out what this was about. Laboriously I started to collect the material to write my history of Egypt: it is not yet finished.

I was not a satisfactory child from my parents' point of view. They were sociable and enjoyed entertaining while I hated parties, pretty clothes and people. I preferred old clothes, animals and solitude. My lonely existence as an only child continued until I was eleven years of age when there was an attempt to make me more sociable. In fact it was to help a friend's child who had been ill that Joan Macrae came to share my lessons and my leisure. This changed my life considerably. Joan was the middle child of a family of five, the rest being boys – Ian, Finlay, Stanley (called Bill) and Don – so that in addition to acquiring a ready-made sister I acquired four brothers. I tended to spend many of my holidays with them and their house became a second home for me. These were probably the happiest days of my life.

In the summer the Macraes took a seaside house at Sorrento on Port Phillip Bay where we spent between three weeks and a month each year. At other times of the year they took a house at Ferntree Gulley in the Dandenongs and we would spend all day either by the sea or in the hills.

I had the freedom of their large square house, Kilmorie, on the corner of Toorak Road and Wallace Avenue just next to Toorak village. And I particularly remember the splendid magnolia tree in the garden. Joan taught me a lot, she was quick, fearless, good at sport and everything else she did; much better than I, who was naturally cautious, not to say timid. Their father had been the Presbyterian minister in Toorak before his early death and the boys went to Scotch College, one of the six Victorian public schools and the largest. It was also the Presbyterian one – all Australian public schools being denominational. The other five were Wesley College for the Methodists, Xavier College for the Roman Catholics, Geelong College another Presbyterian school, and two Church of England schools: Melbourne Grammar School and Geelong Grammar School. Although called grammar schools they were in fact more like English public schools, and it was to the last two that all my family went.

I shall always remember those holidays with the Macraes, swimming in the ocean from what we called the back beaches of Sorrento and Portsea, the long walks through the tii trees, the suppers cooked on driftwood with chops full of sand but delicious, the billies full of hot tea; or the climbs up through the Dandenongs among the tall gum trees, the songs in the twilight, the long walks home. We never made our fortune out of the lump of 'ambergris' we found on the back beach and which turned out to be consolidated engine oil from some ship, but we did save Don, one of Joan's brothers, when he fell overboard from a dinghy on a rough day in Port Phillip, although, in fact, we should never have gone out considering the weather. Ethel Macrae, their elder half-sister, was carried out to sea from the back beach at Sorrento but mercifully was brought back by three gigantic waves at the turn of the tide when we had failed to reach her with everything we had knotted together. We blistered our hands rowing the fishing boats that were let out in the season to tourists, and our backs lying in the sun for the first few days of each holiday, but we were happy.

School had been held over me as a terrible threat for years; each time a new governess had to be found, my parents threatened 'We shall send you to school'. So that when I was packed off to Clyde Girls Grammar School (now amalgamated with Geelong Grammar) in 1925 it was something of a relief to find that I liked it. Clyde was situated halfway up Mount Macedon. It was set in the bush and had its own playing field and golf course. When I was there is was a happy school. We had a good deal of freedom and some girls kept their own ponies. It had been founded some fifteen years before by Miss Henderson at a house called Fairlight in St Kilda. After the First World War she moved the school to Woodend and started the country boarding school to which I went. It was run on the house system of which there were four – Clutha (my house), Braemar, Fairlight and Ingleton. All except Fairlight had a strong Scots connection. It was a small boarding school then with only about 120 girls. Its position on the mountain made it bitterly cold in winter, and the heating system was erratic. But I spent four happy years there and left with regret. My time was enlivened by a bush fire which almost destroyed the school and necessitated the seniors staying up most of the night to beat it out, by trips to Hanging Rock racecourse for picnics, and to Hanging Rock itself, which was the plug of an extinct volcano. I still bear the marks of one of these jaunts when my left leg was pinned between a log and the rock and a deep groove was carved in my knee. This was long before the film *Picnic at Hanging Rock* had been made.

A large part of the school grounds were bush and scrubland and Barbara Davies and I, being good Australians with an eye to increasing our pocket money, decided to trap rabbits for their fur. The wherewithal, the traps, were supplied by Mr Davies. For some time all went well. We set our traps at night and rose early, skinned the animals on the spot and stretched the skins on wire frames placed under the prefects' study, which was well away from the main school building. However, one morning, as we returned bloody and carrying dripping skins, we were met by one of the mistresses who had unfortunately got up at 6 a.m. But even worse from our point of view, she was one of the few English mistresses on the staff and could not understand our treatment of 'the dear little bunny rabbits'. The traps were confiscated and our pocket money after its brief flush returned to normal.

At school I learnt to get up early as there was only hot water for the first three showers each day, and I preferred a hot shower to an extra hour in bed. Throughout my school life I had to work very hard as my earlier irregular schooling had left me with many gaps to make up. I suffered from a kind of word blindness, probably dyslexia, which meant I could not spell, and so had to learn difficult words by heart; and then, if I did not use them for some time, learn them all over again. My mathematics were poor, and were not helped by the teaching that we got. I sat my Intermediate Arithmetic examination thirteen times as without it I could not obtain entry to university. I finally passed after I had left school and was sent to a crammer when all the problems that had puzzled me became quite clear, simply because Mr Coade had the gift of explaining things clearly. I had to work very hard because though I had a good memory I was neither clever nor original. On the whole I had quiet and uneventful schooldays. I was no good at sport: I had thought earlier that if one had two arms and two legs one should be able to do as well as anyone else, but soon discovered that this was not so, so I settled for hockey and long distance running.

On the whole I had few brushes with authority. One, however, was the result of reading the *Witch of Endor*. This was about British prisoners of war getting the better of the Turks in the First World War by means of a planchette board. This seemed to me a good idea, so we got a board. I laboriously learnt the order of the letters, and with the help of a partner, Pat McVicar, proceeded to mislead our friends. In no time at all we had the school in an uproar, as I had just enough knowledge to make inspired guesses in reply to the questions asked. It was not long before I was sent for by the headmistress, Miss Tucker, and told to cease my activities.

I suppose I had the usual Australian childhood with long trips through the bush, holidays at the sea, in the hills, or on my relations' stations. My father would have preferred a boy. He gave me a rifle for my twelfth birthday and taught me to shoot. He also wanted me taught boxing but desisted at my mother's request, so we settled for judo which has proved useful to me several times since.

Our greatest danger living in the country was from fire, and when I was about sixteen we were almost burnt out. One of the men, sent to cut down the blackberries on a torrid summer day, put a match to them instead and went to sleep under a tree. As the wind was directly towards the house, it was no time at all before a sheet of flame was enveloping the edge of the orchard. We all rushed out with wet sacks and started beating, including the old Irish cook, Annie, who had been sitting in the kitchen with her feet in a bucket of water trying to keep cool. She had a somewhat unusual way of fire fighting, as when she approached the flames she used to turn round and sit on them. She was wearing a long black serge skirt at the time and my mother had to persuade her to desist. We would probably not have saved the house if the wind had not changed at the critical moment and blown the fire back on the ground already burnt. My mother later went to thank Annie for her help and to say how lucky the wind had changed at the right moment. 'Lucky', snorted Annie, 'it was all God! I just said to Him "We've done our part – now it's up to you", and He did.'

Once while I was at Clyde fire broke out in the bush below us. School was stopped and we were all sent out with wet bags to beat out the flames. We beat all day, becoming very tired and dirty. As wide fire-breaks had been cut earlier these controlled the fire to a certain extent, so that when night came we managed to have a quick meal in relays before continuing with the fire-fighting. We were up all night and by morning were quite exhausted by the smoke and effort; with our aching muscles we could hardly manage to lift our bags. Fortunately with the dawn the wind changed and blew the flames back onto the ground already burnt so that the fire gradually died out. Since then in the great bush fires of 1984 a large part of Mount Macedon, including the town of Macedon and the many lovely gardens that were such a feature of the area, have been burnt. Originally there had been many more gardens and high on the mountain above the school was one the house of which was burnt down. It was a lovely place with streams and lakes, overgrown boathouses, wild rambling roses and fruit trees. We used to spend many hours wandering round the deserted garden which was out of bounds and so of course more attractive.

We had no swimming pool at Clyde and felt the lack of one in the hot weather, so some of us went swimming in the Woodend town reservoir. It was our bad luck that that was the day some of the town councillors decided to carry out an inspection of the reservoir. Our idea was promptly nipped in the bud.

My father died in 1927 while I was still at school. He had a heart attack while he was out shooting. He had had several attacks before this and by now was only working part-time. He was not a good businessman and, although at one time had had a sizeable legal practice, it had declined considerably before his death, so that when he died he left few assets. As a result we had to sell The Uplands and move to smaller rented accommodation in Melbourne. How my mother managed to send me back to school to finish my education I do not know, but it was certainly quite a struggle. It was not until six years later, in 1933, that my mother managed to buy a small house in Church Street, Toorak, with the proceeds of The Uplands sale and money from another property we had had in Western Port Bay.

I wanted to go to university. Unfortunately it was not possible at that time in Australia to study Egyptology, so I settled for the next best thing, History and Political Science, at the University of Melbourne. This was the only university in Victoria at the time. Here I had the good fortune to be taught by Professor Ernest Scott, who was an unusual, inspiring and unorthodox teacher. He had been a journalist and had written several books on Australian exploration, discovery and history, as well as one on Matthew Flinders, which I had read when young. There was no stuffiness in his approach which suited me well and, under his auspices, the history school became for a few years one of the most respected schools in the University. He disliked students leaving his lectures before they were finished and on one occasion was heard to say 'Wait, I have one more pearl to cast'.

Another don who influenced me was Jessie Webb, the lecturer in Ancient History at Melbourne University. A small energetic woman with a great interest in numismatics, she had travelled extensively on her own in the Balkans, Turkey and Greece before the First World War, and spent a season with Sir Arthur Evans at Knossos. Before I sailed for England she gave me introductions to some of the leading British classicists; these were to prove very useful to me. The vision she had had remained with her, but she was unable to impart it to others. I gradually realised that it is not enough to know your subject – you must be able to impart it to others, as Scott did. My university career was not entirely successful. Professor Scott took a sabbatical in my final year and I lost a whole class in my finals due to my spelling. Also hockey and the social round were always at the wrong time as far as I was concerned, in November and March when I should have been preparing for exams.

To my distress in 1931 my cousin Adrian Mein, who had gone to Cambridge where he got a good honours degree, joined the RAF on a short-term commission, crashed and was killed just about the time of his twenty-first birthday. We had always kept up a firm friendship and till then I had had frequent letters from him. I missed him tremendously and it marked the beginning of my Aunt Tassie's final illness as she never recovered from his death.

In the meantime there were the long lazy days of the summer vacations, swimming at Lorne, or Portsea, or Anglesea in the breakers that came in from the Pacific or from the Southern Ocean, picnics sitting on the cushion bushes overlooking the reefs, long days riding after sheep in the Western District or after cattle on the Hunter River, picnic races (country race meetings to which one took picnics), the dances from which we returned in the dawn after driving over rutted bush tracks for hours – and I still think the call of the magpies in the morning is the most beautiful dawn chorus in the world.

Sometimes our pursuits turned out to be more exciting than we expected. One weekend I spent with the Boyds, with whom I had been at school, at their sheep station, Glenmore. As I have said I did not like horses or riding much but in those days it was a necessity. Most of the Boyd's horses were only half broken but I managed to pick out the quietest amongst them. Gwenda and Mary Boyd and I were going to take a picnic to the other side of the place accompanied by a chap who was staying at a neighbouring station. Our first mischance was with Gwenda's whippet who caught her hind leg when clearing a fence and had to be left at one of the out-stations. Then when we got to one of the boundary fences which we were jumping the chap from the other station went one way over the fence and his horse went another. He landed on a stone and was knocked unconcious. Mary rode hell for leather to the homestead to get a buggy to put him in and we ended up by taking him to hospital.

That evening, for some reason the talk turned to judo and I admitted to having some knowledge of it. I was shouted down by the male members of the party who bet that I could not throw them. This I did, one after another, and earned myself five pounds which I considered a good return in those days. Next day I opted to accompany Mary in the buggy instead of riding. However, this too was hazardous as the ponies were wild and unworked. She managed to take one of the gates at too sharp an angle, hit the gate post a resounding crash and the wheel came off so that we both landed on the ground with the horses trying to kick the buggy to pieces all round us. We had a long walk home. The other thing I remember of that eventful weekend was that they had a Mexican hairless terrier which on an Australian station showed the fleas only too clearly. Many years later Mary was killed in a riding accident.

By March 1934 I had taken my finals and decided to go to England to do the further study I could not do in Australia. In all this I was aided and abetted by my mother who, though she would have preferred me to have been a different sort of daughter, never really tried to put obstacles in my way. I was helped on with my decision by Nancy de Crespigny, a South Australian who had come back from England to retake her finals, and who had been working in England with Mortimer Wheeler. She promised to introduce me to the Wheelers if I came to England with her. So, on 29 May 1934 I sailed on the Orient Line's RMS *Ormonde*, bound for Tilbury.

I little knew, as I saw the streamers breaking and the water widening as we went down Port Phillip Bay which I knew so well from my trips on the paddle steamers *Hygeia* and *Weerona*, how long it would be before I saw Princes Pier again.

Chapter Three
England 1934–1935

The dirty water of Williamstown Bay fell away, the streamers parted and sank in the oily swell. This was not just another trip down the Bay from which we would return in a few weeks, sunburnt and regretful of the return to everyday life: this was going away for one or two years or forever – I did not know then. In a few hours the RMS *Ormonde* was through the rip at the Heads, we dropped the pilot into his oared boat and turned towards Adelaide as night fell. Here Nancy de Crespigny joined the *Ormonde* and we went on through the Great Australian Bight to Fremantle – an enchanting small port where Italian fishermen chased after octopuses in clear water.

Before I left Australia I had decided that I had better learn German because many archaeological reports are written in that language so I had coaching from the lecturer who taught German to the science students and who was himself a German. He quite rightly decided that it would be better if I heard German spoken even if I did not understand it, so invited me to a lecture that he was giving at the University Science Club one evening (all members of the Science faculty had to learn German). To my surprise I found he was giving a lecture on hieroglyphs. I am afraid that that was the end of my German lessons but when I got to Fremantle there was a cable from him in transliteration, the first and only ancient Egyptian cable to be sent as far as I know. I still have it: it reads, 'May all your days be blessed'.

One should always come to places from the sea and preferably in the dawn when the land rises from the mists. Colombo was one such place and even before we arrived there were the smells – the essence of the east, spices and sandalwood and dung fires – all making something indefinable and quite different from the strong smell of the Australian acacias to which I had been accustomed. In Colombo we had time for a day excursion to the famous Temple of the Tooth, but what impressed me far more were the flame and jacaranda trees round the lake and the striking yellow robes of the Tamils. A lot of the drive was up through the tea plantations nestling in the hills. There was just time to enjoy a splendid lime drink on the verandah of the old Galle Face Hotel before sailing.

I had never been particularly interested in the desert, it was the sea which had always fascinated me, but our next port of call was to change all that. It was Aden where the mountains rise almost straight out of the sea like the backdrop of a stage set. It was too spectacular to be real and the heat came out from the land like a sword. What I enjoyed most here was the beach at el-Ma'alla and the large sailing vessels that used to go down to East Africa for timber, round the Arabian Peninsula and up the Persian Gulf with a cargo of mixed merchandise. These were the large baggalas, the booms and the sambuqs, later to be immortalised by Alan Villiers in *Sons of Sinbad* but this was several years before he sailed on these ships. In the coffee houses near the shore the dignified *nakhodas*, or captains, sat exchanging the gossip of the Arabian and Red Seas and waiting for their cargoes to be ready or their vessels to be repaired. These beautiful ships had fascinating names like *The Star of Oman, The Hope of Compassion* or *The Triumph of Righteousness*. God was very close to these Arabian mariners and their vessels still had names like the Elizabethan ships which had sailed into this area four centuries earlier.

We struggled up through the Red Sea with the wind a furnace blast from Arabia, but at Suez I did not have the necessary money to make my first visit to Egypt. Instead I stayed on board the *Ormonde* which stuck ignominiously in the Canal when trying to avoid being run into by a munitions ship. We slewed right across the Canal pulling up cement mooring posts, one after the other, none of them was strong enough to hold us. The cause was the difficult steering of the *Ormonde*, a notoriously tender vessel, to which the Suez Canal pilot had not paid sufficient attention. When we got to Port Said we had to get divers to see if there was any damage to the ship's hull and, as a result, we almost sailed with the divers down below, the captain being unwilling to delay the Royal Mails by even an hour. I am glad that I lived in an era when it was still the custom to travel by Royal Mail steamer, so much more comfortable and relaxing than travel by air.

At Port Said we sampled the joys of Simon Artz, the famous shop that supplied everything for the tourist, and visited an artist with a house overlooking the canal whose rooms were full of watercolours of splendid Nile sunsets and ships of all kinds. However, my penurious state again stopped me from buying anything.

So we steamed on: to Naples, Gibraltar and Plymouth. Plymouth looked oddly small through the rain squalls, but I could only think of Drake and was not really interested in the Plymouth of 1934. From Tilbury I travelled by train to London where I made my first acquaintance with the backs of

England 1934–1935

English houses and the endless chimney pots and the drabness of urban England.

When I arrived in London I went to stay with my cousin, Simon Staughton, who had a house in Cadogan Place near Sloane Square. It was one of those houses that seemed to have only one or two rooms on each floor and stood at the corner of the street. It was a very convenient jumping-off place. My cousin Dora was keeping house for him as he was in the process of divorcing his first wife.

At this point I lost my heart to London. It did not matter that I did not know my way about; the names of the streets and landmarks had been familiar to me since childhood and I felt I had come home. This feeling has never left me each time I have come back to the great dirty, sprawling, friendly city. The first night I took a bus to Knightsbridge and then plunged down the tube to Russell Square to go and visit Barbara Cohen, a friend from Melbourne University, who had a flat in Great Ormond Street and who was studying for a higher degree at the London School of Economics.

However, I did not stay long in London. In fact I had hardly time to register at University College for next term before Nancy de Crespigny and I were whisked off first to York by the Wheelers, where the Royal Archaeological Institute was holding its annual meeting, and then to Maiden Castle in Dorset where Dr Mortimer Wheeler was beginning his excavations. Because Nancy had already excavated with him she was elevated to the position of site supervisor and lodged in a private house with Lesley McNair Scott, an Egyptology student and one of Wheeler's supervisors. Whereas I, short of money as usual, shared a bell tent on the top of the site with Rachel Clay (later Maxwell-Hyslop). Rachel later became part-time lecturer in the Department of Western Asiatic Archaeology at the Institute of Archaeology and was well known for her articles on the metallurgy of the Middle East. At this time she had already dug for several years with the Wheelers and was quite an experienced field archaeologist. I had never liked camping much. My first experience of it in Australia at the age of about twelve had been in a series of thunderstorms in black sand at Frankston, a seaside resort miles away from the sea and with tents collapsing in the night. So I did not look forward to camping at Maiden Castle with any great enthusiasm.

The great hill fort on the Dorset Downs owned by the Duchy of Cornwall was a wonderful place to start one's archaeology. It is a magnificent site with its vast towering earthworks and involved gateways. It dominates the Downs, rising from a saddle-backed hill in the Upper Chalk. As Thomas Hardy had said of it, 'At one's every step forward it rises higher and higher against the south sky, with an obtrusive personality that compels the senses to regard it and consider.' It certainly had a personality of its own: across its green-clad slopes the wind whistled and howled, the rain fell and, as we dug, the yellow clay in the chalk came up to meet us. I had never worked so hard physically before but I found I liked picking and shovelling as long as it was dry. Indeed we could not work when it was wet for fear of messing up the stratification.

The actual direction of the work was initially under the supervision of Mrs Tessa Wheeler with Dr Wheeler in charge of the overall strategy, while the day-to-day arrangements and the liaison with the local society, the Dorset Natural History and Field Club, and the accounts were looked after by Lieutenant-Colonel C. O. Drew, DSO, FSA. He was a first-rate archaeologist in his own right and had partnered Wheeler in all his excavations from Caerleon onwards.

A vast concourse of students came here from Britain and other parts of the world to take their field training. Although they are not mentioned in the final report published by the Society of Antiquaries I remember Chinese, Singhalese, Americans and Indians among other nationalities.

The worst thing about the place as far as I was concerned was the lack of washing facilities. All the water had to be carried from standpipes at the entrance and that first year we campers had no transport. Our evening meals were generally stews of various kinds and we descended on Dorchester to bath where and when we could. I lived largely on bread and cheese during the day neither of which I particularly liked, and which frequently led to indigestion when working long hours doubled up in a cramped space.

We employed a lot of local Dorset labour, mostly men who were unemployed for various reasons. I remember best the foreman Bill Wedlake, who came from Somerset and who had a splendid rich Somerset accent; he had already spent many years excavating in that county. Some of the men had a ripe sense of humour. There was the poacher who always arrived with a hare or rabbit across the handlebars of his bike and who told me about Dorset Horns, the local sheep, remarking: 'No, you would never find another sheep bigger – not for their size.' Or the diminutive workman, whose name I have forgotten, who, when Mrs Wheeler bent over the pit he was excavating and said, 'Careful now, you have a baby down there', replied, 'Oh Ma'am, and I never felt no pain at all'.

I worked for three seasons at Maiden Castle starting as a student in 1934 knowing nothing. At the end of the first year I had become a partial supervisor and for the next two years was in charge of one of the areas as a Field Supervisor. The work had been planned to cover three seasons, but was extended for another, which I did not do.

At the end of the 1934 season I went to Somerset where I had an introduction to Dr Arthur Bulleid who had excavated at the Glastonbury and Mere Lake Villages and who had married a Miss Austen, an Australian and a friend of my family. At Taunton I was joined by an Australian cousin, Rosemary Ross, and for about ten days we hitch-hiked and walked our way through the West Country as far as Tintagel, seeing Lynton and Lynmouth, Clovelly and Bideford on the way. Then at Camelford I had a telegram asking me to go back to Maiden Castle because it was the end of the season and the Wheelers were running out of volunteers. They paid my expenses to return and I took an interminable overland rail journey from Camelford to Dorchester, along lines that no longer exist and which involved endless changes and waiting on little stations with white-washed stone bordered flower beds and cats asleep in the sun. When I got back it was cold and wet and autumn was setting in. The vast hill was almost deserted but a few dedicated students still scraped and dug, recorded and drew.

After this I returned to London and set about finding myself some digs in 4 Handel Street, recommended by the University. This was a rather curious establishment where we got bed and breakfast for about £1 2s 6d a week. Except for breakfast we had to feed ourselves. There was a gas stove halfway down the stairs and a terrible gas geyser which provided baths. Both had to be fed with coins and cost about 1d a go. I had not previously had to cope in this way and knew little about cooking. Our two landladies charged us a shilling for a bucket of coal which could be obtained more cheaply down the road, but there was always trouble if we were caught carrying it in.

I settled down to work at University College under Professor Glanville who had previously been an Assistant Keeper at the British Museum, and was later to become the Professor of Egyptology in Cambridge. The Wheelers had, against my better judgement, persuaded me to abandon Egyptology, for which I had registered, and to go over to Prehistory. They told me that I could never hope to get a job in Egyptology as a woman and promised that they would see that I got something if I changed horses. I did not know then that it is fatal to be persuaded to do something that you do not want to do. I was not really interested in British prehistory for my heart was in the Middle East. But I listened to the Wheelers because I thought they knew better than I did – a great mistake on my part, as it would have been more use to me in my career if I had taken a degree in Egyptology rather than Prehistory.

I shared the top of 4 Handel Street with an English graduate from Cambridge who was doing Librarianship, and an earnest young man who belonged to the Oxford Group and spent his time trying to convert the rest of us to his religious beliefs. All the rooms were let to undergraduates or research students of one subject or another, including a medical student in the basement. People now talk about the permissive society but it was pretty permissive in the 1930s if you wanted it to be. University College had a Free Love Society with everyone changing partners frequently. I was asked to join but declined.

Although nominally attached to University College and given the keys to their Yates Classical Library, we really had no base; this was before the foundation of the Institute of Archaeology and there was nowhere for the archaeology students to be. Wheeler taught at the London Museum, then housed in Lancaster House, but there was no library and nowhere to sit and work except in the Board Room which was not always available. Books were the real problem. It was to overcome this that we were encouraged to join the Royal Archaeological Institute, membership of which gave us reading, but not borrowing, facilities with the Society of Antiquaries.

As well as Wheeler I was grateful to Professor King of University College, the Professor of Geology, who had an immense interest in Quaternary Geology and who lectured to us on this once a week. He also took us through the First Year Geology Course and gave us another hour each week on rocks and minerals. This was an invaluable training for an archaeologist. We also studied physical anatomy in the Medical School, surveyed the quadrangle of University College with plane table and theodolite and did a kind of social anthropological course with Dr K. de B. Codrington, later Professor of Indian Archaeology. Wheeler taught the main outline of British prehistory and the Aims and Methods of Archaeology as well. In our spare time, if we had any, we were supposed to get up to the top of the London Museum and help Delia Parker and Ione Geddye with mending the Maiden Castle material.

Perhaps the over-riding reason for my switching courses was that, as a postgraduate, I was allowed to do the Prehistoric Postgraduate Diploma in one year. This was not the usual arrangement and I could not have done my course in Egyptology in that time. But though I had given up straight Egyptology I still retained my connection with the Department, then under Professor Glanville and housed under the dome in University College. I went twice a week to learn hieroglyphs from Dr Margaret Murray, the Assistant Professor of Egyptology at University College, and to study the small antiquities. This was in addition to doubling up on all my other studies to enable me to do the two-year course in one.

One day the medical student from the basement of 4 Handel Street told me that when out in the country at the weekend he had passed a barrow which was being excavated and had come away with a skull. I was horrified at such desecration but he wanted to know the age, so I agreed to take it to Wheeler to date. I managed the outward journey all right with the skull wrapped in a piece of newspaper; but on the return, after Wheeler had said he did not want it anyway, it slipped out of my hands on the top of a No 14 bus in Piccadilly and I had quite a lot of explaining to do as the conductor called a policeman. I had not yet finished with that wretched skull as, returning home, I left it on my table that night and quite forgot about it. The first thing I knew in the morning was a terrible crash and my breakfast had fallen on the floor. The Irish maid had brought it in and, seeing the skull, dropped everything. Thinking to reassure her I said, 'Oh Annie, it is very old – about eighteen hundred years before Jesus Christ.' To which she replied, 'How can you be such a liar when he was the first man.' I could think of no suitable reply. I had to pay for the broken china, too.

The London of those days was a very different place from now: it was much quieter, I will not say cleaner, but certainly cheaper. My chief items of expenditure were fares from University College to the London Museum. Bread was 1½d a loaf, butter 10d a pound, sugar 2½d a pound, cauliflowers 2d or 4d each and sherry 1s 8d a bottle; eggs were a penny each and chops 3½d. Clothing was equally cheap: £4 16s 6d for a top coat, a guinea for a felt hat, half a crown for a scarf; trousers were 3s 11d, a shirt 5s and socks 6d. On Sunday I allowed myself a treat and bought muffins at 3d for six from the muffin man who came round every week with his bell, carrying on his head the tray of muffins covered with a white cloth.

I also used my time to wander about London at the weekends when it was quiet, visiting the Wren churches in the City, the pubs and other monuments. With my fellow students Molly Cotton and Dorothy Marshall, I explored many neighbourhoods including Windsor Great Park in the snow. Molly was later to make her name in Roman archaeology. Dorothy was the daughter of a Scots doctor with her home in Rothesay. Peggy Preston, who later married Stuart Piggott, and is now Margaret Guido also joined us. Working with the Wheelers one was in the centre of the British archaeological world, and by attending meetings at the Society of Antiquaries I gradually met all the leading figures in British archaeology. Later, in the 1940s I became a Fellow of the Society of Antiquaries myself.

I also had various relatives living in England: my aunt Tasmania, another aunt who had been married to my mother's brother Tom and who was a Spensley, firmly rooted round South Kensington. She had a large flat in Queen's Gate and often had me round to a meal. She was keen on science and made me a Fellow of the Royal Geographical Society as well as taking me to the Royal Institution where I heard Rutherford's classic lecture on splitting the atom. Her brother, Howard Spensley was High Sheriff of Bedfordshire and was a collector of Chinese celadon and Italian bronzes, with a choicely furnished flat in Montpelier Place. He too asked me round but could not understand why I did not wish to possess the objects that I excavated. He had a country house, Westering Manor, Bedfordshire, an old house which he left to the Australian Government as the country residence of the High Commissioner.

He asked me down for Christmas but before this I went to the Saar, Germany, and Belgium in the vacation with four friends Rosemary Ross, Elizabeth Agar, Peggy Preston and her sister Pamela. We went to examine the material in the museums at Cologne, Frankfurt, and Heidelberg, including the famous Heidelberg jaw which took quite a lot of finding. It was eventually fetched from a remote drawer in the University and dusted down for our inspection. This was the winter of 1934 when the Nazis were in the ascendant. Peggy spoke excellent German and got on well with people, but I found all the heel-clicking and 'Heil Hitlers' nauseating. We visited the Saar which the Germans were taking over, and there we saw them marching through the streets with torchlight processions: it was all very alarming and a portent of things to come. It is useless to say people in the 1930s did not know what was happening: they did but were powerless to prevent it. We had learnt at the Melbourne University about Fascism and Hitler's Nazis and it was very disquieting to see it in operation.

That winter I was cold as I had never been cold before. After all I had been at school on a mountain where the snow fell every year, but the bitter piercing cold of the English winter was something I had never felt before, and the thick grey-yellow pea-soup fogs shrouding London like the beginning of a Sherlock Holmes mystery had to be tasted to be believed; they smelt and tasted awful.

By the spring Nancy and I decided that we must have some fresh air. She was at Cambridge to do her Diploma under Dorothy Garrod, the Disney Professor of Prehistoric Archaeology, so we decided to go off to the South of France and Spain to see the caves. In order to do this we bought a cheap second-hand Chrysler coupé with a soft top. In this we enjoyed travelling to the caves in both countries. In France we visited the cave called Trois Frères on the estate of the Béguin family and were taken round by the young Comte de Béguin who, like his father, was a keen archaeologist. He apologised for the lack of bats in the caves and explained that they had died for some unknown reason and that he had had to go to Algeria and import larger and more imposing bats to restock his caves. I never could see the necessity for this.

The Spain that we visited was much more primitive than it is today. No-one knew any other language and a woman driving a car was a source of astonishment. When we arrived at Puente Viasgo, in northern Spain, we had trouble finding the small hotel and equal trouble next day in getting someone to show us the caves nearby. When we did get in, we had to leave cork branches at every junction to find the way back, and the only man who would accompany us was the local idiot.

To complicate our Spanish visit further, we arrived while they were having a general strike and could get no money, so had to sleep out in the car in the Pyrenees – in fact lack of funds dogged our entire trip, a not unfamiliar experience for me.

On our return I had decided to go to Russia and had already booked myself on a Russian boat leaving London Bridge on the morning of 20 April 1935. To get back we had to hurry rather more than intended and finally arrived in Calais with the headlamps turned round the wrong way and the front bumper off, as a result of fast driving over poor roads, but I caught my boat all right.

The trip to Russia was one I shall never forget. I was one of sixty-four passengers travelling hard class and when I say hard I mean hard. We slept six to a cabin and not only did the cabins have no amenities, there was only one sink for washing between all sixty-four of us. As the Russians did not see the point in separating men and women, we were in equal numbers in the cabin and you cannot, of course, separate a single sink. The lavatories were completely blocked from the first day out and the crew never attempted, as far as I could see, to clear them.

Although it was 20 April when we sailed from London Bridge, spring had not come to the Baltic and twenty-four hours out of Leningrad we stuck in the ice and icebreakers had to be sent out to free us. I had no idea that ice made so much noise grinding against the ship's side. I was, in fact, quite glad when we stuck fast because then the noise stopped and we could sleep at night. Our ship, which had specially reinforced bows, charged at the ice, ran up on it and by its sheer weight broke down the already disintegrating floes. The two icebreakers from Leningrad were most impressive, carving away the ice in large slices and leaving a clear channel behind.

We stayed only a few days in Leningrad – but long enough to get involved in a difficult situation. We had had on board a man who claimed to be an English communist and whose name was George. Also on board was an Australian communist called G. Ryland, who had taught himself Russian, and an American, Frances Farmer, who had won a trip to Russia in a beauty competition at Seattle University (she later became a minor film star). She knew nothing about communism and did not know what she was in for. There was another passenger, also called George, who had been born in Russia and spoke Russian but who had left there when a child and was now a British subject.

The first George said he wished to show us some of the real Russia but that, as he did not speak Russian, he wanted the second George as interpreter. He took along Frances and myself as cover – though we didn't realise this at the time. We went to a rather decayed house in a bullet-torn street in Leningrad. (I was amazed to see traces of the 1917 Revolution still apparent all over Russian towns.) After a good deal of difficulty we were admitted to a flat. It was quite large and rather dilapidated and I chiefly remember a huge samovar in an overcrowded room. Everything had to be translated from English to Russian so we got the full gist of the conversation. George One started: 'Tell her we come from Ivan.' Answer: 'Do not mention Ivan.' George One: 'Well what about Boris?' Answer: 'No, no, do not ask about Boris.' After a few more exchanges of this kind I turned to George Two and said, 'I don't think we should be here; this is the wrong kind of Russia to get mixed up with.' So we rapidly withdrew in spite of George One's protests.

George Two and I decided we had got mixed up with the White Russians – not what one wants to do when paying one's first visit to Russia. We went back to the hotel in rather a chastened frame of mind and I said to my room-mate, who worked in a birth control shop in the Charing Cross Road, 'If we are taken away suddenly by the police, do not be surprised.' To my amazement she flashed a badge at me and said, 'I am a member of the Communist Party and we have been watching what you have been doing. I am so glad you told me.' The wretched George One disappeared after all

The Road to El-Aguzein

this and I never found out what happened to him. Frances was terrified and would not go out anywhere at all.

On 1 May we had excellent places in Red Square to watch the might of the Red Army goose-stepping its way through the streets and the endless tanks rumbling across the square at full speed. It was an alarming display of might; even if the uniforms were ill fitting, the weapons looked excellent.

In Moscow I met many other students from various part of the world and we used to go and talk for hours in the Parks of Leisure and Rest where the public could learn parachute jumping from the top of high towers! Space was at a premium, everywhere was crowded with several families to a room and there was no privacy. There were queues in the streets for bread and people would stop you in the street and ask how much your clothes cost. It was still bitterly cold although it was spring, and there was snow on the ground in Red Square on 1 May. I also joined the crowds shuffling past Lenin's tomb and saw for a brief moment the waxy features of the man who made Soviet Russia into a reality.

There were no public bathrooms in the Russian hotels in those days: you were either lucky and got a room with a bath or not as the case might be. Even if you did achieve this, it was not much use as there were no plugs anywhere. The Russians considered it dirty to wash in anything but running water, or so they said, but I think there was a shortage of all commodities. The food was bearable but took hours to serve so that we were barely in bed by midnight and had to be out early to go on our excursions about 8.30 a.m. Breakfast was rye bread and sweet black tea. Rye bread, dumplings and borsch seemed to be the main ingredients of all our meals. I bought a bottle of vodka to keep out the cold but there was no proper rate of exchange and one could only officially buy at the tourist shops which accepted only foreign currency.

When we got back to Leningrad to catch the boat we found it had sailed two days before its scheduled departure time. This put some of us in difficulty. I had come to Russia without telling the Wheelers or my mother as I was sure they would not approve. The Intourist Office offered us accommodation to wait for the next boat but this was not due until almost the end of May and I had examinations in June. In fact, as it was, I was missing a good deal of the term. Other thwarted passengers included an English army officer who had been to Russia to see the May Day parade and the Russian weapons, a representative of the AA hoping to open up Russian roads to tourists, an American booked to catch the *Queen Mary* at Cherbourg in a few days' time and several others. In all there was a group of about eight people who could not wait for the next boat.

We finally persuaded Intourist to send us back overland. They agreed to give us tickets but no food. As none of us had any money to speak of we finally persuaded them to let us have some rye-bread sandwiches, some filled with caviar and some with smoked salmon, and some tonic water. Thus equipped we set out. The first night was not too bad as they gave us sleepers but as usual mixed up the sexes. After crossing the border we were in the Baltic States which had not then lost their independence. We pooled our resources and were just able to buy the necessary visas at the frontier. Everything seemed to cost one lat or two lits in these strange currencies.

We arrived in the morning at Riga, which I still think is the cleanest town I ever saw – one could have eaten a meal off the pavements. Our next connection did not leave till midnight. So we left our luggage at the station and walked round the town and down to the port before catching the next train. From Riga we went on through Latvia and Lithuania to East Prussia and the Polish Corridor where all the carriages were sealed. The British officer hid his notes in the lavatory but I could not help thinking that that would be the first place they would search. There were armed guards all through the train. As we went through eastern Germany we could see the blast furnaces roaring all through the night as Germany rearmed. We continued via Konigsberg to Danzig and from Stettin to Berlin. On the Berlin platform we pooled our remaining resources and bought several plain omelettes. This was the first food, except for the caviar, smoked salmon and rye bread, we had had since leaving Russia four days before. It was the best meal I have ever had in my life.

One of the members of the party was a chronic alcoholic and spent the time drinking brandy and lying on the floor of the carriage. We had to lift him in and out every time we changed trains and I do not know why we did not leave him behind somewhere. In between we rested our feet on him.

It was now three nights since we had slept. We had been sitting up all the way and I had collected a cold and lost my voice. On reaching the Hook of Holland we took ship for England and arrived at Harwich. It was a rough crossing but I started to revive. However, when I reached England I could only croak and slept for twenty-four hours. This was the first journey I had done entirely on my own and I was surprised to find how easy it all was and how helpful people were.

Russia was what you liked to make it. If you were a communist you came back more so: if you were not, you could see nothing good. I remembered the clerks in the hotels working their abacuses to do the accounts, the old mandarin from Outer Mongolia in his magnificent robes of golden spun silk, paying in pre-Revolution gold roubles, the domes of the Kremlin in the sun above the snow, the anti-god museums with their crude caricatures and the Hermitage Museum with bullet holes still in its walls. I met George Two again many years later when we were both working for the Ministry of Information and he was in the Crown Film Unit. Later still I got a letter from Ryland in Australia to say he had remembered me after forty years.

After I got back the examinations moved towards me inexorably. I really had not done enough work and I knew it. The written papers were comparatively easy but the viva was daunting, particularly as I had never done one before. My examiners were O. G. S. Crawford, the pioneer of British aerial photography and ordnance survey maps dealing with archaeology, Sir Cyril Fox and Dr R. E. M. Wheeler. Crawford stumped me with the first question: 'Why do we have poppy days?' I knew perfectly well that it was to commemorate the fallen of the First World War, but what he wanted was the reply that poppies grow in disturbed ground and so could serve archaeologically to outline ditches or other holes cut in the ground.

Somehow I passed my examinations. During this time Mrs Wheeler was immensely kind to me. Many nights I had dinner with the Wheelers at the large Lyons in Piccadilly where I regularly ate a chicken omelette costing about 1s 3d. Mrs Wheeler wanted me to move into their flat in Park Lane but I wished to preserve my independence.

That summer I went back to Maiden Castle as a fully-fledged site supervisor earning the princely sum of £3 a week. I was in charge of Site E, a section twelve feet wide cut through the innermost western defences in a well-preserved stretch just south of the western entrance. This section showed six main phases of rampart construction and under the original turf line there was a Neolithic working floor. I had the largest force of workmen, under the charge of Bill Wedlake, the foreman, as excavating on this sloping surface was very hard work. The original bank was about nine feet high but had long since been cut away. It had been raised slightly by about another two feet twice and then entirely rebuilt at the time of Rampart Four. The top had a palisade of stout posts set back from the crest and at the rear was a small limestone revetment. Inside was a considerable area of Iron Age occupation right up to the edge of the bank with a series of hearths and postholes. There was even a clay oven which we fortified with paraffin wax to preserve it. I shall always recall one of the visitors who asked what it was and when told said in wonder, 'Did they have bees in those days?'

The earliest settlement at Maiden Castle was a Neolithic A occupation of c. 2000 BC on the eastern part of the hill. This took the form of two parallel lines of interrupted banks and ditches covering an area of about 12 acres. The Neolithic village was occupied by downland farmers similar to those at Hembury in Devon and other Neolithic sites in England. After a time the village was deserted and before the beginning of Neolithic B a large long barrow was constructed. In the eastern end of this was a burial of a man about 25 to 35 years of age, approximately 5 feet 4 inches tall with a long skull. The skull had been broken and the brain extracted; the reason for this is obscure. There were vestiges of Bronze Age material on the site, but no permanent occupation on the hill until well into the Iron Age in the fourth century BC. At this stage the Iron Age people built a single line of fortification with timber revetted ramparts enclosing 15 acres. There were two entries to this, the eastern and the western, the eastern being double and overlooking a paved market place with traces of cattle pens. Subsequently the main enclosure was extended to the western end of the hill enclosing an area of 45 acres. At the western end a new double enclosure was built on the model of the origianl eastern entrance. It was later revetted with stone and timber. The main enclosure had a considerable occupation within the walls. In the middle of the first century BC it was inhabited by different groups of people who took over this desirable hill fort. The first were a group of people called by archaeologists Early Iron Age B. Outer lines of rampart and ditch were added and the height of the original rampart was doubled. This seems to have been done because the incomers were slingers – I found 450 slingstones in one pit alone. It is possible that the people who did this were the Veneti from southern Brittany, as they had been displaced by Julius Caesar's attack on them in 56 BC. Then the multiple earthworks were enlarged to form the vast defensive system now visible. About AD 25 the fort changed hands and it was taken by the Belgae from south-eastern Britain. The main ramparts were slightly modified. In AD 43 Vespasian, before he became emperor, stormed the town. Evidence of this is shown in the Belgae war cemetery cut into the remains of the East Gate which the Romans must have stormed. The huts inside the gate had been burnt, and the graves cut into the burnt debris. There were at least 28 graves, some double, containing pots of Wessex B type and joints of meat instead of grave goods. The skeletons exhibited extensive and fatal cuts upon their skulls and spines. One was killed by an arrow of the type shot by the legionary *ballista*. The stone revetments of the gate had been thrown down, and a new metal road built, probably by the Belgae, with no protective gates or other means of defence. This was in use for about 25 years. Roman Dorchester seems to have been founded then and the partly Romanised Belgae moved there. The hill top lapsed to pasture until *c*. AD 370 when a Romano-British temple and priest's dwelling was built in the eastern end. This was only occupied for about 150 years and was abandoned sometime in the fifth century AD. After that the great hill fort with its astonishing ramparts was deserted save for the sheep, the rabbits and the calls of curlews and whimbrels. Indeed, when excavation of the site began in 1934 none of Maiden Castle's early history was known.

I had kept the Chrysler I had gone to Spain in with Nancy at Easter and now shared it with Rachel Clay. We lived first in rooms in Dorchester and then outside in a small village. We had to leave our digs in Dorchester rather suddenly. The food was awful, we could not eat most of it. The end came when Rachel threw her pudding out of the window right onto our landlady who happened to be passing by. It was the same landlady who, on seeing the GB plate on the back of the car, explained to a friend that it stood for Gone Abroad.

This was my happiest and most successful year at Maiden Castle. Having passed my examinations, I knew more or less what I was supposed to be doing and everything seemed set fair. However, my mother, alarmed by my trip to Russia alone, decided it was unwise to leave me alone and came over from Australia to look after me. She came down to stay in Dorchester and her worst fears were confirmed when, looking round the church with the verger before going up to the site, she discovered that I had been at his house the previous evening drinking. The reason was simple: his son was one of my workmen and the old man specialised in home-made wines, so we were asked round to sample some. These home brews are notoriously strong and some of the students failed to find their way home through the ramparts that night.

After Maiden Castle was over, she and I had about a fortnight driving through the West Country and Wales. At Broadway I stopped off to see Toti Navarro, the lecturer in Bronze Age Prehistory at Cambridge, and spent a few days digging at Shenbarrow with him and group of his students.

In the autumn there was a decision to drive a new road through Whitehawk Neolithic camp at Brighton and Dr Curwen, who was the local Sussex archaeologist, asked Wheeler for some of his students to do a rescue dig. So Lesley McNair Scott, Peggy Preston, Bernard Sturdy and I were sent down to clear the site. Whitehawk Camp is situated on the Brighton race-course. It covers an area of some 10 acres. Much of the site has been levelled by the construction of the race-course and by allotments. The site consists of four concentric rings of interrupted ditches on the eastern edge of Brighton. Excavations were carried out first in 1929 by the Brighton and Hove Archaeological Club under the direction of Mr R. P. Ross Williamson. Further emergency excavations were undertaken under Dr Cecil Curwen in December 1932 as the race-course's pulling-up ground was to be extended. A third season was carried out in October 1935, lasting for five weeks. This was undertaken urgently because it was proposed to construct a new road connecting the Manor Farm housing estate with Freshfield Road. As Whitehawk Camp is a scheduled monument, permission had to be obtained from HM Inspector of Ancient Monuments. This excavation was on behalf of the Sussex Archaeological Society under the overall direction of Dr Curwen. It was this third rescue dig in which I was involved. The area excavated took the form of a wide section following the line of the proposed road right across the centre of the site, the section being more than 800 feet long.

It was early October when we arrived and the weather turned very cold, some snow fell and visibility was bad. I was employed by Brighton County Council in the post of ganger. You can imagine the time we had with the Brighton navvies. They tried every kind of joke on us, mostly of a rather crude kind. However, they were using the light railways or Decauvilles, to move the material and knowledge of how these operated was to prove useful to me later in Palestine and Egypt.

While working at Whitehawk I heard that I had been accepted to go and work with Sir Flinders Petrie in Sinai, so that I should really be going to do some Egyptology at last. Lesley was going out to Southern Palestine to excavate at Tell el-Duweir with John Starkey, the director of the excavations.

England 1934–1935

My mother meanwhile had taken a flat in Curzon Street and it was from there I left for Egypt. All the London Museum staff came to Victoria to see us off. We were the first of the Wheeler students to spread our wings beyond England.

Chapter Four
Sinai 1935–1936

In 1935 Sir Flinders Petrie required more staff for his excavation of an Egyptian frontier fortress at Sheikh Zuweyed in Sinai. Dr Murray and Mrs Wheeler were both on the committee of the British School of Archaeology in Egypt, and I was one of the students chosen for the work. Here for the first time I was doing what I really wanted to do – excavating on an Egyptian site, even if not strictly within the bounds of the country itself. I only regretted that I had not devoted myself entirely to Egyptology during the year I had spent in England studying. At least I had learnt the elements of hieroglyphs, thanks to Dr Murray, and had also acquired a certain knowledge of the objects, due to my studies in the Petrie Collection at University College. But, perhaps everything had turned out for the best, for if I had done the Egyptology Diploma I should still have had a year to go and so would not have been able to go to Sinai.

Lesley McNair Scott and I left Marseilles for Alexandria on 9 November 1935, aboard the ss *Champollion*. I remember little of the journey save that the ship was full of English grocers on their way to the Sudan to supply the British troops there, and also French troops and horses on their way to Syria. It also rained excessively at Marseilles and melted my rather cheap cardboard suitcase waiting on the quay, and I had to get another from a vendor in Alexandria before I could land.

In Egypt we were caught up in the riots and troubles that were the result of pressures put on Egypt by the Italian–Abyssinian war. Egypt was afraid of being drawn into the conflict whether she wished to or not. British naval units had been moved into Alexandria harbour without prior consultation with the Egyptian authorities, and Sir Samuel Hoare, the Foreign Secretary, rode rough-shod over Egyptian susceptibilities. A speech he made at the Mansion House in London on 9 November led to riots in Cairo and Tanta on 13–14 November. There were further disturbances on 19 November at the funeral of one of the students killed in the earlier affray. A day of national mourning throughout Egypt was declared for 21 November. Hoare spoke again on 5 December and there were further riots in Cairo, Tanta and in Assiut on 8–9 December. The background to all these disturbances was the impending revision of the Anglo-Egyptian Treaty which was finally signed the following year.

However, we managed to go to the Cairo Museum and visit Giza and Saqqara – tantalising glimpses of what the country had to offer. We then left Cairo and went to Kantara to catch the train to Palestine. Our overnight journey through Sinai was dusty and sandy and our companion was a French prostitute whose activities in Cairo had been interrupted by the troubles and who was going to Jerusalem in search of peace and quiet. In my innocence I imagined prostitutes would look different, and was shattered to find she looked like everybody else.

Lesley and I should both have got out at Gaza to go to our respective expeditions, but when I got there the station-master pressed a cryptic note into my hand, which read 'Go Jerusalem'; so I remained on the train through Lydda junction, now Lod, to the capital. This route lay mainly through the coastal plain and it was not until after Ramleh that the line began to climb into the hills. This journey cost about another 60 piastres, or 60p. During the journey one of the Arab passengers invited me to his daughter's wedding in Jerusalem, which I duly attended.

The start of the expedition was delayed which gave time for John Waechter, another member of the party, to join us, and together we explored Old Jerusalem and visited the Palestinian sites with some of the American students. Professor W. F. Albright, that doyen of Palestinian archaeology, was at that time Annual Professor of the American School in Jerusalem. The Petries had made their headquarters in the School so we were lucky enough to have access to their activities and their library. In the basement of the school Dr Clarence Fischer, an American archaeologist who dug at Beth-Shan-Beisan, was pursuing his gigantic task of preparing a corpus of Palestinian pottery, sadly still not complete. John and I stayed at the Swedish consulate with Mr and Mrs Larsen.

The Petries were a striking looking pair. He was over six feet tall and resembled, when I knew him, one of those patriarchal figures with a black beard streaked with grey, hawk-like eyes of brown and beautiful hands with long, slightly gnarled, artistic fingers. He wore somewhat old-fashioned clothes – dark suits of broadcloth and a wide-awake hat. He is the only man whom I have ever met who was a genius, and one knew it. He carried an immense store of information in his head and when he wanted to relax he did not read a book or go to the cinema, but took up a fresh subject. He was, as anyone who has read his *Seventy Years of Archaeology* will know, almost entirely self-taught. As relaxation he had taught himself chemistry and physics. He was a fine draughtsman with a good line which was still quite firm even though he was now in his eighties. If he had a fault it was an almost complete lack of a sense of humour. He lived an austere life with few comforts, although by this time he could no longer face the English winter and spent the whole year in the Middle East based in Palestine. He was an indefatigable worker. Never did I see him idle. In Jerusalem he was always preparing reports; his publication rate of a volume a year was phenomenal when you consider all the drawing, annotating and proof correction involved. It was this genius which drove him forward even in his old age to accomplish as much as possible. But it was more than that: there was an indefinable spark which went straight to whatever was the heart of the matter. I remember Rik Wheeler describing his visit to him on his deathbed in Jerusalem in 1942 when, as he told me, 'His mind was running even faster than it was wont, as though it still had a great distance to cover before the approaching end'. Wheeler left, his 'brain stretched by the immensity of the impetus of a mind for which there were no trivialities in life and no place of respite'.

Petrie never did anything on the spur of the moment. He even stirred his tea one way rather than another because it was more effective. I never heard him raise his voice either to us or to the workmen, but they respected him as a great man. He was always the Pasha, or rather el-Basha as they have no P in the language.

On the excavation he confined his attention entirely to the work in hand. Because the site was some distance away and up a lot of loose sand, he did not visit it every day but spent a large part of the time in the site hut drawing and comparing what we were finding with other material. However, he had his telescope which he kept trained on the work and woe betide us if we were seen talking to one another. This was regarded as unnecessary and a waste of time and if observed, was followed up by a brisk note to get on with the work. He took all the photographs on the site. The objects and pottery were arranged on shelves draped with a black backcloth against the sides of the hut. Then the stand camera would be set up; this had no lens – only a piece of cardboard with a pin-hole through it. The exposure could take anything up to half an hour, but the film was so slow, speed 40 H & D (the emulsion speed named after Hunter and Duffield) made specially for him by Kodak, that it did not matter if the whole expedition passed between the camera and the objects, as they sometimes did because the camera was set up in the only passageway into the mess room. He developed at night and describes how he did it (*Methods and Aims of Archaeology*, p. 83) where he says he placed a red envelope round the chimney of the ordinary lamp to provide a darkroom light. By the time I knew him he had dispensed even with this and developed by the light of a candle with a red piece of glass propped up in front of it. Because the film he used was so slow this diffused light was quite adequate.

Sinai 1935–1936

Lady Petrie was also very striking looking. In her youth she had been known as one of the Three Graces of Hampstead. Since her marriage to Petrie she had devoted herself whole-heartedly to his work. Now well over sixty, she still had a good figure and splendid dark eyes. She ran the camp, saw to the workmen's pay, and did part of the shopping in Gaza as well as visiting the bank. She was an excellent fund raiser and an adequate draughtswoman but was lacking in practical skills. Or perhaps she just did not wish to exercise them. It was, I think, a matter of principle with her that she never did anything of a practical nature if she could get anyone else to do it. This applied to everything – winding the camp clock, opening a tin or anything else. She could not cook but this hardly mattered when all the food came straight out of tins. One day when Major Jarvis, the Governor of Sinai, arrived for lunch at short notice, for some reason Lady Petrie felt she could not offer him the normal camp fare of sardines and bully beef and suddenly remembered that when in Gaza a few days before she had removed the drumstick of a chicken she had been eating and put it in her pocket. This she pulled out, gave it a dust and placed it in front of him – I understand that was not the first time she had done that sort of thing, as I heard a similar story when I was working at Tell Duweir.

She did, however, spend a lot of her time doing the accounts in four different currencies at once – Palestinian, Egyptian, Syrian and British. The Syrian was a hangover from an expedition they had done the year before looking for sites, but somehow it was never eliminated. The first two currencies were necessary because although we drew the money in Jerusalem and Gaza and had to change it into Egyptian currency to pay the men, some of them came from Palestine and so had to be paid in Palestinian currency.

When we got to Jerusalem, the other two members of the expedition, Jack Ellis and Carl Pape, were already at Sheikh Zuweyed. Jack, who was in his early thirties, was a thin, fine-drawn ex-RAF fitter who had left the air force at the end of a twelve-year engagement, most of which had been spent in the Middle East in Iraq and Palestine. He was Petrie's *mudir*, or head-man, who arranged everything and who spoke quite good Arabic. Carl Pape, a few years younger, was the architect. He was a Lancastrian with slow speech and a passion for fire-arms and polar exploration. Although John Waechter was only seventeen, he was completely adult and fitted in well. He had already done a certain amount of medieval archaeology in England and a lot of travelling. He had a passion for cars and had worked for some time with his brother-in-law on some garage venture, having left Westminster School, where he was not particularly suited very early. He was interested in everything – birds, animals, insects and reptiles as well as archaeology. He was a good companion with whom to explore the country. He later became Lecturer in the Palaeolithic at the Institute of Archaeology.

When we finally left Jerusalem it was in an old bus sufficiently decayed to have been withdrawn from service on Palestine's public roads, and which

The Road to El-Aguzein

the Petries had bought and already used for their Syrian survey. We went first to Tell el-Ajjul where the Petries still had an excavation house and where they stored much of their heavy equipment. This was kept under the alert eye of their guard Abdulla who lived in a tent just beside the expedition house with his wife, many children and numerous animals.

The first night Lady Petrie suggested that she and I should sleep in the bus to guard it against robbers. She slept soundly, but every time I fell asleep I fell off the narrow seat. Next night I opted to sleep on the old kitchen table in the expedition house at Tell el-Ajjul. I awoke in the middle of the night to hear odd crashing sounds from the next room which I had not investigated before I went to sleep. Turning on my torch and opening the door I found that it led to one of the storerooms. It had been used as the skull repository; there were racks from floor to ceiling and the skulls were stored on these in boxes. The noise was made by huge monitor lizards which had made their way into the store and were in the process of knocking the skulls on to the floor. As I watched fascinated, a skull on the top of the pile tilted towards me and fell. Hurriedly shutting the door, I went back to an uneasy rest on the table.

The next morning the Petries and Jack Ellis, who had come up from Sinai, went down to Sheikh Zuweyed leaving John and I to pack up the heavy baggage and get it loaded on the baggage camels. This presented some problems, as neither of us knew very much Arabic, having been in the country for less than a week. We had a most uncomfortable journey to Sheikh Zuweyed as baggage camels are not suitable for riding.

The hamlet of Sheikh Zuweyed (it was hardly more than that) was situated in the sand-dune belt of Sinai, close to the northern coast and on the overland caravan route to Egypt. Here there was nothing but sand-dunes rising to between fifty and sixty feet in height and a salt marsh with some date palms, a few wells, and a concrete police post and the railway siding. The police post, with its concrete cell for prisoners, I was to get to know pretty well in the next few months.

The camp had been planned by Pape the previous season, and Jack Ellis had built a mud-brick expedition house in front of, but at a little distance from, the police post. At the beginning of the 1935 season Ellis had gone down alone to prepare it for the Petries, and while doing so had developed one of his recurrent attacks of malaria. There was, of course, no doctor and his Arab hosts called in the local sheikh when he became delirious. This man wrote out a section of the Quran on a piece of paper, caused his host to wash it off in water and then gave the water to Jack to drink. The fever broke and he recovered. This kind of treatment is very common among the Arabs.

None of the rooms in the expedition house was more than five feet wide, because that was the maximum width of roofing iron that could be carried on a camel. All supplies had to come down by camel as Zuweyed was no longer a rail stop and the station had fallen into disuse. The expedition house (see plan), had one long room running along most of its width which was used as the mess room.

Because I had been sleeping in the bus the first night at Tell el-Ajjul my kitbag had been left in the room with John who saw, but did not mention, that a field mouse had entered it during the night. It lived there undisturbed for some time till it had eaten its way from one side of my Bradleys coat and skirt to the other – which led to difficulties when I wanted to go back to England as I had nothing else suitable to wear.

The expedition house at Sheikh Zuweyed had a table in the mess room, a trestle supported on boxes – in fact we lived, ate and slept on boxes. They contained our provisions so that whenever a new supply of bully beef or some other vital material was required, one might have to dismantle a bed or the table. All we had in our rooms was a bed, a basin on a box, a bucket for slops, and a water container. We had blankets, not sleeping bags, and sheets, though a change of these was not provided. We supplied our own towels.

For our WC we had a palm leaf hut out in the desert. This was all right at the beginning of the season but by the end one was sitting in a kind of palm wickerwork box with very little to protect one from the passersby as the palm leaves had disintegrated.

There was, as Lady Petrie frequently assured us, £100 worth of stores. These consisted of tins of bully beef, sardines, herrings in tomato sauce and plain herrings, jam, treacle, marmite, tea and sweetened condensed milk – a sore trial to me as I do not like sugar. We got our bread made locally – flaps of Arab bread made of flour, ground up not in the local mill but on one of the saddle querns with which the site abounded. The result was that the bread was extraordinarily gritty, large lumps of the quern coming off daily, so that the enamel wore off our teeth, and I ceased to wonder at the worn state of the prehistoric teeth I had previously examined. Bread and grit were the answer.

Breakfast consisted of tea and condensed milk, small local eggs, bread, butter and jam. Lunch was sardines or herrings, bread and tea. Dinner sometimes had the addition of lentil soup, to which I fortunately became addicted, rice, bully beef, bread and tea. I do not remember any vegetables, or any fruit except an occasional orange someone bought on a shopping trip into Gaza. My diet was supplemented by hampers from Harrods sent by my mother, which caused me great embarrassment as I feared that the Petries would think I had been complaining to her about the food.

Lady Petrie, although she wore riding breeches, considered it unladylike to wear one's shirt tucked into the waistband. She tried to persuade me to do as she did and leave it out, but as my shirts were boys' blue cotton ones with tails, they looked distinctly odd so I kept them tucked in. She also had a theory that it was unladylike to go into Gaza in trousers. But she did not

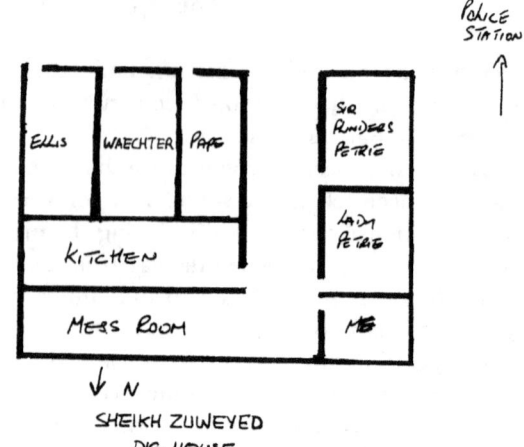

SHEIKH ZUWEYED
DIG HOUSE

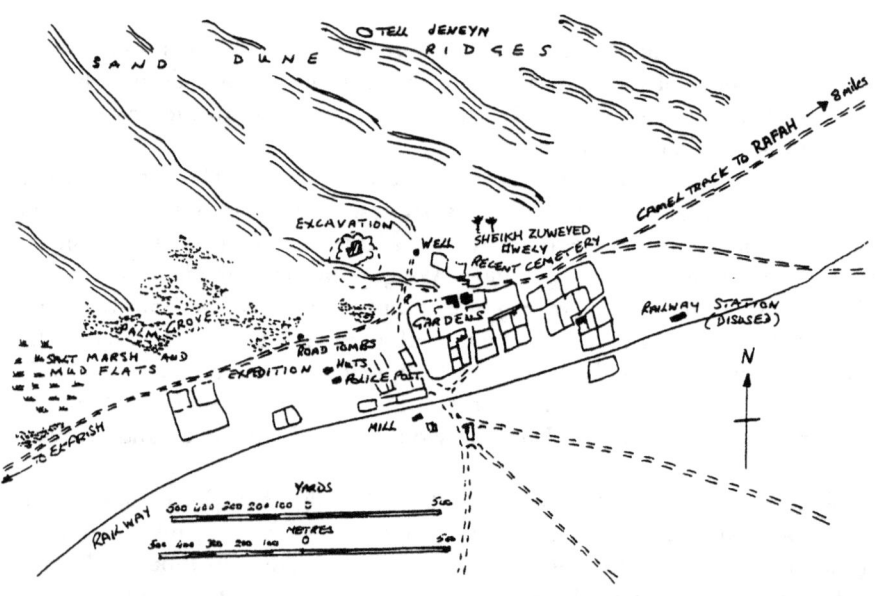

start from the camp in her town outfit; she stopped the car on the outskirts of Gaza and in the Muslim cemetery, a most unsuitable venue, she put over her head a black embroidered dress from Bethlehem. As she was wearing a shirt that stuck out of the top and breeches and socks that came out underneath, the total effect was rather strange. She was also seldom seen without her topee. She even wore it in bed. I now know that the reason for this was because fragments of mud kept dropping from the walls and she wished to keep them out of her eyes and hair; but the effect, when you saw her sitting up in bed doing the accounts, was definitely odd.

The cook was limited in his repertoire. I only remember him trying to cook one chicken which came to the table complete in its feathers and, presumably, undrawn. All he could do was make tea, soup when he felt like it and boil rice. When I left I got a chit from Lady Petrie which said in part, 'Williams is a good girl – she can cook'. I do not remember that I ever had much opportunity. The camp was strictly teetotal as the Petries did not believe in wine or song. However, the staff decided to celebrate Christmas and bought a pudding and some brandy in Gaza. Neither Petrie would eat the brandy sauce though they enjoyed the pudding. I have a feeling that left to herself Lady Petrie would have quite enjoyed the sauce. Poor Lady Petrie: the thing she really enjoyed was helawi – the Arabic name for halva, that very rich Middle Eastern sweetmeat made with honey and sesame seeds. When we really wished for a quiet time someone bought a slab of this in Gaza and left it in the mess room. Next day there was never anything left and Lady Petrie was ill with a bilious headache for the next three days. Poor dear, she never associated it with the helawi, but we did.

Our rather badly balanced diet led to everyone, except the Petries, getting influenza, and not being able to shake it off; as soon as one recovered another went down. The cook started it and was found blowing his nose on the tea towel which helped to infect everyone. By this time we had been joined by a couple called Teasdale, both doctors who had previously worked in India. They had never excavated and seemed nervous of the local inhabitants: they kept asking if they were friendly. They slept in a small tent nearby and John amused himself by firing his revolver near them at night. They left after a few weeks. Meanwhile I had got influenza so badly that it turned into pneumonia and I ended up in the Gaza hospital which at that time was run by the Church Mission Society. Dr Hargreaves, who ran the hospital for the Society, was a good doctor and provided a lot of much-needed medical care in Gaza but he made only one convert – the houseboy. The nurses were all Armenians, orphans who had lost their families in one of the Turkish massacres earlier in the century. To recover I went to Jerusalem for a few days and while there was asked by Professor John Garstang to join him at Jericho. This move was to alter the whole course of my future.

However, before that and despite our frequent bouts of illness work had been going well. The site, Tell Sheikh Zuweyed, was also called Tell Abu

Selymeh. It lay among sand-dunes in the area between Rafah and el-Arish. Originally when these coastal cities were built the area had not been as sandy; in fact it was a garden area. This was reflected in the name of one of the mounds – Tell el-Jenayn (Tell of Gardens). Now this and all the other mounds, of which there were many, were buried under sixty feet of dunes. Petrie had originally been on his way to the Garden mound when he heard of another at Sheikh Zuweyed and turned aside to examine it. He chose it because it was the only one in the neighbourhood not covered in Roman remains and part of the side was also easily accessible.

The 1935/36 season when I was with them was their second. The site was one of the Egyptian frontier fortresses built during the XVIII and XIX dynasties to guard the road and the wells between Egypt and Palestine. This route was called 'The Ways of Horus' according to the papyrus Anastasi I. The Bible, Exodus 13.17, refers to it as the 'Way to the Land of the Philistines'. The north wall of the hypostyle hall at Karnak depicts the route and the names of the forts with their wells at the time of Seti I. The forts are shown as crenellated towers and the wells as pools. The route began at el-Kantarah, where the modern railway line used to start, close to ancient Pelusium on the border of Egypt proper and ended at Rafah, ancient Raphia. The first fort at el-Kantarah was called 'The Dwelling of Sese', an abbreviation of Rameses II's name, and is identified with Tell Abu Sefah. The fort before Raphia is called 'N h s of the Prince' and the well was called 'The Well of Menma're', the prenomen of Seti I. It is shown as a small fort S on the plate, the pool marked T. This is almost certainly Sheikh Zuweyed, which in its Hellenistic Period Petrie identified with Anthedon, 'The City of Delight'. But the exact location of this site, as with so many others, is still uncertain and the ancient descriptions have discrepancies not easily reconcilable.

When we were there an area about 100 by 90 feet was cleared at the top of the tell and was gradually extended northwards so that, even as we went down, the exposed area never contracted to less than about 88 by 80 feet. As soon as one level had been cleared, planned and photographed, it was removed and we went down to the one below. The site was dug in occupation layers numbered from A at the top to N at the base. The water level was reached at 112 inches under M, the penultimate layer because N did not run under all the part we were excavating. There were three levels below the earliest building. First a clayey turf line four inches deep which overlay a dark layer of sand, and then a clean layer of sand overlying the water level. The earliest settlement level, N, seems to have been destroyed by fire, this was well over 50 feet below the surface. The earliest fort that we could date belonged to the late XVIIIth Dynasty, to the time of Horemhab. Above this was a XIXth Dynasty fort of Rameses II with alternating black and light bricks in a checkerboard pattern. One of the curious things we found in the early levels was a hunchback skeleton with his hands tied behind him;

lying beside him was a set of dice in a box decorated with blue glass and containing a scarab of Rameses II. One of the dice showed a six on all sides. It would appear that he had tried to cheat the garrison, had been found out and met a summary punishment.

Zuweyed was not a main fort or trading post and its name has not been identified with certainty. It was, however, used as a fort on the desert route between Egypt and Palestine. All this work was very good training for a student, anxious to learn stratification. Perhaps I was lucky, too, in that I had to learn the hard way by unscrambling a buried site with many superimposed layers, pits, granaries and all the other complications that this entailed. I was also fortunate to begin my career with Sir Flinders Petrie, a man already a legend in his own lifetime, with whom I have always been glad to have had the privilege of working.

Petrie, who liked to be called Prof, was the grandson of Captain Matthew Flinders the circumnavigator of Australia. Petrie was very proud of this and on one occasion we had an argument about what his grandfather did or where he went. I have forgotten the exact details but having read history at Melbourne I was quite certain that I was right, I had nothing in Sinai to check this so I wrote to Professor Scott asking him to clarify the matter, as he had written the definitive life of Captain Flinders. I always remember the beginning of his reply which went approximately 'How you had the temerity to argue with a man of Sir Flinders Petrie's authority I do not know – unfortunately you were right and he was wrong.'

It was here that I fell in love with the desert. It was always changing and when there was a wind the sand spurted off the tops of the dunes like foam off the crest of a wave. When there was an occasional shower of rain, and we had a wet winter, there were the changing patterns of damp on the face of the dunes, again so like the sea. I learnt to walk along the crests of the dunes and avoid, if possible, the long climb up their sides. I loved the clear cool air at night. Whoever was foolish enough to say the sands of the desert never grow cold could never have lived in a desert. When it rained the Bedu rushed to plant their grain in the well-manured camel track to el-Arish and it grew while we watched, almost overnight. On one occasion when it rained really hard there was a flood, not where we were but further inland, where several villages were washed away and where the Colt expedition had to stop their work. H. Dunscombe Colt was an American who undertook the examination of four large towns in the Negeb; these were Sbeitah (ancient Subeta), Auj'a el-Hafir (Nessana), Khalasah (Elusa) and Abdeah (Ebod'a). These towns did not all flourish simultaneously. The expedition's most important find was a quantity of Greek papyri.

When it blew and there was a sandstorm, we had to suspend the work and the sand poured into the holes we had dug. Our food became so full of grit as to be uneatable – that is if we could keep the primus alight. The corrugated iron roofing which was pegged to the expedition house with iron or wooden pegs and wires, could not withstand a really hard wind, when it tended to blow off, much to our discomfort.

It was here, too, that I learnt that archaeology is not all stratification and assemblages of objects, but welfare and life. Every evening we had a sick parade when the men would be dosed by Lady Petrie or myself with Epsom salts (English salts) as they were known to suffer terribly from constipation, or given burn dressings, or have their wounds dealt with with permanganate of potash. Burns, usually caused by exploding primuses or flaring oil lamps, were the worst. The family of one of the workmen who had been badly burnt did not fancy our sterile dressings, so they went down to the railway line and collected the diesel oil that had run out from the engines and by now was well mixed with sand and dressed his wounds with this. Next time we saw our former patient he was a hospital case.

The local fishermen provided us with other types of casualty to treat. They nearly all had injuries to their right hands and some had lost an eye or an arm, due to their habit of dynamiting the fish. The explosives they used were mainly from old ammunition from the First World War. They would prise the explosives out of shells, which sometimes exploded, and load them into empty tins – our condensed milk tins were much in demand for this. The shells were readily available for there were still many old ammunition dumps scattered about in the desert. (They also used this ammunition for their rifles, but often it was of the wrong calibre and the rifle would explode.) The trouble with fishing with dynamite is that it destroys not only the larger edible fish but all the marine life in the immediate vicinity, including the food that the fish live on. Several of our men had been injured in this way.

We worked from sunrise to sunset and as the season advanced so did sunrise, so that in the end we were doing well over twelve hours a day and saw the advance of sunrise each day with distaste.

We rose half an hour before sunrise so that when the rim of the sun appeared over the horizon we could blow whistles on the Tell for work to begin. However, we too were summoned in this manner by Lady Petrie blowing a whistle in the camp. I would not have minded being called or shaken or knocked up, but I could not stand whistles blown in my ear when asleep; and we were all so tired that we were still deeply asleep around 4.30 in the morning. The floor of the mess room, like that of all the other rooms, was just sand so every now and then I gently brushed Lady Petrie's whistle off the table onto the floor and stood on it. Then there was peace till the next week when she got another. At the end of the season I dug about eight or ten of these out of the sand.

We had half an hour for breakfast and an hour for lunch and worked a six-day week. One day was spent in getting provisions from Gaza and our men had to walk into Rafah, 8 miles away, on that day to get their supplies. The pickmen were paid 10 piastres a day, about two shillings. They worked in gangs made up of a pickman, a hoeman (*tourier*) who placed the sand in baskets with a wide-bladed hoe, and a bunch of boys who varied in number according to the length of the run, that is, the distance the earth had to be carried away from the site. Some of the men were semi-settled Bedu from the Wadi Ghuzzeh area who were used to doing a little cultivating for catch crops and knew the routine well as they had been working for the Petries for the last ten to twelve years. Others were pure Bedu of the Terrabin, Sawarka or Bayyadin tribes of North Sinai. We employed about two hundred men and they always arrived armed. To avoid trouble if there was a dispute we got them to stack their arms at the edge of the excavation.

Everyone was armed in those days but it was not only here, as I was reminded later when reading St Exupéry's *Wind, Sand and Stars*, where he writes of the surprised comments of the Moors who went to France: 'In Paris you walk through a crowd of a thousand people and nobody carries a rifle.' this would have been the reaction of our Bedu, for a world without guns was to them unthinkable, as the gun was the sign of manhood.

Water was one of our main problems, both for ourselves and the men. In the beginning our only supplies were the local wells. Anyone who has had any dealings with desert wells knows what this means. As the season progressed the water got lower and stronger. It also tasted strongly of ammonia because it was impregnated with the droppings of camels, goats and occasionally an animal who had died in it. The wells were deep and we had to keep a man continuously at the bottom scraping out a sandy strong-tasting brew. By the time it got to the site the men were usually very thirsty and made a concerted rush for it, spilling as much as they drank. Fights sometimes broke out and to quell these we had the water points placed below a bluff from which we could jump onto the struggling figures below. The water got better if allowed to stand, but the smell could not be eliminated and it quite drowned the taste of the tea. Although the men were used to drinking this kind of water we were not. Finally our well got so bad that the Petries arranged for the Palestinian Government to supply us with a water tank from Gaza which stood in the railway siding and from which we got our supplies.

While we were working in Sinai the Italian–Abyssinian war, which had started in December 1934 and was to go on till October 1936, was taking place. As a result there was a large demand for camels and vast quantities of these animals used to pass through Sheikh Zuweyed. These camels caused Major Jarvis, the then Governor of Sinai, considerable trouble, although Sinai itself was not a camel-breeding area to any great extent. The frontier between Sinai and Egypt was at Rafah but the customs post was at the Suez Canal because the Egyptians did not like the desert much and had difficulty in finding officials to work there. All camels are marked with *wasms*, tribal marks that indicate to the initiated the tribe that owned them. The system was that if they were foreign camels their owners paid customs dues at the

The Road to El-Aguzein

Canal, whereas if the camels were locally bred they passed freely into Egypt. It was rather surprising to find that in one year Sinai had produced 100 000 camels whereas Syria and Arabia – both great camel-breeding regions – had only managed 40 000 between them. What was happening was that the brands were being changed by the Bedu of North Sinai from foreign to local and then the animals were kept about ten days, after which they went across the border free of customs dues. Nobody ever discovered how much the local committee of experts (one Egyptian official and two Bedu sheikhs) made in bribes out of the practice.

After my influenza I moved out of the camp and into the cell in the police post because Dr Hargreaves said I must have fresh air and there was no window that I could open in my room. The cell in the police post was very comfortable with a high barred window and cement walls. Of course, with me inside, the prisoners, when there were any, had to be outside which was usually two or three times a week. I would have to step over sleeping prisoners outside my door when I went to bed. There was, unfortunately, one distinct disadvantage in the jail – there were far more camel ticks than in the camp and the crickets were very noisy. However, otherwise I was very comfortable and the police sergeant was very helpful, teaching me Arabic in his spare time.

The men over whom I stepped were the hashish smugglers with whom the police were most concerned at this time. It was a trade that the Egyptians, inspired by Russell Pasha, chief of the Cairo police, were very anxious to suppress. No thought then that it was a soft drug – they had seen far too much of what it did to their own people to be lenient. The police used to pass long metal rods through the camel loads looking for the small packages of hashish, but the drug was sometimes carried inside the camel itself or tucked in a slit in their skin. Sometimes bulk packages were brought in by sea and dropped, buoyed off the coast, but these were difficult to pick up. Most of the supply came overland by camel. But this was also difficult for the smugglers, as the Bedu are expert trackers and could tell at a glance to what tribe the camel belonged that had passed that night; besides, no-one but a smuggler would travel by night or on the less frequented routes. Both smugglers and police were armed and there were often gun battles in which people were killed. Many of the smugglers were caught through informers; others got through by keeping to little-used routes, but none the less there were always a lot outside my cell door. When I was there there were about 150 police for the whole province. They were Sudanese and very smart, all were mounted on camels and had been trained by an ex-Guards NCO. A similar number of foot police were stationed in the main settlements. In addition there was a separate Sudanese camel corps and light car patrols largely engaged in suppressing smuggling. These police were recruited from round el-Arish or from the Neklawi Bedu of central Sinai. They were local Bedu and supplied their own camels, saddles and trappings. They were paid

E£2.50 per month. On Friday, which was our official day off being the Muslim rest day, I noticed with interest that the *shawish*, or sergeant of police, held a local court outside the police station. Here the same men came week by week and here they would sit all day, sometimes disputing angrily. Once I asked him why the same people came week after week. 'I never settle their cases,' he said. 'If I did, they would only go away and commit some other crime'. Some of these cases had already dragged on for several years.

I used to enjoy watching the police setting off for their patrols on their splendid riding camels each equipped with beautiful camel trappings. The saddle bag, *al kharj*, used to be put right over the frame of the saddle and had two holes to permit the high saddle pommels to pass through. An ornamental piece with two tails hung from the rear of the saddle, these tassels fell to the same length as those falling from the saddle bag, which was always richly coloured, violet, black, red, yellow and white with a woven design. Over this a black or white sheepskin was often laid on the unlined wooden saddle, or *shadad*, to make a more comfortable seat for the rider. The real pommel was often finely inlaid with metal simulating silver – usually either lead or soft steel. Traditionally these saddles were made of tamarisk wood, as were the baggage saddles which had much smaller pommels.

Sometimes the police patrols went into Rafah and when they did they often brought back our mail. All the time I was in Sinai I never wished to leave the site and go to Gaza and sample the doubtful joys of civilization. I was quite content to walk the dunes; sometimes we went as far as the sea about 3 miles away. Other times we just lay on the sand watching the dunes or the camel caravans going down to el-Arish. They used to start shouting greetings to us as soon as they heaved in sight and they were still shouting the last as they disappeared over the horizon. Then there were the pottery and objects to be drawn, Arabic to be learnt, photographs to be taken of the site and the objects with the plate camera that Rik Wheeler had lent me.

Carl Pape was a keen photographer and I learnt a lot from him. We used glass plates, not cut film, for though the plates were very easily broken, they gave a fine negative. We had no ice and the water was often so hot that much of the emulsion used to peel off the plates in spite of our efforts at putting hardeners in the water which made developing very difficult. I found an unexpected use for hyposulphate in Sinai one night when I was developing the plates: I spilled it over my trousers and it took off all the stains caused by fish oil and tomato sauce from our unending tinned foods, that had accumulated gradually over the season. Unfortunately, however, the hypo also rotted the material away.

As the season drew to a close we gradually uncovered part of the outer walls of the XIXth Dynasty fortress with its well constructed courses of alternating coloured bricks. This was a most beautiful and effective piece of construction and gave me great respect for Egyptian military architecture,

The Road to El-Aguzein

later enhanced by seeing more complete specimens in Nubia.

Although the Petries invited me to return for another season, I finally left at the end of March 1936 as I had accepted Professor Garstang's offer to join his excavation at Tell Keisan in the plain of Acre. I left Sheikh Zuweyed with regret. It was a splendid site and the desert by day and night was the most beautiful thing I had ever seen. But it was the Sinai Arabs that I missed most – with their friendliness and their willingness to meet one halfway whatever mess one had made of their language.

Two particularly interesting things happened to me in Sinai. The first was that I had my first real Arab meal, sheep's eyes and all, with the tribe all seated on the ground. The eyes I could have done without, but treated them rather like oysters which I don't like either. The second thing was more important. The Terrabin decided to make John and myself members of the tribe, this entailed having our wrists ritually cut and our blood mingled with that of the Terrabin. So that I like to think there is some Arab blood flowing in my veins. This was a very unusual thing for them to do for a woman, but then Arabs do not always follow the expected pattern.

On the way into Gaza my kitbag, which had been insecurely attached to the back of the car, became detached at one end and trailed all through the streets of Gaza. As a result, until I left for Jerusalem, small boys were running up demanding bakshish for returning articles of clothing – all very embarrassing. I could not get the bag repaired in Jerusalem and so ended up by making a white 'sausage' bag which my mother 'lost' on my return to England.

Chapter Five
Palestine, Turkey and England 1936

It was my illness in Sinai that brought me first to Jerusalem and then to Jericho. When still in England I had applied to go to Jericho to join Professor Garstang to catalogue his flints, but fortunately for him Joan Crowfoot (later Joan Crowfoot Payne), who had dealt with these the previous year, decided to return and do this work again. However, when he heard that I was convalescing in Jerusalem, he asked me down to join his dig. I was extremely glad to do this as it reduced my financial liability for board in Jerusalem and enabled me to take part in the excavation of the pre-pottery Neolithic levels of Jericho.

It was a large camp with a large staff. G. M. Fitzgerald (called Fitz), who had already dug Beisan (ancient Bethshan, a large site in central Palestine), was in charge of the Late Bronze Age levels; Alan Rowe, who had been George Reisner's assistant in Egypt, was in charge of the field work; Immanuel Ben-Dor, who was attached to the Department of Antiquities, dealt with the pottery; Joan Crowfoot examined the flints; there was a Dane, Dr Aage Schmidt, who helped with the pottery and photography; Botos, the Arab surveyor, did the plans; Meroe Garstang, the professor's daughter, kept the records; Mrs Garstang managed the housekeeping and John Buxton assisted with the field work. We all lived in a complex of large houses near the spring at Jericho called Elisha's Fountain, except for Fitzgerald who preferred the comfort of the Jericho hotel.

Garstang was working for Liverpool University with funds provided by Sir Charles Marston. Because of the various disputes about the dating of Jericho Garstang had brought in Fitzgerald to excavate the Bronze Age levels, and settle the controversy about their date which had arisen as the result of an earlier season's work. Garstang has been criticised for his methods but, when I worked with him, his records were meticulously kept. Room cards were made for each room or area excavated with a note of the dimensions of the walls, material and state of the floors, or any constructions, and a list of the main contents of each room. Then each type of pot was entered on its own special card after having been drawn and photographed.

In the mild air of Jericho I soon recovered and was able to help with the field work, for two weeks. Garstang was not the first to excavate the mound which had been extensively dug before the First World War by an Austrian expedition. 1936 was his final season on the site. The previous year soundings had been made into the Neolithic levels so that we were opening up areas already tested. The soundings in 1934–5 had revealed two metres of Mesolithic occupation resting on sterile marl and natural rock. The mound of Jericho was a long low oval, it had been gridded in twenty-metre squares, and the area we were excavating extended on the east of the mound towards the modern road. In fact the early levels extended considerably beyond the ancient mound, indicating that the earlier settlement had a wider extent.

In the 1936 season, an area of about two thousand square metres was uncovered; allowing for a certain batter on the sides of the cutting as we went down, even at the base there was an area of about a thousand square metres. All this work was carried out under the direct supervision of Alan Rowe, who had the reputation of being a very careful field archaeologist. The cutting revealed seventeen levels, of which the upper seven were Early Bronze Age, and had already been cleared before I arrived. While I was there we were going through eight metres of Neolithic houses. These had burnished floors covered with red and cream plaster; the whole floor was beautifully constructed, with carefully rounded corners and set on 4 to 4 centimetres of limestone chippings. The buildings were made of a type of plano-convex brick of which Kathleen Kenyon later made great play when she came to work the site. Although Kathleen Kenyon's archaeological methods were impeccable her domineering character and the behaviour of her dogs often made life at the old Institute in Regent's Park unbearable. The dogs were strays from the Battersea Dogs' Home who kept on straying, were extremely vocal and over whom she had little control, so conversation when they were around was difficult.

Already in the seventh millennium columns were in use in the small megaron-type building which had served as a shrine. Two columns stood in the porch and both engaged and free-standing columns were also found. The rooms of Level XI showed evidence of earthquakes as burials beneath the floors had earth fissures separating the bones. In Levels IX and X the earliest pottery was appearing as built-in furniture in the form of basins scooped in the ground and lined with the local marl, the rim carried above the level of the ground to form about one-third of the vessel. All these were unbaked. The idea, however, of making free-standing vases was clearly already present. Kenyon in her later excavations has discounted this evidence and claims the pottery was brought in from outside, but anyone who saw this material *in situ* could not doubt that it was formed on the spot. Here were the first fumblings towards free-standing objects, not only pottery but statues and models, all of unbaked clay. One of the models we unearthed, was a house with two storeys, was shaped somewhat like a beehive; but unfortunately because of its fragile nature it collapsed.

The workmen we employed here were very different from the semi-Bedu that I was used to in Sinai. Here for the first time I met the Kuftis, those Egyptians from Upper Egypt trained by Petrie who had become the *reis*, or foremen, of so many excavations in the Middle East. With Petrie we had had no foremen and dealt directly with the men ourselves. I did not like these Upper Egyptians walking about with their sticks and shouting at the men when they saw one of the staff approaching. They were centres of corruption, taking a percentage of each man's wages, and often introducing the younger men to hashish. The men were either locals from the Jordan Valley or Druzes from the neighbouring hills.

This was, as I have said, the last season at Jericho and Professor Garstang intended to move on to Tell Keisan, a large mound near Acre, when he had finished. When I was about to return to Sinai, Garstang asked me if I would join them at Tell Keisan when I had finished my season with the Petries, and I had gladly agreed. I was to be given the position of Assistant Field Director to work under Alan Rowe. At Acre we lived in a house on the walls of that ancient city called 'The House of the Four Winds', which had a wonderful view over the harbour where we used to take out a boat and swim in our time off.

Tell Keisan was a huge square-topped mound, which had already been surveyed by Garstang and Rowe, with a view to their future operations, in a short preliminary season in the spring of the previous year (1935). It had a large Middle Bronze Age II glacis and ditch, but the upper levels in which we were working were Hellenistic. We now started to clear the site from the top, level by level, while some investigations were carried out on the glacis area and in the ditch below. I was in charge of the work at the top of the mound. This had already been surveyed in the usual twenty-metre square grid by Botos, Garstang's Arab surveyor. As soon as we started work we came on houses, kilns, floors and other structures. There were a very large number of Greek wine jar stamps, mainly from the islands and dating to the second and third centuries BC. Many were Rhodian or Chian, indicating the importance of the wine trade between the Greek islands and Palestine in the fourth century BC.

Tell Keisan was a splendid site and I used to stand on the top of the mound with my workmen, many of whom knew a few words of English. These, I was intrigued to find out, were confined to 'Stand up' and 'Sit down' – terms not particularly useful in archaeological work. When I asked them how they had acquired this vocabulary they explained that they had been in jail for murder and that, when they assembled in the morning for the governor to inspect them, this was what was said. They were quite good workmen, though untrained in what we required, but as they came from different villages, were usually hostile to one another, and fights were frequent. If Garstang was there all was well as the workmen all liked him and respected his authority. However, Alan Rowe did not have the same ability to handle them, and occasionally ugly situations arose when one man would attack another with a knife or pick and the rest of the gang joined in. Rowe nearly always felt impelled to go and have a cup of tea when these fights broke out, leaving me to deal with them. There is nothing like archaeological excavations for bringing out the strength and weakness of the protagonists.

However, our work at Tell Keisan did not proceed undisturbed. We had started work about 15 April and a week or two later riots broke out in Palestine. At this time Palestine was under mandate to Britain from the League of Nations. The riots were due to local Arab fears of the greatly increased Jewish immigration into Palestine, largely as a result of the pressures in Western Europe, and Germany in particular, caused by the rise of National Socialism. The Jews were not slow to defend themselves and crates of merchandise being unloaded at Jaffa and Haifa had burst open showering out rifles, machine guns and hand grenades consigned by the Zionist authorities in Europe to their more belligerent cadres in Palestine. The Arab *fellahin*, deserted to a large extent by the landowners who were making a profit out of selling land to the Jews, turned to force and tried to take the law into their own hands: after all it was they who were being dispossessed of their ancestral homes. These troubles were the beginning of six months' almost uninterrupted riots throughout the country.

I, like most of the other British who worked in Palestine, was strongly pro-Arab. Finally things became so bad that the men were afraid to come to work, we had difficulty in getting the money to pay them, and Garstang decided to stop work until things were more settled. The end of the season was anyway rapidly approaching as he had only planned a short session in 1936 as preparation for a full-scale excavation the following year.

However, Garstang was a far-sighted man: he had been largely responsible for planning the foundation of the British School in Jerusalem after the First World War – a point now often forgotten. He saw at once, when law and order began to break up in Palestine, that it would be a long time before the status quo was restored, and he made his plans accordingly. When I worked with him he held the post of Professor of Methods and Techniques of Archaeology at the University of Liverpool. He had had a wide experience of field work in the Middle East and Africa. He had worked in Turkey, Egypt, the Sudan and Palestine. Before 1914 he had been in south-western Turkey working at Sakce Gözü (Sakce Geuzi). This was a mainly prehistoric site with a Syro-Hittite palace on the top of the mound, and Garstang had been reminded of this work when he found the prehistoric deposits at Jericho. He therefore decided to make arrangements to go back to Turkey for a while, at least until things settled down in Palestine, and to look for a site which would link Palestine with the Aegean. He did not, however, confide to us his entire plans.

He always believed in going to the top, so he made arrangements before he left Palestine to have an interview with Kamal Ataturk. This was because he did not want to have any trouble with his concession and this was almost certainly as a result of his earlier experience when Turkey was the Ottoman Empire. Before 1914 Garstang, who was very interested in the problems of Hittite geography and who had travelled widely in the country, obtained a *firman*, or permit, to excavate at Boğazköy (Hattušaš), the Hittite capital. Germany was at that time wooing the Turks and Kaiser Wilhelm II visited the Ottoman Empire as a friend of Sultan Abdul Hamid. The German orientalists approached the Kaiser and persuaded the Sultan to revoke the British *firman* and grant it instead to a German expedition under the direction of Hugo Winkler. Now Winkler was a philologist and not an archaeologist and the story goes that, fascinated by the discovery of the Boğazköy tablets which were the Hittite archives and written partly in Akkadian, he remained in his tent deciphering them instead of directing the work and noting what they were found with. The result was that as late as when I went to Turkey in 1936, the Phrygian painted pottery that came from the layer above that in which the tablets were found was thought to be Imperial Hittite ware, which it was not – the latter being plain red. This mix-up was not discovered until Von der Osten, another German but working for the Chicago Oriental Institute, sorted out the Alishar Hüyük excavations which had been carried out for the Institute between 1927–32 by E. Schmidt, also a German. The revision must have cost the Oriental Institute dear as they had to republish their expensive Alishar volumes. It was also a lesson in archaeology: showing how even an experienced archaeologist can be misled by mound stratification and its complications.

But when Garstang was first in Turkey it was the period of the *Drang Nach Südosten*, when German engineers were building the Berlin-to-Baghdad railway and the Kaiser had visions of an empire extending eastwards to the Euphrates and beyond. The agreement for the German concession for the construction of the railway line was signed on 14 June 1914, but in fact the Germans had been in charge of the construction work long before this, as witness Leonard Woolley's stories of his dealings with them when he was excavating at Carchemish in 1912. Woolley fell out with them primarily because the German engineers wished to remove quantities of earth and stone from the ancient mound of Carchemish which lay within Woolley's concession and which was part of the ancient town. Woolley was particularly annoyed with Contzen, the German engineer in charge, who tried to remove the Carchemish fortifications after Woolley had returned to England at the

The Road to El-Aguzein

end of the season. How Woolley and T. E. Lawrence, who was then his assistant, settled the matter is amusingly told in Woolley's *Dead Towns and Living Men*.

Before we left Acre news came of the death of Mrs Wheeler. This was totally unexpected and great loss to me as she had always advised and helped me in my archaeological career, and I had a deep affection for her as a person. She had been unsparing of herself in her archaeological work, an excellent organiser and was very good with people. She had been a great help and support to Wheeler in his early archaeological career. They had met at London University where they were both students prior to 1914. Rik was in Palestine at the time of her death and it was not until he arrived in Paris that he read of her death in *The Times*.

We set off by road from the House of the Four Winds for Ankara. It was with genuine regret that I left Palestine, Sinai, the Arabs and the impending 'troubles'. We went first to Beirut and then up the coast visiting Byblos and Ugarit on the way seeing René Dunand and Claude Schaeffer, our French colleagues who were working in Syria and the Lebanon, then held as a mandated territory by France. This trip was of tremendous use to me as I saw other archaeologists' techniques.

Professor Garstang was the epitome of the absent-minded professor – he lost everything he put down and he had a passion for unpacking his suitcase at every overnight stop and hanging his clothes in the wardrobe. When we left Latakia, where we spent the night before visiting Schaeffer, Garstang left behind the trousers of his dress suit; formal attire was very important in the 1930s, one could not visit a head of state incorrectly dressed and Garstang was due to see Ataturk. Garstang had a rather difficult figure, being short and plump, and was travelling in a pepper and salt knickerbocker suit which was highly unsuitable for official visits. The loss was discovered when we arrived in Ankara where Sir Percy Lorraine was serving as ambassador. He was a very tall man who tended to wear wide-awake hats and cloaks and who did not like archaeologists. The British Embassy was ransacked for clothes then we tried the French Embassy, but none of the right size was forthcoming. So in great haste we had to simulate a diplomatic infectious illness and leave Turkey on the Orient Express without further delay.

We had in fact already travelled on the Asiatic part of this train, the Taurus Express (or Toros Express), from Aleppo to Haidar Pasha. Aleppo, set on its hills with its buildings of honey-coloured stone, seat of the first British consulate in the Levant, was the great trading city of Syria, with its mixed population, its streets crowded and humming with life, life not only of the town but of the desert. Ibn Jubyr, the Arab historian, has said 'Aleppo is one of those cities of the world that have no like', and anyone who has seen it will agree.

The Orient Express, when it existed as a regular train, had for me a certain charm and I viewed its passing with sorrow, as the end of an era. It was wonderful to board this express at Aleppo and see on its sides the nameplates of its destinations – Ankara, Haidar Pasha, Istanbul, Salonika, Sofia, Trieste, Milano, Paris, London. It split somewhere along the line and one could go either through central Europe and Germany or via Italy and France as we did. Mrs Garstang was French so we naturally took the route through France. I remember most the dun-coloured plains of central Europe, almost as never ending as the steppes. I never quite got used to the platforms – or rather the lack of them – on European railways and how one had to swing oneself up from ground level onto the train instead of stepping in as in England or Australia.

On my return to England I went back to excavate with Wheeler at Maiden Castle. The death of his wife had made life very difficult for him, and Molly Cotton and I had quite a time organizing things so that they worked smoothly.

I became one of his site supervisors on trench H cut across the edge of the rampart where the early and the later camps joined. We stripped a large section of turf off the inner side of the ramparts and uncovered the curious casemate construction by which the ancient builders had prevented the chalk blocks from slipping down into the ditches. Down into the ditches we went as well, for, as the Director pointed out, we were only volunteers and if the sides slipped in and we were injured it would cost less than the workmen. Many of the men that we employed were out of work and we were fortunate in getting the same men year after year. One regular was an old soldier who had lost a lung and could only do light work; another was the local poacher whom we had to bail out of jail each year but who was a great character. Another was Bernard Sturdy who lived in a caravan and only ate porridge, but nevertheless worked steadily through the season. But the best, of course, was the foreman, Bill Wedlake, who became more of a friend than a workmate.

In the four seasons the Wheelers had worked at Maiden Castle they employed more than one hundred volunteers a season. Many of these have gone on to make their names in archaeological history in fields across the world: Dereck Allen, Peter Shinnie, Molly Cotton, Kim Collingwood (later Lady Wheeler), Gus Bradford, Joan du Plat Taylor, Lesley McNair Scott, Rachel Clay and Barbara Parker (later Lady Mallowan). But for me by 1936 the magic of the great hill fort had gone; Mrs Wheeler was dead. Rik Wheeler was in many ways a perfectionist with drive and ambition but no patience with the minutiae of the day-to-day running of things. He was a difficult man to work with and one of the reasons I did not do the last season with him was because of a disagreement we had about the rampart stratification I was excavating at the southern junction between the original eastern earthwork and the western extension, site H. Here we found what Wheeler described as 'a series of dumps each rammed hard behind retaining walls of limestone'. Although I was unsure as I had never seen anything like it before, I regarded it as a series of casemates and said so. This Wheeler strongly denied. I later learnt that this sort of casemate construction was frequently used in building ramparts, and I saw it at Tell Duweir and Boğazköy. It was after this incident that he said to me 'I can see what I wish to achieve but when I fall short of this I tend to lash out at the nearest person.'

My heart now lay not in British prehistory but in the ruined cities of the Middle East, with the Arabs and the Turks, excavating under blue skies but under difficult political conditions. The freedom and camaraderie of the English excavations might be lacking but there we were professionals – the few directing the many.

Chapter Six
Turkey 1936–1937

Archaeology is not an end in itself but is an index to human behaviour with its failures and human progress.

Garstang, *Prehistoric Mersin*

The expedition to survey and excavate in south-west Turkey was made possible by the generous help of Mr Francis Nelson, a Liverpudlian who had migrated to America when a boy and made a fortune. Generously and spontaneously he offered to finance Professor Garstang's work there when he had had to close down his work in Palestine owing to the troubles.

The staff for his initial season consisted of Professor and Mrs Garstang, John Waechter and myself. Towards the end of the season we were joined by Alison Dunn, the daughter of an old friend of the Garstangs. This time, instead of going out on the Orient Express, we went out by train to Venice where we joined a Lloyd Tristino steamer (this Italian firm later changed its name to the Adriatic Line). John and I were supposed to meet the Garstangs in Venice or, failing this, on the boat or in Istanbul. But they were held up for some reason and we were always going round railway stations, hotels, shipping offices, wharves and embassies asking fruitlessly in various languages for them, and attempting to describe a short bearded man. We did not finally catch up with them till Ankara.

Madame Garstang, who I think had met her husband in Egypt before the First World War, was the daughter of a Pyrenean hill farmer. They were not rich people and her father regarded her lack of dowry as a problem – dowries were still then customary in France. So Garstang asked for the hill behind the farmer's house. The farmer replied that this was quite useless, as he had never been able to grow anything upon it. Garstang said that was all he wanted. He had seen that it was made of marble; he quarried the stone,

The Road to El-Aguzein

shipped it from Marseilles to Liverpool and had it made into headstones for cemeteries, and so made his fortune.

In Istanbul we stayed at the Londra Palas Oteli on the hill of Pera overlooking the Golden Horn. In the 1930s Istanbul was far more decayed than it is today, but then as now it is one of those towns that looks its best from the sea, with the towering minarets of the Sultan Ahmet, built in 1609, and the Suleymaneye, built some fifty years earlier, though I have never like the vast bulk of Ayia Sofia. The many Osmanli mosques and the splendid fortifications at Rumeli Hisar and the journey by boat to the Black Sea I found fascinating. Here again the Garstangs eluded us but we had enough to do; they had set us the job of cataloguing all the Syro-Hittite sculpture in the Istanbul Museum and other useful tasks. I still have the notebooks I filled so laboriously there.

John and I thought that we were going to Turkey to look for the town and temple of the Sun Goddess of Arinna, one of the principal deities of the Hittite pantheon – indeed, Garstang had written an article in *The Times* describing his plans on these lines, but it did not turn out like that at all. Great was our surprise to find when we reached Ankara that far from working on the plateau we were off to southern Turkey to explore the plain of Cilicia, known to the Turks as the Chukur Ova, for a prehistoric mound that would link Thessalian material with prehistoric Jericho.

In the 1930s Ankara was still largely in the process of construction. Many of the great boulevards were not yet made and, though part of the embassy quarter was built, they had forgotten to put in the drains in the streets and houses. So it all had to be torn up again with the inhabitants camped uneasily in the houses.

Staying in our Ankara hotel John and I got tired of the then unrelieved diet of rose petal jam for breakfast, so that we decided to get some honey for a change. With this in view John drew a bee on a piece of paper and waved away the jam; the waiter looked surprised, and sent for the head waiter who spoke French and asked 'Why did you say that there was a fly in the jam?'

The town was full of cats and dogs as the Turks never kill animals but just leave them to die. We stayed in a hotel whose name I have mercifully forgotten. It was infested with cats. If one opened one's window the merest fraction, the cats were in. All ravenously hungry, they were apparently all over the hotel and waiting for any opportunity to gain entrance and food. The drainage was also elementary and water from the room above was always descending in sheets all over everything. I left with no regret at all.

Although I spent some time in Turkey, I spent most of it in Cilicia, the Chukur Ova, which the Turks claimed was not the real Turkey. Turkey, they said, was confined to the plateau, the heartland alike of the Turks and the Hittites, comprising the great area lying inside the Kizil Irmak, or Red River, with Ankara, ancient Angora, at its centre. It was here that the Levant merchants came to exchange their broadcloth for the wool of the goats of the Anatolian plateau, and built up the British connection with the Middle East which has lasted ever since the sixteenth century when coffee was introduced from the coffee shops of Istanbul.

The splendid mountains of the Taurus, the Anti-Taurus, the Kurt Dağ and the Amanus dwarfed any mountains I had seen until then. Their passes wound for miles through snow-clad mountains, with the mountain streams running beside the tracks. I took with me Xenophon and Arrian and read on the spot of the struggles of the Greeks over two thousand years earlier.

The Chukur Ova, freezing cold in winter and boiling hot in summer, was inhabited by a mixture of peoples: Kurds, Circassians, Arabs, Bulgars and Turkomans, so that each village had a different language; these were Muslims from the remnant of the Ottoman Empire in Europe settled in the unhealthy plain where life expectancy was but a matter of a few years and most succumbed to the endemic fevers of the plain. Yet the Cilician Plain is one of the richest areas of Turkey with its cotton crops, and with Adana, the town founded on a Hittite site, and Tarsus, the city of Paul.

In due course John and I were dispatched thither by the Posta – the local train that ran on the days when the Taurus Express did not run, which was every day of the week except Mondays and Thursdays. The Posta was a train to which I was to become devoted, with its high banshee wailing whistle as it approached each unguarded level crossing, but this was my first experience of it and I had no idea how it would behave. In the Posta there were no sleeping cars and no restaurant and we sat up all the way in bug-infested carriages built before the First World War by the Germans when they were pursuing their *Drang nach Südosten* – their push to the east to reach Baghdad.

Turkey in those days bore very little resemblance to the country today. We had to have a photograph attached to our railway tickets. Numerous photographs had to be submitted in London when obtaining the original visa. I took this all as routine: but I had two sets of passport photographs and to my surprise I found that the ones I had submitted in London were the ones returned to me in Adana, not those I had also given up in Adana on arrival. After this I had rather more respect for the efficiency of the Turkish Secret Police who really checked on everyone very thoroughly.

When John and I finally left on the Posta we were seen off at Ankara by what seemed to be most of the British Embassy staff. Somehow in the 1930s the embassy staffs were more cooperative to people travelling and working in the Middle East than they are today, perhaps because there were not so many. The Embassy, knowing the foodless condition of the Posta, had thoughtfully provided a vast hamper of food, for which John and I were more than grateful on our thirty-six-hour journey. When we got to Kayseri they took off the engine and used it to shunt other goods wagons so that we were in the siding for about twelve hours. We did not know enough Turkish to make them understand when we asked how long we were staying so we

The Road to El-Aguzein

remained rooted in our carriage the whole time. Then we moved on through the Cilician Gates down to Yenice where the line branched to Mersin and so to Adana.

In Adana we lived in one of the many Yeni Palas Otelis which are to be found all over the country. They usually belie their names as they are neither very new (yeni means new) and most certainly are not palaces. I notice that the guidebooks say that the Cilician Plain has a mild winter climate. I can only conclude that the winter of 1936–7 was unusual as it was anything but mild. Professor Garstang, who had worked in Turkey before the First World War, obviously remembered only the sunny days and had assured us it was hot, so that John and I had few warm clothes. The only heating in the Adana hotel was a charcoal brazier that stood on the main landing. This we used to remove to one of our bedrooms to make Turkish coffee in a vain attempt to keep warm. Then there would be loud cries from the Turkish staff and the brazier would be whipped away, usually before the water had had time to boil. For some reason we had little to read and the weather broke soon after our arrival. As the main roads were not then tarmacked it was difficult to make excursions round the Plain though we did accomplish some by araba (horse carriage) which did not stick quite so fast in the mud as a car would have done. There were few English people in Adana but from one, an engineer, we were able to borrow a book *The Handbook of Natural History: The life of the Bedbug* which began, 'The bedbug is a friendly little creature devoted to man . . .'. We had more than enough evidence of this throughout our stay in Turkey.

The Garstangs had remained in Ankara to pay their long delayed visit to Ataturk, and we had no idea when they would arrive. So we religiously met the Toros Express every time it came in, only to be disappointed. Finally, they joined us and we decided to concentrate on making soundings on four mounds and to decide after that which one to investigate fully. The sites were: Chaushli, a small site some six kilometres from Mersin, undoubtedly prehistoric but with disturbed stratification; Souk Su Hüyük, near Mersin; Kazanli, a beautiful flat-topped mound near the sea between Mersin and Tarsus, with its main occupation in the Bronze Age; and Sirkeli, a large mound, probably once the local Hittite capital, situated on the River Ceyhan. On the rocks overlooking the river was an Imperial Hittite inscription from the time of Muwatalis (1296–72 BC). This was extraordinarily difficult to photograph and record as the rock overhung the river. To do this I was swung out on ropes over the river which was in flood at the time.

When we began our excavations at Sirkeli, we continued to live in Adana and take the early morning train to the town of Ceyhan. It left Adana at 5.30 a.m. and the only food available at Adana station was semolina flavoured with rose water – an acquired taste at the best of times. We took bread and cheese for lunch, but again by the time we got back to Adana in the evening, dinner was long since over as the Turks tend to be early eaters. For some reason the only food we ever found in Ceyhan was aubergines fried in fish oil.

To avoid the daily journey with its considerable disadvantages, we moved to the khan at Ceyhan, as there was no hotel. This was a typical, old-fashioned Turkish khan built round a square with a well and a trough in the middle of the yard. The lower rooms were for storing goods, the animals lived in the courtyard, and we lived in rooms on the upper floor. There were no washing facilities so we had to fight it out with the camels and donkeys at the trough in the yard and could not clean much beyond our faces, hands and teeth. No women ever stayed in the khans and no provision was made for them. One could not just buy a basin and retire to one's room as one might have to share the room with a large number of other people. If one wanted privacy one had to buy all the beds in a room; which were really large dormitories. It seemed to rain almost continuously during our stay there and most nights were spent moving beds round the rooms looking for a dry place, as the roof leaked extensively all over our beds, clothes and equipment. All that was provided in this khan, as in hotels, was a worn pair of Turkish slippers under the bed, very necessary in view of the mud outside.

The flooded river and the relentless rains finally forced us to abandon our work at Sirkeli after only a few weeks. First we went back to Adana, but the old Roman bridge spanning the river there acted as a dam and a large part of the town was flooded. As most of Adana was built of mud brick many of the buildings collapsed into the streets and many people were drowned. So we decided to withdraw to Mersin on the coast.

Fortunately for us the railway line ran on a raised embankment clear of the floods. Conditions at Mersin were much better and we settled with relief into the Toros Oteli overlooking the sea. So civilized was it that there was even a WC with a seat, something hitherto unknown in our travels. The elements, however, had not yet done with us. Hardly had we settled into the hotel than a tidal wave smote the open roadstead that served as a harbour and quite large coasters were swept up onto the road. All this was connected with the latest eruptions on the island of Thera/Santorini in the Aegean. Unknown to me this caused my mother much anxiety when she read about it in *The Times*.

Near Mersin was the site of Souk Su Hüyük or Yarmuk Tepe, the mound marking the place of prehistoric Mersin. This mound was half cut into by the Souk Su or Cold Water River, and this was the site that Garstang finally decided to excavate. This had a Hittite fortress near the top of the mound and then proceeded down through many layers to the Neolithic, ending below the present water level at a date of about 6000 BC. Here we dug a series of trenches down the sides of the mound to date it, as we had at Sirkeli, because, as Garstang pointed out, it was difficult to date the Cilician mounds by surface material as the soil was so glutinous and clayey. Cold Water Mound was a good name for the site as it was bitterly cold – the

The Road to El-Aguzein

wind blowing straight off the Taurus Mountains which were covered with snow. We had to wash all the sherds in cold water in the bitter wind, so that my hands became chapped and bloody. As I have said, Garstang had not prepared us for this cold. I only had one suit of warm clothes and one sweater and it was a great contrast to Sinai and Jericho. The Garstangs believed in sending their clothes by trunk via Thomas Cook and Son. This was a long slow process in Turkey so that the season was well advanced by the time they arrived. The Customs had carefully unpacked my trousers and put them in Professor Garstang's trunk as they did not believe in women in trousers, although the peasant women wore them.

The Adana Museum was at this time housed in an old Greek Orthodox church with the director's house in the courtyard. The museum director, Ali Bey Yalgan, was originally of a tribal family and proud of it and he erected a nomad tent with all its equipment in the museum grounds. It was he who acted as our inspector and our general mentor all the time we were there. We owed him a lot: he struggled with our inadequate Turkish, he told us where to go and what to do, but he had one habit I found hard to forgive: he would take our choicest painted sherds and write their provenance on them (in the Arabic script which was more familiar to him than the new Turkish) on the painted side and in indelible pencil. In many countries the government appoints an inspector to accompany foreign archaeological expeditions 'to facilitate their work'.

In Turkey I acted as field supervisor as well as photographer. Garstang's camera, a half plate Saunderson, had belonged to his brother-in-law, Robert Gurney, who had used it for photography in the Red Sea when he was studying the habits of fish. As a result the camera had got wet and was slightly warped. There was of course no dark room in the hotel so we had to develop the films at the museum. The dark room in the Adana Museum was on the first floor and had been a Turkish lavatory. It still had its hole in the floor above the lavatory below – which was still in use. The smell was such that neither John nor I could remain in there with the door closed for more than a few minutes. The water was also very cold and we found that the emulsion, instead of frilling off with the heat as it had in Sinai, rose in blisters with the cold. We had a kettle on a primus boiling beside us but even so it was a tricky business getting the right temperature without a thermometer.

At Mersin, as we dug down to the lower levels, my room in the Toros Oteli became full of sherds. It was a great disadvantage not having a proper dig house for our equipment and for the material, so we used the floor of my room instead of a table. My room had a number of rat holes and rats and to stop their activities I stuffed the holes with the largest of the prehistoric sherds which I heard them vainly trying to tear their way through at night.

I had never liked oil with my food, having been born with jaundice, and by now the rich Turkish food laced with oil was having a bad effect on my inside. The Garstangs' only remedy was liberal doses of castor oil which did not alleviate it. In an attempt to obtain something plainer, I noticed that on the menu there was a salad of cold cauliflower. I thought that if I could get this without the oil just after it was boiled, it might help. So I asked for it plain. The waiter, always anxious to please, arrived with the cauliflower on a plate swimming with oil, saying, 'I knew you did not mean plain, so I have put on three times as much oil as usual.'

Mersin was a polyglot city with Bulgars and Kurds as well as Turks; it was also then the third largest port in Turkey. The longshore men were Arabs or Egyptians, many of whom lived in thatched houses down near the shore. They had been left behind when Ibrahim Pasha retreated after his abortive attempt to conquer Turkey in the last century. Then there were the red-tiled houses and villas like many of the Mediterranean ports. From Mersin was shipped the produce of the rich plain – the cotton and grain – and the produce of the silver mines of the Taurus; and yet a large part of the Chukur Ova was at that time still swampy and undrained – and the haunt of the malarial mosquito.

In Mersin every evening at about five o'clock, a carriage with two kavasses, splendid in red and gold uniforms, and a large man sitting alone within, was to be seen driving through the streets of the city. This was Matthews, the English consul. Well known and respected by all the merchants of Mersin, carts drew aside at his progress, shopkeepers came to the entry of their stalls to bow for he was a great man and all the town knew and respected him. The kavasses were Turkish subjects but were Lars from the Black Sea coast, non-Turkish ethnically and proud of their long association with the English. In my early days in Turkey, the Levant Consular Service had not long been amalgamated with the Diplomatic Service, so that the officials had all been trained in the old way and were expert in the language of the countries in which they worked. Matthews spoke Turkish, Arabic and Persian fluently, as well as French and Italian, and therefore had no difficulty in communicating with the merchants and officials. He also had a wide knowledge of Turkish customs, literature and Muslim practices, as had others in the Service. He had two stations: in the winter at Mersin (Icel) and in the summer on the Black Sea at Trebizond (Trabazon). But personally he was a broken man with no future in the Service. He had divorced his wife, which was not allowed in the 1930s, and had married an English girl he had met in Istanbul. She never went out in the streets unless accompanied by a kavas and was terrified, as far as I could see, of Turkey, the Turks and everything else. He was quietly drinking himself to death, as I have seen so many others in the Consular Service doing in the Middle East. We had nothing but kindnesses from the Matthews and I respected his wide knowledge of the country and its inhabitants; but they were lonely, bored and unhappy and we could do nothing for them except lift their minds for the moment from their problems. Matthews did not come into the category

The Road to El-Aguzein

of consul described by Doughty in his *Travels in Arabia Deserta*: 'A consul is a man sent to play the Turk to his own countrymen.'

It was the consul who introduced me to Nasreddin Hoca, the Turkish folk hero whose stories and anecdotes are well known to all Turks. Whether he was a real figure or a myth is disputed. According to the official version he was born at Hortu on the plateau and buried at Akshehir in *c.* AD 1284 (AH 683). The earliest-known text of his works dates from 1658 and was published in Leiden. An example of his kind of story is, 'that one day the Hoca was chopping wood near the track to Akshehir when a man came along and asked how long it would take to walk to the town. The Hoca heard him, looked up but said nothing. The man repeated his question but still the Hoca said nothing, so that the man decided he was deaf and walked on. The Hoca watched him and when he had gone a certain distance shouted after him, "It will take you about one hour." "Why could you not have answered in the first place?' asked the man. "Because I had to know how fast you walked," replied the Hoca.'

The other folk hero known all over Turkey was Karaoğlan, a kind of Turkish Robin Hood who was the leader of a band of robbers fleecing the rich and giving to the poor and who was the source of many songs sung by the local minstrels.

Mersin was in many ways still a medieval town. The town watchmen used to go about in pairs at night blowing whistles at all the street corners, and chanting the equivalent of 'All's well' in Turkish, giving ample warning of their approach so that all thieves could make off well in advance.

About two and a half months after our arrival in Turkey it was Christmas. John and I were by this time quite exhausted, what with the work and weather, and asked if we could go across to Cyprus for a few days to stay with Joan du Plat Taylor who was then the Assistant Director of the Cyprus Museum. We really enjoyed our Christmas. My dysentery responded to the ministrations of an English doctor and proper medical remedies and Joan took us all over the island in her car visiting sites of all periods. I quite lost my heart to this lovely island in the Mediterranean set so close to the Turkish coast.

Although we were lucky going over, when we tried to return to Mersin it was not so easy. There was no regular passenger service between Cyprus and Turkey but after about ten days we finally found a small Italian cargo boat of about 2000 tons with no passenger accommodation at all, so that we had to sleep in the crew's quarters. We sailed from Famagusta in a full storm, taking about sixteen hours for the crossing instead of eight. John caught cockroaches all night, of which there was a wonderful variety, but the captain assured us these were the sign of a clean ship!

Professor Garstang was not very pleased with our somewhat protracted holiday and had gone ahead and dug Kazanli on his own. This meant all the plans, drawings of sections, photography and pottery had to be done on our return, so we had plenty of work. All this time we continued to live in the hotel in Mersin. After Kazanli was finished we started on Mersin, or rather, Souk Su Hüyük, and worked on that for the rest of the season.

> *O Kazanli itself is a beautiful site*
> *with a nice level top and a comfortable height;*
> *and its stratification a joy to behold*
> *tho' the way it was dug leaves us both rather cold.*
> *For we sailed away to Cyprus – left him sitting on the shore –*
> *thinking 'O, he can't go digging with Serkeli on the floor.'*
> *We were wrong, all along,*
> *for the old man's proved too strong.*
> *For no sooner did we leave*
> *than Kazanli did he grieve;*
> *and he took a little spade*
> *and the holes that he made*
> *are still there for all to see.*
> *Woe is me, woe is me.*
> *For he found some painted pottery*
> *which greatly him delighted*
> *but their intricate patterns*
> *our sad young lives have blighted.*
> *And under it was Hittite and the Bronze Age came as well,*
> *but in spite of all our searching there's no Neo on the tell.*
> *So it's draw, draw, draw, till the light fades in the sky,*
> *and it's wash, wash, wash while the bitter wind blows by,*
> *and it's mark, mark, mark with fingers numbed and worn*
> *and describe each ruddy little sherd till you wish you'd not been born.*
> *And if you see us later on with chilblains on each hand*
> *and peering through dark glasses, perhaps you'll understand.*
> *For the moral of this story, if it's not already shown,*
> *is never take a holiday and leave your boss alone.*
>
>   V S-W, Mersin, January 1937

Finally Garstang decided that he had enough material to indicate on which mound he should concentrate his efforts the next season, and made up his mind to return to England about the beginning of March 1937. Just before he left, John, Alison and I thought we would like to visit Yilan Kalisi or Snake Castle, which we had seen across the River Ceyhan when we were excavating at Serkeli before Alison arrived. This fortress guarded the passes of the River Ceyhan and the Mountains of Light as well as the main route between Adana and Iskanderun. We went by train to Ceyhan with the idea of hiring a taxi to go to Yilan Kalisi but every time we started off from the station we were picked up by the police for identification. This caused considerable delay and it was quite late by the time we got to the castle. Yilan Kalisi is briefly dealt with by Robin Fedden and John Thompson in *Crusader Castles*. They failed to ascertain its medieval name though it must have had one. It is, however, an outstanding example of Armenian military architecture, but as they could find no trace that it had been sacked they thought that it must have been evacuated after the fall of Sis to the Muslims, though it may have fallen earlier as one cannot imagine that the Egyptians would have left a fortress of this magnitude still occupied on their flank. It is very well built with seven horseshoe-shaped towers in the upper ward. Today it has an evil reputation for snakes and sorcery.

There are several stories about this castle which were well known in the coffee houses of Adana and Ceyhan. According to these Yilan Kalisi was ruled by Sheikh Merun who was half snake and half human. The king of Tarsus suffered from leprosy and was attended by a Jewish doctor who told him the only cure was to catch Sheikh Merun, cut off his snake's tail and boil it. The only person who could do this was the snake king's shepherd who was recognisable by a black mark between his shoulder blades. The snake king was, of course, a magician so knew the danger he was in. He sent away his shepherd for seven years as he knew that only through him could he be captured. But finally the shepherd came back, went to the baths in Tarsus and was recognised from his mark by the doctor. He was forced to divulge the whereabouts of the snake king's hiding place. The snake king Merun knew that this was foretold for, as he said, 'No one can escape one's fate'. So he said to the shepherd when he was captured by him, 'I have allowed myself to be taken, and have ordered my servants not to bite your men, but the doctor does not want to cure your king but to have my tail for his own ends. My head is as poisonous as my tail is beneficial: therefore when he boils the tail see you get it and he does not, by changing cups with him.' This is what the shepherd did and when the doctor was dead the shepherd returned to Yilan Kilasi where, by means of his magic powers, he understood the language of the birds and the plants and realised which was useful and good for treating people's ailments. However, the shepherd was illiterate and had to employ a public letter-writer to write out his prescriptions, with the result that the letter-writer derived all the benefit and not the shepherd.

By the time we had climbed all over the castle it was dusk but we were not worried as John had enquired at the station the time of the last train back to Adana and understood it was 7 p.m. Unfortunately for us 'seven' in Arabic is the same as 'morning' in Turkish and in fact there was no train till the next day. This would not have mattered if Alison had not been leaving next day with the Garstangs to return to England on the Taurus Express. The taxi refused to cooperate or rather he broke down when we tried to get to Missis, the next station on the line, so we hailed a passing oxcart and travelled for some hours by this, a most slow, uncomfortable and bone-bruising method of transport. We arrived at Missis to find there was no hotel and everything was shut as it was by now so late at night, that we ended up going to the barracks. We spent some time in the barrack room where all the soldiers, who had gone to bed, hastened to get up to examine the strange creatures who had arrived in their midst. They rang their officer upstairs and we finally got up to his room. He was in bed but got up and put on his boots and cap though still in his pyjamas. We tried to persuade him to ring Adana as we were afraid that the Garstangs would be worried about Alison. He did so but the line only went as far as the station and, as he was convinced we were Germans and nothing we could say to the contrary would make him change his mind, the message never got through to the Garstangs who spent a worried night. Finally we spent what remained of the night in a Turkish house eating honey and cakes and sleeping for a few hours in one of those vast brass beds common in the Middle East. Next morning we got a train leaving at about 5.30 a.m., which in fact gave ample time to catch the Taurus Express. (Speaking of honey there were few tins or bottles in Turkey in those days so that if one bought honey it was given you in a screw of newspaper. On later visits I brought my own containers.)

The Chukur Ova is full of castles of which Yilan Kalisi was only one. There was Sis, the old Armenian capital, Toprakkale, the earth castle and Anazabus or Anavaza, which was a curious island-like rock set in the plain thirty miles from Ceyhan, in the midst of marshes and swamps; at the foot lay a Roman city of which this was the citadel. This site was later investigated by Michael and Mary Gough in the 1950s, but when we visited it, it was comparatively unknown. We took some lunch with us and offered a small boy from the few huts at the base of the citadel some chocolate, but he did not know what it was. Nor did he know what paper was as he came and asked us what we were doing making notes – all this within sixty miles of Adana – the fourth largest Turkish city. Things are very different nowadays: the swamps have been cleared, and many of the narrow dirt tracks have been tarmaced.

Caesarea by Anavazus, to give it its full name, also had a legend attached to it. This was about the building of the aqueduct that supplied the ancient city with water as the Romans could not drink the local swamp water. The story goes that two young men were engaged on building the aqueduct and the king of the city had promised his daughter to the winner. She was in love with one of them and he was leading until he stopped for a moment to drink of the flowing water and let the other man win. The princess was so upset that she flung herself off the northern tower, and the stain of her blood in the form of a great red streak can still be seen on the limestone rocks to this day.

After the Garstangs and Alison Dunn left for England, John went back to Palestine where he joined the police as it was still in the time of the 'troubles', and I went back to Cyprus because, as I have already said, I felt strongly drawn to this beautiful island. I stayed with Joan and worked in the Museum for the next few months. At this time Cyprus was an extremely peaceful place with the Turks and the Greeks working together in harmony. It had been in English hands since 1888 when Disraeli obtained it from the Ottoman Sultan as a result of the Treaty of Berlin. It had good agricultural land in the great central plain or Mesorea, and much mineral wealth in the form of the copper from which the island obtained its name. The Americans ran the copper mines and operated a model complex with their own hospital and built whole villages for their workers.

At this time I was extremely interested in flints and spent a certain amount of time cataloguing and classifying the material that Porphyrios Dikaios, the Cypriot Keeper of the Museum, had excavated at Erimi and Khirokitia. In between working in the Museum we went about the island examining reported finds and doing small rescue digs. I would have liked to remain where I was, but the previous year I had agreed to excavate in Ireland with the Harvard Mission to Ireland. This meant I had to leave the island, to my great regret, by the end of April; by 4 May I was in Paris and a few days later in London.

Chapter Seven
England, Ireland and Greece 1937

On returning to England I went to work for the Harvard Mission to Ireland which was one of the schemes set up to help deal with the very bad unemployment in Ireland in the 1930s, and the men who worked for us were all unemployed Irish labourers. The Mission was a mixed one, mainly American but also including Irish, English and Australian. It was under the directorship of Hugh Hencken with Hallam L. Movius Junior as the field director.

The Mission was engaged in excavating a crannog in Meath, once the stronghold of the Irish kings of Lagore who had taken to the bogs to escape the Viking raiders. A crannog is an artificial island made of alternating layers of peat and brushwood set in the middle of a bog. The weather was extremely wet: the local Irish called it soft but that was an understatement. It meant that we were pumping nearly all the time just to keep the site clear of water. When it rained hard the whole area turned into a lake. It was very easy to pierce the blue clay sealing in the water table and when this happened the whole trench filled up in a matter of minutes, sometimes even before we could get out of it.

This excavation presented many difficulties, both of stratification and preservation. Because of the very wet nature of the soil many things were preserved that would normally have disappeared. Thus wooden bowls, buckets, paddles, spoons and handles had all survived well, but had to be dried out gradually and then treated. This meant that in the beginning they had to be placed in buckets of water with labels on wires hanging out of the bucket indicating their find spots. Sometimes these came off or got hopelessly tangled up, which led to confusion. The contrast with work in Sinai and Turkey could not have been greater. Here we had a small number of men, we could only move about the site on duckboards which were very slippery,

The Road to El-Aguzein

there was no pottery and what there was had the surface almost rotted away. The animal bones, on the other hand, were splendidly preserved and, as the ancient inhabitants seem to have lived on an almost unrelieved diet of meat there were plenty of them. One got the impression that life in the bogs must have been noisome in the extreme as the inhabitants just threw their bones over the stockade wall, where they must have rotted with a very bad smell.

Sean O'Riordain, our liaison with Dublin, was the equivalent of a government inspector in the Middle East. A fanatical Irishman who could see nothing good in England, he had had his training in prehistory in Germany. He spoke Erse and when we went on a trip to Connemara and the west of Ireland which was Erse-speaking he agreed to act as interpreter. But as he talked to an old peasant woman in fluent German by mistake there was remarkably little result. The man who dealt with the animal bones on behalf of the Dublin Museum was a real enthusiast for his job, so much so that while he was dealing with one of the dog skeletons a workman remarked 'He spoke powerful lovingly of that dog'.

While we were in Meath we accidentally became involved in a milk war. The farmers were not receiving what many of them considered they should be getting for their milk, so some of them lay in wait for the milk lorries sent to collect the churns from the farms and shot at the drivers. This did not go on for very long but while it was in progress milk was in short supply. Sometimes shots were taken at anyone who moved on the road and sometimes we got mixed up with this.

At that time Lord Dunsany, an Irish author, lived near where we were working and was busy writing a not very flattering account of the expedition in which he changed the nationality of the Americans to black Liberians come to explore Old Ireland. It had its humorous side but was not too popular with the American members of the expedition.

I went from Ireland to London as Nancy de Crespigny, who had worked in Ireland the previous season, was marrying Hallam Movius in St James's, Piccadilly, where I acted as her bridesmaid. I went to Liverpool afterwards to work on the publication of the material that the Garstang expedition had found in Turkey. I had not been feeling very well in London but put it down to the transition from the heat of the Middle East to the damp of Ireland. However, in Liverpool I became really ill with a high fever which came and went. The local doctors could make nothing of this, and it was not until I went up to Scotland for a few days to stay with Dorothy Marshall with whom I had studied in London and worked at Maiden Castle, that the problem was diagnosed. Her father was a doctor and recognized the fever as undulant or Malta fever, which he had seen in the Mediterranean during the First World War. I had got it from eating goats' milk and cheese in Turkey.

This illness put paid to me returning to my work in Turkey with the Neilsen Expedition under Garstang as I was obviously in no fit state to go back. However, Garstang did send me to Germany to examine the Tell Halaf material as he was republishing his pottery from Sakce Gözü in the light of finds made at Nineveh and Arpachiyah after he had concluded his excavations. For the next three years I had recurrent attacks of the fever, but fortunately wore through it by about 1940 when it disappeared as suddenly as it had come.

The Tell Halaf material was in Berlin in the collection of Baron von Oppenheim. The Baron was an extraordinary character. A diplomat by profession, he had become interested in archaeology before the First World War when he was posted to the Ottoman Empire. He had obtained a *firman* to excavate at Tell Halaf, now in northern Syria but then under Ottoman control, which he had found in 1899 when he was serving with the German Diplomatic Mission to Egypt. In 1902 he was sent to the United States to study railway development in dry conditions, because of the German wish to build the Berlin-to-Baghdad railway. Von Oppenheim was consulted as to what line the railway should follow because his travels in Syria and Turkey had given him an unrivalled knowledge of the terrain. In 1899 he travelled along the tributaries of the Balikh and Habur – an area later explored by Max Mallowan in his search for the Mitannian capital Wassukanni. In the 1890s this area was under the control of Ibrahim Pasha, the paramount sheikh of the Milli, who held a *firman* from the Turkish Sultan, Abdul Hamid, to raise his own force of irregular cavalry, known as the Hamidiye Regiment. It was really an independent area within Ottoman control. While staying with Ibrahim Pasha von Oppenheim heard of some remarkable statues found on a mound near the village of Ras el-Ain at the headwaters of the Habur. He had a certain amount of difficulty in persuading the Checkens (Circassians) of Ras el-Ain to say from which mound they had obtained the statues, because after finding them by accident when trying to use the mound as a burial ground, they had been visited by a series of disasters including a drought, cholera and swarms of locusts. All this the superstitious Checkens put down to disturbing the figures which were rather terrifying in aspect, made of basalt with inlaid staring eyes. The villagers thought they were afrits, or spirits, in the same way that the Arabs in Mesopotamia had regarded the Assyrian winged bulls from Nimrud. Von Oppenheim made a sondage (a test trench) at Tell Halaf and in three days uncovered the façade of a palace belonging to the first millennium BC when Tell Halaf was known as Gozan. This so interested von Oppenheim that on his return to Istanbul he requested and was granted permission to excavate the site. Some ten years later he was informed by the Ottoman authorities that someone else wished to excavate there, so von Oppenheim resigned his diplomatic post and took to archaeology full time. He worked at the site for several years before the war and when this broke out he returned to work for the German intelligence. He was an expert in Arab affairs and spoke Arabic fluently. He was captured by the British while disguised as an Arab

The Road to El-Aguzein

in Cairo during the war. He was a very rich man and had built a museum to house the Tell Halaf material. Unfortunately it was situated near the Berlin marshalling yards and was destroyed by Allied bombing during the Second World War, so I was lucky to see the material when I did. It was the only time I remember seeing a museum in complete comfort as von Oppenheim was followed round by a manservant and every time we stopped a glass of wine was poured out for us. By the end of the day I saw the Halaf culture through a happy haze. Von Oppenheim also had a very large flat in Berlin, with every room a replica of a different Arab room or tent, completely furnished and equipped with the right material.

After Berlin I went to join Joan du Plat Taylor and her mother in Vienna. We went down the Danube by steamer stopping in Belgrade, in Buda-Pest for several days and for some time in Sofia before finally getting off the boat in Varna. We then went on by train to Istanbul. I have no happy memories of this journey as I am not good at sleeping sitting up in trains. We spent some days in Istanbul sightseeing. Then we went to Athens to get a boat for Cyprus, as there was no ship direct from Istanbul. Here, however, Cooks had slipped up and booked us on a boat that did not exist – the boats went fortnightly, not weekly. This meant that we had a whole extra week in Greece which Joan and I used to take a trip round the Peloponnese. Travel in Greece was very different from today; the roads were bad, the hotels were poor and there were no buses to every corner of the country. Instead we had to ring ahead for mules to wait for us at the railway stations, so it was on muleback that I first saw Mycenae and Tiryns, Delphi and Olympia. It was most delightful travelling round in this way. At Delphi we met John Forsdyke, the Director of the British Museum, who was staying there with one of the Benakis (whose home is now the Benaki Museum in Athens). Delphi was a charming little place with only one hotel and no shops to speak of.

Greece is a most beautiful country but it is really a place for the young, so that I was glad that my first visit was when I could enjoy it to the full. We were fortunate also in knowing many of the British and American archaeologists working there. Many of the Americans in particular, such as Virginia Grace and Pete Daniels, were also working in Cyprus. Somehow it was all one world with old Dr Hill, an American, Homer Thompson, a Canadian, and his wife, Dorothy, who was an American, digging in the Agora at Athens; Saul Weinberg, with whom we stayed a night at Corinth, Tom Dunbabbin with whom we spent a night drinking in Cretan tavernas in Athens, old Theodora Benton digging at Ithaca in her bathing gown because she could not get to the site except by swimming, and Alan Wace at Mycenae. The British School at Athens was full of students and there were even more at the American School. It was all new and exciting and we were young.

We sailed from Piraeus in a ship with a deck cargo of timber loaded in a manner to give us such a list that even the Greek port authorities could not bring themselves to give us clearance. In those days the Greek maritime marine were known as coffin ships. No one else would touch the vessels which the Greeks bought up cheaply and sailed, sometimes to the bottom of the sea. On board was O. G. S. Crawford, whose question about poppies had discomfited me when I had the oral for my Diploma three years earlier. He had at that time a house in Cyprus on the Kyrenia range, and was going out for a holiday. After some hours' delay, the harbour-master at Piraeus gave us clearance and we sailed. Fortunately for us it was a still passage. If the cargo had shifted, I am sure that the ship must have sunk. So, by the end of August, we were back in Cyprus where I stayed with the Taylors for about a month, working in the Museum in Nicosia, before going on to Tell el-Duweir in Palestine.

Chapter Eight
Palestine, Trans-Jordan, United States 1937–1938

Because of the recurring fever there was no chance of my returning to Turkey, so I had to look round before I left England to see what further archaeological work I could find. I was lucky to be offered a post as a field supervisor with the Wellcome Expedition to Tell el-Duweir in Palestine. This expedition was financed by Sir Henry Wellcome who was very interested in archaeology and had supported several expeditions in the Sudan and Palestine. The director was John Starkey who had been one of Petrie's assistants, but he had fallen out with Lady Petrie and had left Tell el-Ajjul, taking the rest of the staff with him.

Palestine was by this time in the grip of the Arab Revolt. I crossed from Cyprus to Jaffa and went up to Jerusalem by road. I stayed, as usual, in the Swedish Consulate in Jerusalem, at Larsen House, as the Larsens had by now become good friends of mine. I then went down to Tell el-Duweir where I remained for the next six months. This site, set in the southern Palestinian hills, was a very large mound, one of the most extensive in Palestine, and was the ancient city of Lachish. There were two other field supervisors as well as myself: James Kirkman was in charge of work on top of the tell, Warren Hastings supervised work in the temple area of the fosse, and I looked after the cemetery. As well as my field work I also took all the photographs. Charles Inge was in charge under Starkey as *wakil*, or head man, Olga Tufnell looked after the pottery (and, for that matter, the sick), while an American called Holbrook Bonney was the surveyor.

On this expedition we all had separate rooms arranged rather like cells in a row behind the main building of the compound. We used to entertain some of our Arab workmen to coffee in the evenings, so I had to lay in a complete coffee-making apparatus consisting of a pot, roasting arm, *mudd* for grinding and pestle, because traditionally all coffee had to be freshly roasted before making and then ground at once. The beans came overland in small green sacks from the Yemen. After work the men used to congregate – it was recognized that only the pickmen had this privilege – and they settled in for an evening of smoking, drinking coffee and story telling. We used to go off to dinner leaving them in our rooms and then come back and carry on till we wished to go to sleep, when we threw them out.

Here I met again many old friends from Sinai whom I had first met excavating with Petrie and who, when the work had come to an end at Sheikh Zuweyed, had moved back into Palestine. These were mainly semi-settled Bedu of the Gaza Strip, nomadic Bedu of the north Sinai tribes such as the Terrabin, my brothers, or the local tribesmen like the Amorine. These men used to come with their tents and some of their families and settle in for the whole season. Many of them had been doing this work for about ten to twelve years, as they had started as small boys with Petrie when he was digging the sites in the Wadi Ghuzzeh area in the late 1920s. As well as this trained elite, we employed local labour from the surrounding villages as basket boys, shovellers and workers on the light railway. These villagers were a constant source of trouble, as they were usually at loggerheads, one village with another, and they did not leave their disputes at the side of the trench.

On one occasion a fight broke out between rival groups of villagers that had nothing to do with the work but was caused by someone's donkey straying onto someone else's field and eating part of their crop (just as in the well known Egyptian Story of the Eloquent Peasant). The women in the village started to keen and the men on the site came to blows with anything that came to hand, such as picks, staves and hoes. Fortunately for us at that moment an RAF plane flew overhead, and the fighting broke off, as the Arabs thought that we had called it up to bomb them. We had of course no means of communication, and would not have done this anyway, but it showed how frightened the villagers were of the retaliatory tactics used by the Mandatory Government in those days.

One day when returning from the site at lunch time, I was joined by some of the local Amorine sheiks. The path was very narrow and I was uncertain about the order of precedence. But when I drew back they pressed me to go forward as they said 'You are the Mudir who is in charge of our men so you must go first'. This was an interesting sidelight on the Arab attitude to women; it was not the sex but the job which mattered to them. I wish I could have put this idea over to some of my more anti-feminist colleagues.

The tombs at Tell el-Duweir ranged from the Chalcolithic to the Iron Age. The Chalcolithic ones were cut in the soft limestone and were multiple burials in quite large tombs. The smallest were the Hyksos, into which one could hardly crawl and where work was impeded by having a primus to

The Road to El-Aguzein

melt the wax with which to coat the skeleton to preserve it. As well as tombs there were other rock cut structures in my areas such as an Iron Age dyeing works, *c.* 400 BC. One of the most interesting was Cave 6013 of Chalcolithic date where a pillar had been left to support the roof and the adze marks still showed very clearly how it had been made. Many of the photographs that I took that season appeared later in Vols III and IV of the Lachish publications.

The main thrust of the work was not in the cemeteries which lay at the edge of the mound and were only being cleared to provide a dumping place, but on the top of the mound where the Iron Age Levels of the eighth to sixth centuries BC, were being excavated. This revealed a palace of the Persian period, Guard rooms in the eastern towers flanked the outer gate Level II where the Lachish Letters were found in a burnt layer. The destruction was probably the work of the Neo-Babylonian king Nebuchadnezzar who sacked Lachish shortly before he destroyed Jerusalem in 586 BC. The gate had been burnt by cutting down the surrounding olive groves and piling them against the gate which calcined the limestone of which the walls had been constructed. The letters in ancient Hebrew were written shortly before the sack of the city and Letter IV refers to the 'Lights of the other Judean watch towers going out' as they were captured by the Neo-Babylonians.

Tell el-Duweir, ancient Lachish, was an important city both in Iron Age and Bronze Age Palestine. Before the final destruction the city had been sacked and burnt by Sennacherib of Assyria about 700 BC. Evidence of the sack is shown on the reliefs from Nimrud in Mesopotamia now in the British Museum.

Work started, as it had with Petrie, at sunrise, but it was a better system in that we got up in turns and did a week at a time on the early shift. This meant that we had to get up well before dawn so as to be ready on the top of the mound to blow a whistle when the rim of the sun was seen to be crossing the horizon. It was bitterly cold and those who could afford it invested in the Arab *farwah* – a long-sleeved garment with a sheepskin lining, which could be worn either inside or out. However, I had as usual no money, receiving only my fares out and back and my keep while there, which left little to live on. My work on the tombs lay on the opposite side of the mound from the dig-house and necessitated a walk of about 20 to 25 minutes back after the whistle had gone, so that breakfast and lunch were always finished by the time I arrived, and I seldom saw the other members of the expedition except at dinner. Most of my time was therefore spent with my workmen which was very good for my Arabic. As I was also the expedition photographer this meant developing shots at night, which also tended to isolate me.

In the evening my men used to tell various local stories and tales from the *Arabian Nights*. I could never remember these complicated stories in detail but I could oblige with the *Tales of Baron Munchausen*, and a certain number of Hoca stories that I had learnt in Turkey. At that time there was no wireless or radio to distract people and story tellers were in great demand among the tribesmen.

They also told me the local village or tribal news and talked about their camels, their lives and their work. One man was unlucky: first his wife died, then his camel; there was no doubt about which he missed most. Another whose camel had a sore pad where it knelt was told by Olga to bathe the place with hot water and disinfectant. Next day he arrived looking very part worn and when we asked what was the matter he explained that he had been holding up a basin of hot water under the camel all night so had got no sleep.

Our chief assistant and general dogsbody around the house was Diab who had only one arm, not that that stopped him doing anything. The other had been bitten off near the elbow by an angry camel when he was a small boy. One of the villagers, Abu Tawil, a very tall thin man, was our explosives expert. The site was a stony one and large boulders were always having to be removed. If possible they were got out of the holes they were in by putting soil first under one edge and then the other so that they gradually rose to the surface. However, sometimes they were too large to shift in this way, or else the rock was too solid. In the cemetery area the roofs of the old tombs had often collapsed under the weight of the earth and sometimes this, too, had to be blown away. So we were always taking refuge from flying stones after the danger signal had gone up. One day, however, Abu Tawil, who was a bit absent-minded, did not get away quite fast enough and blew himself out of one of the holes, coming out arms and legs flying. Surprisingly enough, he did himself very little harm.

Tell el-Duweir had a curious atmosphere and was not a happy camp. Starkey lacked the greatness of Petrie and the humanity of Garstang. Only at Christmas when Gerald Harding, who had been appointed Director of Antiquities, came over from Trans-Jordan was there any attempt to get together; otherwise we all seemed to lead separate and isolated lives.

In December after Ramadan came the Aid, the great Muslim holiday of the year when work stopped for several days. Some of us decided to go down to Egypt. James Kirkman, Bonney and myself took the expedition pick-up through Sinai to Cairo, where we met Starkey, who had travelled there by train. Crossing Sinai was splendid: with the stark contrasts of the colour, the bare hills and the deep wadis. We spent the night in one of the government resthouses. When we got to Egypt we went down to the Fayum, to Hawara and Lahun as well as visiting Saqqara and Giza. Starkey knew everyone, and as an old Petrie man many of the officials in the Museum and the Department of Antiquities, like Brunton and Engelbach, were his friends with whom he had worked in Egypt. After a few days we drove back through the Mitla pass and after another night in a resthouse got back to Palestine. The roads through Sinai were largely the work of Major Jarvis the British

The Road to El-Aguzein

Governor of Sinai whom I had met two years before while working with the Petries. The pick-up was ideal for this work as it had large desert tyres, but the roads were cleverly constructed with tarmac laid on wire netting over the worst of the sand patches.

That year, 1937–8, Dr Margaret Murray and Donald Mackay had opened up Tell el-Ajjul on the Petries' behalf. Petrie had fallen out with the Palestinian archaeological authorities and they would not let him excavate on his own. Towards the end of the season at Tell el-Duweir John Waechter, who by this time had joined the Palestinian police, came over for the weekend and took me over to Tell el-Ajjul. We spent a pleasant day and on the way explored one of the many prehistoric sites to be found in the wadi beds in southern Palestine. At the Wadi Nakhabir we found some splendid hand axes.

We had a Chinese archaeologist for part of the season at Tell el-Duweir excavating one of the caves. When he left I took over his work. He left me his notes but they were more concerned with the flea population than with the archaeological evidence, as I was to learn to my cost. The caves had been used by local shepherds to shelter their sheep and were alive with fleas. We found the only way to cope was to spread a sheet on the ground, stand on it and hundreds jumped off; one was then only left with the residue. It was, apart from that, an interesting site and the scene of an early pottery workshop dating to the Late Bronze Age. Much of the pottery had not been baked when disaster fell upon the Tell which was sacked by the Assyrians, so that it was neatly stacked for firing but still in biscuit form. The stone base of the potter's wheel was also still in position, although the wooden base had long since rotted away.

Many of the local Arabs had curious customs. Those from Jebrin ate snails, the large edible snails introduced by the Romans. They were also splendid slingers and could easily throw from the plain up over the ramparts. It made one realize what an asset the slingers must have been to siege warfare.

At the beginning of January our quiet routine of work was destroyed by the murder of John Starkey on his way from the camp to Jerusalem. He was going up to collect the men's pay and to attend the opening of the new Jerusalem Museum. He always travelled with just an Arab driver. The car was stopped before they reached Hebron and he was hacked to pieces by an axeman. His murderer was a gaol escapee who had already committed a similar murder. This man was caught again but never came to trial as he was killed trying to escape. The cause of Starkey's murder was never satisfactorily cleared up. With his short thick-set figure and beard he certainly could have been mistaken for a Jew but this is unlikely as he spoke fluent Arabic and, according to his driver, had had quite a long conversation with his murderer before his death; nor was robbery the cause, as he was not robbed and anyway the return journey would have been the time for that for then he would have had the men's pay. His Arab driver was unharmed and allowed to go with the car. The men on the work certainly knew something had happened to him before we received official notification, for news travels fast in an Arab country. The murder was certainly committed by someone who knew of his movements and the local Arab landowners claimed to have had a grievance as he had expropriated some of their land. Gerald Harding came over from Jordan to try and clear things up, and Charles Inge took over the direction of the excavations. For protection we were given a posse of six Palestinian police and a truck, and all of us laid in small-arms for our defence. So the season passed uneasily to its close, and without Starkey's drive, energy and enthusiasm all hope of continuing the clearing of the great mound vanished. It was the last season at Tell el-Duweir: all that equipment, all that money and all those hopes had been destroyed in a few moments on the Hebron road. And next year the war would be upon us.

In April, when the season came to an end, I went with John Waechter to Trans-Jordan to survey and excavate the Wadi Dhobai on the way to Qasr Azraq in the Jordanian desert. Situated to the east of Amman, the Wadi Dhobai was one of those watercourses where water collected in the winter, so that in the spring there was quite a deep pool which lasted for some months, until used up by the Bedu. We were there from the end of April until the beginning of July.

Wadi Dhobai was in a flint desert, or Hammada in Jordan – miles and miles of country with the underlying limestone scattered with flints. As a result it had a rather forbidding appearance as the overall picture was of black overlying a dusty yellowish-white. This was the area where the Ummayad caliphs had had their hunting lodges, as a good deal of game had once existed in the desert, although this has to a large extent been eliminated by the introduction of the car and the high velocity rifle. The ibex and the gazelle were rapidly becoming extinct, although in the 1930s quite a number still survived. Hyenas, jackals, foxes, hares and sand rats were common. The striped hyenas were in fact quite a nuisance, sniffing round the tents at night. Once I shot at one which put his nose under my tent flap at night. There was also the *warral*, a snake-headed monster lizard reaching 3 feet in length. Among the birds the only ones I remember clearly were the great bustard, the lesser bustard or *habara*, the kestrels and the vultures. However, it was really the insect life that was amazing; every stone had its inhabitant, each more extraordinary and horny than the previous one. We took quite a number back to the Natural History Museum, to learn that we had found several new varieties. One would not imagine that they could survive out there in the desert, with no moisture but the dew and no vegetation, but they must have preyed upon one another. Scorpions were also present in large numbers, and we had to turn out our shoes each morning to check that there were none inside. This Ali, our cook, failed to do one day and was bitten, and he suffered a very swollen leg for several days.

We had supplied ourselves with a box of bully beef, onions and tea. Ali made a sort of gritty Arab flap for bread – his previous job had been watchman for a road gang. When we first arrived at Wadi Dhobai we lived on the water from the water hole, filled by the April rains. However, we had not been there long when we were joined by the Beni Sakr on their seasonal migration. We were really the intruders as they had marked the rock with their *wasm* or tribal mark, but they were very good about it and did not seem to resent our presence. After they had been in residence for some time using the water became more and more of a problem. They drank it, watered their flocks in it, swam in it and washed their clothes in it, so that it gradually changed its colour, taste and smell. It turned from brown to green with a thick scum on it, developed a strong flavour of camel, and was covered by a variety of small red spider.

We got on well with the Beni Sakr who used to offer us camel's milk and spent many hours drinking our tea. However, we had one strict rule: their camels were not to come into the camp as they tended to trip over the guy ropes and bring down the tents. One morning just after Ali had brewed up our morning pot of tea there was a particularly strong smell of camel, so I said to him, 'Ali you have let the camels into the camp again.' To which he replied, 'No, it is the tea' – and it was. After this, remembering our experiences with the Petries, we decided to go to Amman and get some tanks. None were available there, so we went on to Jerusalem where we bought some old oil drums. We washed them out with petrol, and then to air them we left off the caps while we returned by road through the Jordan valley. Unfortunately we had not succeeded in washing out all the heavy oil and when we filled them with water in Amman we found we had three distinct layers – oil mixed with red dust, water and petrol. Before we could drink this liquid we had to strain it through our handkerchiefs, which acquired a reddish stain that never washed out. The taste of the tea also left a certain amount to be desired as it had so much diesel oil in it.

The Beni Sakr could not understand that we were not Muslims and kept asking us when we were going to make the pilgrimage to Mecca. They came carrying ostrich eggs and young gazelles which they tried to get us to take but we had no means of feeding them. Ostriches were long since extinct in this part of the world, although occasionally found in the Nufud Desert near Hail, but their eggs could still be found in the desert. In Jerusalem Edward Keith-Roach, then District Commissioner of Jerusalem, had a flat in the garden of Larsen House where we used to stay, and when we went back to get the water tanks he presented us with some extra food – quails in aspic which he had had sent out from Fortnum and Mason; they formed an interesting contrast to our usual diet! It was extremely hot, and we had a series of sandstorms which almost blew down the tents. We suffered from a shortage of reading matter too. For some reason we only had Reeds' *Nautical Almanac* so that we became very conversant with the lights and markers of most of the English coast; this was to serve me in good stead during the war when I became a press censor dealing with nautical almanacs. The other work we had was Doughty's *Arabia Deserta*, and I am always glad that I read that great master's work in the area in which he had travelled.

> To Charles Doughty, on reading *Arabia Deserta*
>
> *You knew the limestone hills*
> *And black the desert flints*
> *Reflected rays;*
>
> *As slow your camel paced*
> *The unmapped tract –*
> *Arabia's desert ways.*
>
> *Arabian father – we salute as such*
> *One who knew those lands*
> *And suffered much*
>
> *You saw twixt sky and sand*
> *The mirage grow*
> *The minarets and domes*
>
> *Yet by Arabian mirage*
> *Not deceived*
> *You saw beyond – and what*
> *You saw bequeathed.*
> V.S-W. Sinai, April 1936

As you may imagine, we had no visitors in this remote place and the only tracks were those to desert landing places, cleared by the RAF. One day we saw a cloud of dust, indicating a vehicle heading past us out into the desert. Beyond there was nothing – no water and no supplies – so we sent the cook's boy to head it off. To our surprise it turned out to be an English artist in a small car, with no water, supplies or petrol, travelling with a school atlas and heading east on what he thought was the road to Amman. If we had not seen him he would have died of thirst in the desert when his petrol ran out. He was not at all grateful for our help. It is people like this who make desert travel a menace and cause trouble when search parties have to be sent out after them.

As June wore into July the power of the sun increased. I had not realized before how desiccated one could get when the only water one took in was by the mouth and washing was at a minimum. Also the sun had rotted my shirts after six months at Tell el-Duweir combined with the none too gentle ministrations of the washing girls who tended to rub them on stone and pound them to get out the dirt. So I was now almost in rags. By July we thought that we had had enough and decided to go down to Akaba to see the port and have some swimming. We had been excavating prehistoric hut circles for about six weeks, and published an account of our work in 'Excavations at the Wadi Dhobai, 1937/38', Journal of the Palestinian Oriental Society, 1938.

First we went to Petra where we walked through the Sik and got to the Cooks camp which was then established there. We slept in the tombs and ate in a large marquee. Here we met again a Crown Film Unit engaged in making one of the numerous films about Lawrence of Arabia as we were now in Howeitat country. The unit was run by a German producer with an English camera crew who were extraordinarily unsuited where they were. We had already met these types in Amman where they had been staying in the same hotel, the Philadelphia. After dinner the German, who was a Prussian of the Junker class, pressed a crème de menthe upon me. Though I was not very fond of liqueurs I did not like to refuse. I woke up during the night in my cave completely paralysed – quite conscious but unable to move hand or foot. I was suffering from the effects of wood alcohol poisoning, though I had not until then heard of it. John strapped me onto a horse and we left Petra. I was still unable to move that night but gradually the effects wore off. I have never drunk crème de menthe again.

We worked our way down to the Gulf of Akaba and had a few days' well earned rest in the government resthouse at Akaba. There were no hotels at that time and the permanent population of the tiny port cannot have numbered more than two hundred. The way down to Akaba was most spectacular when one got to the spot where the road dipped off the plateau into the Wadi Araba. The colouring was like Petra, all muted pinks and yellows, but I thought far more effective. Akaba was famous to us for Lawrence's attack on it in the First World War. It still holds an important strategic position on the borders of Saudi Arabia, Sinai and Israel. The village lay within the area controlled by the Howeitat Bedu. When we were there it was under the military command of the Arab Legion, run from the old square fort at the southern end of the village. The ancient town of Ezion Geber, where Solomon had his fleet, was nearby in Palestine and we went over the excavations. (This area has since been greatly developed by the Israelis.)

Akaba's main industry was fishing and we went out several times, also sailing and swimming, but the coral reefs were hard on the feet. One of the fish that they used to catch and eat was, I think, called Bint el-Bahr. It was pink with blue spots and if one had seen it anywhere else one would have thought it inedible.

After our trip to Akaba we returned to Jerusalem, John went to Rhodesia and I went back to Cyprus. After a short time in Cyprus I returned to England to see my mother in the flat in St John's Wood, which she had rented from an actress. Its *pièce de résistance* was the bath which on pressing a button miraculously revolved from the bathroom to the bedroom.

In the autumn for some reason I decided it was necessary to go to America to study the material excavated by the Chicago Oriental Institute in Syria. However, I also decided to visit Boston and see the Peabody Collection, New York for the Metropolitan Museum and Philadelphia for the Pennsylvania Museum collection. At that time I had many American friends whom I had met when excavating in various parts of the Middle East. There was also my old friend Nancy de Crespigny, who, after her marriage to Hallam Movius, had settled outside Boston. Hugh Hencken, with whom I had worked in Ireland, was at this time the Director of the Peabody Museum, and his wife Thalassa (Cruso) who had been one of the members of the London Museum staff in charge of costume when I had first arrived in England. Barbara Parker, who had studied Mesopotamian archaeology under Sydney Smith while I was doing Egyptology, also wanted to visit the American collections so that in October we crossed the Atlantic in the ss *Georgic*. We had six and a half days of misery travelling steerage with no money as usual. The cabins in that class were only to be reached via the galleys and dining saloon, so that we lived in a perpetual smell of boiled cabbage, which had bad effects on seasick passengers. Also, in the few years since I had travelled on a British ship, I had forgotten the passion that the British lines had for organized games, bets on the distance travelled and gala dinners, all of which I had been spared in my Mediterranean voyages. Most people go on a sea voyage to relax, but this is very difficult on a British ship. The *Georgic* also creaked like a basket so that at night one awoke wondering if she was really waterproof or not, and the condensation below was so great that rusty water dripped all over one's clothes staining them. I did not really like the *Georgic* and nor did Barbara.

No country looks its best in its customs sheds but New York seemed to me to be particularly disorganized. Nowhere else have I had to hump my baggage into the middle of the street to get a taxi. The prices of everything in the United States seemed to us astronomical, so that we were not able to afford an hotel room and had to find lodgings in the YWCA. Neither Barbara nor myself were actually YWCA types, but we were very grateful for these hostels in New York and Philadelphia. We travelled to Philadelphia by Greyhound bus, but unfortunately it had a defective heating system and the hot water ran into the luggage compartment turning the contents of my suitcase into a soggy mess and although the company paid for cleaning my clothes they were never the same again.

We spent several days in Philadelphia, mainly in the Museum, and became acquainted with the remarkable kindness and hospitality of the American people. For instance, a woman in the store where Barbara went to buy moccasins insisted on shutting the store and driving us all round Philadelphia because she had once received a kindness when in England. The next day

The Road to El-Aguzein

she came and took us to the train. The train trip was interesting, as we moved from the richer Eastern seaboard to the Middle West.

When we arrived in Chicago we went to stay at the International Students Hostel attached to Chicago University. This was a great improvement on the YWCA, but we were rather surprised when we arrived to be asked if we had not been afraid to come from the station. It was then in the midst of the gangster era, and I must admit that we had not given it a thought. Here as usual the American archaeologists were very good to us and Bob Braidwood had the stores opened for us which enabled us to examine the Syrian material. I remember Chicago mainly as a very windy and cold city, where I ate a solitary Thanksgiving dinner in a drug store, Barbara seeing no reason to rejoice at American survival.

From Chicago we went to Boston where we stayed with the Movius's. At that time old Mrs Movius was still alive. Boston society I found extraordinary as they still went in for routs and assemblies, things that had gone out in England in the last century. I there saw old Mrs Movius take down the *Social Register* and solemnly check if someone was fit to be asked to the house. Every second person we met seemed to be a Daughter of the Revolution, and we were solemnly taken to Bunker's Hill and to follow the course of Paul Revere's Ride. However, I liked the colonial architecture, both here and in Pennsylvania, with its white columned porches and dignified proportions. But there was much about American life that I did not like and I knew that personally I would never be happy there. I did not like the lack of privacy, the convention by which people could come and throw a party in your house bringing their own food and drink without previous notification, the made-up food, the packaged food, the vast helpings, the early meals – 6.00 or 6.30 for an evening meal – the passion for culture to the point of taking classes in it, the terrible smell of skunks on the night air though they might be passing several miles away down wind, and the grossly overheated houses.

On 29 November 1938, we sailed from New York for Cherbourg on the *Aquitania*, a very different proposition from the *Georgic*. To begin with she was a proper Cunarder and had never been anything else, she had a good crew with a high morale, and she was a beautiful smooth ship. At Cherbourg I got off and proceeded to Paris to await my connection with the Adriatic Line ship I was to go on from Marseilles to Cyprus. There was a few days' overlap and Cunard put me up in a small third-class hotel near the Gare du Nord. I stayed here several days and then went on to Marseilles to get the boat.

At this time the Adriatic Line boats went on to Haifa after Cyprus, so they were full of refugees going out to Palestine. This mid-December voyage was very rough, particularly in the Gulf of Lyons and rounding the toe of Italy. My recollections of the trip were first an extraordinary proposal of marriage that I received from a Lebanese Arab on board whom I had helped with some difficulty about his ticket. He approached me and suggested that I should accompany him to Beirut and marry him as he lived in one of the villages up in the Lebanese mountains. He was on his way back from the Argentine where his family had business interests. He said that he could see me in the family courtyard with him, each smoking our hubblebubble. As I did not like tobacco, I could not quite envisage the scene. So I told him that as I was a Christian I was sure that his family would not approve. However, he brushed this aside as of being of no importance as, he said, his mother had been a Christian. However, with the aid of a White Russian friend of mine whom I had met in Cyprus earlier I was able to persuade him that my family would never agree, which fortunately he took as a perfectly valid reason for refusing the proposal. It was on this voyage my judo proved very useful, the ship's photographer seeing me with a half-plate camera offered to show me his cameras but we ended up in a dark room where I had to resort to judo in order to escape his clutches. I arrived in Cyprus just at the beginning of 1939.

Chapter Nine
Syria, Cyprus, England and War 1939–1947

For the next eight months I was based in Cyprus. After a few weeks I found a small house to rent on the Prison Road in Nicosia. It was a pink and white bungalow, nestling in newly planted orange trees and the rent was £50 for six months. The du Plat Taylors were selling their house and Mrs du Plat Taylor was returning to England so that in due course Joan moved in to share the bungalow with me. I also inherited Katrina, the du Plat Taylors' old cook who was excellent. Here I was more comfortable than I had ever been, even though the furniture was distinctly sketchy; a couple of camp beds, a few Cypriot rugs, some chairs of the du Plat Taylors and a dining-room table made in the bazaar. During the summer Lady Petrie stayed with me in Nicosia for two or three days while she was checking something for 'Prof' in the Cyprus Museum. During the day I went on working in the Museum where Joan and I were engaged on making a catalogue of the pottery. This required a detailed description of each main type and photographs to match; it was a slow business but very interesting. I was also engaged in writing papers for Porphyrios Dikaios, the Curator, on his flints from Erimi and Khirokitia.

In April, John Waechter, Joan and I carried out a survey of sites in the plain of Jabbul in northern Syria. I went first to Jerusalem to join John and pick up the transport. My aunt Tasmania had given me £100 without which I could not have done this work. This was to help me to 'go underground' as she used to say. Quite what she envisaged I did I shall never know. We were allowed to borrow the Tell el-Duweir Ford pick-up and the old bus called Elijah used by the British School of Archaeology in Jerusalem. We hired an Arab driver, who was actually half German, to drive

Syria, Cyprus, England and War 1939–1947

this old bone-shaker while John and I drove the pick-up to Beirut to collect Joan and the equipment arriving from Cyprus. Palestine in the spring of 1939 was still in rebellion. I had to get a military pass to get about in Jerusalem where a curfew was in force. John, who had been living in Jerusalem since he came back from Rhodesia, already had one.

While waiting in Beirut for Joan we stayed in the Grand Hotel Bassul in the centre of the town and overlooking the sea. Here began my long association with this hotel for which I still retain the greatest affection. Before the First World War it was the only European-style hotel in Beirut. It was a family affair and here the Kaiser Wilhelm stayed on his memorable journey to the Middle East. Now it was rather faded and decayed but you were always assured of a warm welcome and excellent service. Madame Bassul, who presided over the whole affair, sat in awful majesty in an inner sanctum encased entirely in black and as a great privilege one was invited in to see her. Here in the hotel there was ample space to store our expedition equipment, unlike modern hotels which seem to have no storage space at all. The rooms were high and the beds draped with mosquito nets on a magnificent type of brass bedstead. Here we stayed while we visited the offices of the French High Commissioner (the Lebanon and Syria were still under mandate to the French) for the requisite permits. We went to the Museum to see the collections and the Curator, the Emir Maurice Shehab, who belonged to one of the principal Lebanese families.

Beirut was much more a Mediterranean city than an Arab one although its taxi drivers drove then as now with a wholly Arab verve which was often lethal. We only stayed in Beirut long enough to make the necessary arrangements and then proceeded to Aleppo via Damascus. We made Aleppo our headquarters for the whole period of the survey. Here we stayed at the Hotel Claridge Palace – a vast gloomy pile built round a courtyard with a fountain. It was a rabbit warren of a hotel, run by Armenians. They also had an hotel in the Lebanon and to this they ultimately retired when things became too difficult in Aleppo, but that was not for some time to come. It must have been quite cheap as we acquired a whole suite with bedrooms opening off a central hall where we took our breakfast and any other meals we wanted if we did not wish to go down to the main dining-room.

When we arrived, Aleppo was having one of its anti-French strikes and riots. This rather delayed us as we could only collect our stores intermittently when one of the shops opened, and most of the buying had to be done surreptitiously because of the strikes. Here we met for the first time the Altounians, that Armenian medical family who have done so much for Aleppine health by building the Altounian Hospital. They extended almost unlimited hospitality to any British subjects who were passing through Aleppo, particularly archaeologists, as Mrs Altounian was English; her father R. G. Collingwood was one of the great experts on Roman Britain. The Altounians had fled from Turkey at the time of the Armenian massacres before the First World War and settled just over the border in Aleppo which had a large Armenian population. The late 1930s in Aleppo are vividly described by Freya Stark in *Letters from Syria*; I never saw the violence that she described although there was some shooting.

We had trouble with the Elijah bus and its gearbox and the whole engine had to be stripped down. The mechanics replaced it the wrong way round so that we had three reverse gears and one forward, which caused some difficulty when we tried to drive out of the garage. This error was unusual as the Armenians were on the whole good mechanics. The hotel was well placed, being in the Armenian quarter on the edge of the suqs and the car repair district, but there was always a background of hammering, so it was hardly quiet.

I had first felt the charm of Aleppo when I had stayed there briefly in the same hotel with the Garstangs before catching the Orient Express in 1936. It is a honey-coloured city built around the Ayyubite citadel with fine modern stone buildings and old covered bazaars, with the citadel dominating the town. Long ago Abraham was said to have pastured his cows there, thus giving Aleppo its Arabic name of Halep, meaning milk. Aleppo, in fact, has a long history for on the surrounding hills remains of Chalcolithic settlements have been found. It was a great city in the second millennium BC when it was the capital of the country of Yamkhad. It has always been an important commercial city catering for the needs of the Bedu of the desert and at the crossways to Mesopotamia and Anatolia. It was here that the English set up the Levant Company in the sixteenth century and it was the site of the first British consulate abroad. Aleppo is one of those cities in which one can spend an infinite amount of time and always find something new and delightful – its mosques, its gardens, its vast spice bazaars, the dervishes with their tall tarbushes and the Arab tribesmen coming in for their annual purchases.

We had tents and only used the town as a base, spending most of the time camped in the plain and returning only occasionally for supplies. The Plain of Jabbul, with its great salt lake from which most of the neighbourhood received its supply, was full of ancient mounds and modern beehive-shaped houses closely clustered at their feet.

One day when we returned to Aleppo we were surprised to find Rik Wheeler there with his new wife, Mavis, on their honeymoon. They were staying at the Hotel Baron and we were even more amazed when Rik asked if he could join us at the Hotel Claridge. And join us he did; he was down for communal breakfasts and he joined us on trips to several sites including Eski Membidge on the Euphrates and Qalat el Nedjem (the Castle of the Stars), just to the north. Rik had lost his heart to the Middle East when he had visited it for the first time in 1936 and indeed I had seen him there briefly between my work at Sheikh Zuweyed and Tell Keisan. So perhaps it was not altogether surprising that he had decided to spend his second

The Synnot children painted by Joseph Wright of Derby in 1781. Walter, the central figure in the group, was the author's great-grandfather. Reproduced by permission of the National Gallery of Victoria, Melbourne.

The author after graduating in 1934.

Work in progress at Sheikh Zuweyed. Beyond the excavations workmen are taking baskets of soil to the waste tip.

John Waechter and Jack Ellis beside the Petries' car at Sheikh Zuweyed in 1935. In the background are our living quarters.

The excavations at Maiden Castle, 1936; the author measuring at site H.

Aerial view of Maiden Castle from the south-east.

The camp mess room, complete with field telephone exchange, at Tell el-Duweir, 1937.

The excavation team at Tell el-Fara'in, 1966. Back row, left to right, Pud Darvall, Peter French, our inspector, Joe Clarke, Stephanie Gee, our foreman Ismayin Ibrahim Fayid. Front row, left to right, Joan du Plat Taylor, the author, Dorothy Charlesworth, Angela Kenny, Ann Darvall.

The author at her childhood home 1917.

The author lecturing at Deir el-Medina.

Sir Flinders Petrie at Jerusalem 1938. (Photograph: Carl Page)

Lady Petrie

The author and Mrs. Garstang watching excavations on the Neolithic levels at Jericho 1936.

honeymoon in the Orient. However, it was not his wife's milieu and she was bored. When we saw them off on the Toros Express I did not think that the marriage would last very long, which it did not.

After finishing our survey we decided to go down the right bank of the Euphrates and visit Baghdad. In this we would be following in the footsteps of Gertrude Bell who went that way in 1910. On this trip our staple diet was bully beef and local bread. The latter used to get so hard after several days that we had to make a kind of stew or soup out of it which was the only way it could be softened. While we were doing this survey we had a remarkable instance of how good the local Arabs' memories were. We were camped by the mound called Beske when we were visited by an old Arab who asked us about David Hogarth an archaeologist and Keeper of the Ashmolean Museum who had visited the area before the First World War.

It took us about three days to do the trip of about 950 kilometres to Baghdad. We arrived at night and the last part of the trip was a nightmare as there were so many car tracks crossing and recrossing one another on the face of the desert. When it rained people used to take off to get as firm a surface as possible so that a large area was scored with wheel marks. As Cook's *Handbook* said when referring to the area from Abu Kemal to Ramadi, which is approximately 300 kilometres, 'The track is very undependable'.

On the way to Baghdad we visited Dura Europos, a Seleucid town on the Euphrates, excavated by the Americans. They told an odd tale about their labour troubles. They kept on engaging men at a fixed rate but the men never turned up for work. When they went down to the village to enquire why, the men said, 'Because the soldiers never came to fetch us.' So used had the inhabitants become under the Turks and then the French to arbitrary government, that they could not believe in the free engagement of labour. At Hit, with its famous bitumen wells, we saw the pillar of smoke by day and the fire by night that are mentioned in the Bible. According to Herodotus it was from here that the pitch used in the building of the walls of Babylon came.

At Baghdad we stayed in the Tigris Palace Hotel near the Maude Bridge, the pontoon bridge built by General Maude in the First World War and named after him. We had the greatest difficulty making the night porter understand that we had come by road from Aleppo as this was obviously not the usual route. Indeed there were only three accepted routes then: Imperial Airways, Nairn Transport from Beirut, or rail from either Mosul or Basra.

We stayed several days in Baghdad visiting the Museum which was then in the Government Press Buildings in Bridge Street. Seton Lloyd was Director-General of Antiquities and as I knew him he kindly looked after us, arranging various excursions to sites such as Babylon and Ctesiphon. I did not like Baghdad much. After Aleppo it was hot and dusty and nothing was left of the fabled circular city of the Caliphs. The hotel was dusty and

The Road to El-Aguzein

dirty, too, with trains of ants running across the floor and Indian punkhas suspended from the ceiling which were the only means of keeping cool. Although it was only April it was already extremely hot and summer time had begun in shops and offices which meant that they only functioned in the morning. I quite understood the value of the old houses with their cellar-like basements for use in the hot weather. Baghdad contrasted ill with the stone-built cities of the Western Arab world – Jerusalem, Damascus and Aleppo.

Our Arab driver, August, was always in trouble in Baghdad because, though he was a Palestinian, he could hardly understand a word that the Baghdadis said. Even the word for bread was different and he came to us almost in tears wishing he could go home. When we came to leave, we wanted to go back across the Great Syrian Desert and had to obtain a certificate of desert worthiness from, of all people, the Baghdad Fire Brigade. They looked with distaste at 'Elijah', but fortunately for us the certificate was granted in the end. This system was in fact a very sensible precaution as the authorities did not want to have to waste time, money and sometimes lives looking for ill-equipped travellers crossing deserts.

We took the desert route to Damascus which lay about 850 kilometres to the west. The first night we spent camped at Rutbah Fort where Nairn Transport kept a small resthouse open to all who had passed the Iraqi Customs post at Ramadi. The next night we camped between Rutbah and Damascus. Here we were visited by several Bedu of the Shammar, the great Arabian tribe who roam over much of the Syrian Desert. They looked with dislike at our bully beef and were only reassured by the picture of the bullock on the tin. They were afraid that as *Nasarinis* (Christians) we might feed them pork. August gave them nearly all our water while we were pitching the tent pouring it literally over their hands; he was as improvident as they were. However, we finally arrived in Beirut and sank thankfully back into the Grand Hotel Bassul while awaiting a ship to take us back to Cyprus. John and August meanwhile departed for Jerusalem to return the transport.

The ship we finally got was a Romanian cargo ship with passenger accommodation for only about six people. They insisted that we had to be on board by five o'clock. She lay out in the harbour, not alongside the wharf, and the crew refused to start the winches to load our heavy equipment. If it had not been for the strength and agility of the Beiruti porters we should never have got on board. We had nothing but trouble with the Romanians. We had been issued with tickets all inclusive for the overnight run to Cyprus but, having got us on board, they refused to let us land again or to give us dinner. We had a furious row involving the local Beiruti agent before this was settled in our favour. This did not give us a very favourable impression of the Romanians. They seemed an extraordinarily mixed race if our crew was anything to go by, some dark, some fair and nearly all unpleasant. We were delighted to get back to Cyprus.

Syria, Cyprus, England and War 1939–1947

That year we dug in Apliki, a Mycenaean mining settlement in the mountains above Morphou. It was situated in a fold of the hills which were splashed with bright reds and oranges from the detritus of the previous workings. Here for the first time it was possible to establish the Bronze Age date of many of the great piles of slag connected with the copper mines that had previously been attributed to the Phoenicians or the Romans. The pottery of the houses was definitely Mycenaean in date as were the *tuyeres*, the clay tubes through which the furnaces were heated.

We lived in a house provided by the American Mining Corporation who were mining the copper at Morphou and whose men had first come upon the ancient workings. While I was there I had an accident. While crouching down to give directions to some of the men in one of the trenches, a large thistle spike went through the muscles of my left leg and did not stop till it reached the bone. I had to be taken down the mountain on a donkey and had half a dozen stitches put into my leg by one of the American doctors attached to the mine. The scar and the hole made through the muscles are still with me.

This excavation was most interesting and satisfactory, because mining shafts and adits are difficult to date as the mining tools do not change very much over the ages. Cyprus had been an important source of copper for the ancient world and at much the same time that we were working at Apliki Dikaios was investigating an Early Bronze Age mining village at Ambelikou, whose exhibits, like ours, were later housed in the Cyprus Museum at Nicosia. My leg injury hampered my work for the next few days on the dig but by the end it was possible to get about fairly reasonably.

Meanwhile the summer of 1939 was drawing on. All through the long hot days we drew and photographed, described and catalogued in the Cyprus Museum. At the end of July I left for France to join my mother in Paris. We had been going to have a short holiday in Brittany but everything went wrong. We booked through Cooks but they became confused between St Brieux and St Briaux and we landed up in the middle of the night in a remote village in the Station Hotel which was the only one. We then returned to the right place to find it full and spent an uneasy ten days in very crowded conditions. All the time the European situation was getting worse and worse. The French were mobilising with troop trains everywhere and all the roads crowded with military vehicles moving east. We therefore decided to go back to England, but this was not so easy either, as by then all the cross-Channel boats were packed with people also trying to get back. However, after a few days we were able to make our way to London and find some rooms there.

The last few days before the war were filled, as far as I was concerned, with trying to find something useful to do. Ever since my teens I had been expecting this moment: the question was not 'Will there be a war?' but 'When will there be one?' The previous year I had seen the fiasco of Munich

The Road to El-Aguzein

and Chamberlain's stupid promises and had also seen the rich packing their cars with goods and heading out of London.

After the First World War, when so many intellectuals and graduates had been killed, the government determined that this should not happen again and a list of reserved occupations was drawn up. Archaeology I found, belonged to one of these reserved occupations, along with farm workers and other useful animals. We were all entered on a vast register but this did not help me find something useful to do. So I decided to apply for the Censorship as I knew several foreign languages including Greek, Arabic and Turkish. To my amazement, on sitting for the examination in Turkish, I was handed a paper in the old Turkish script that Ataturk had abolished in 1926. I then realized that all the authorities had done was to bring out the censorship papers that had been used during the First World War for us to do. This rather dented my faith in the efficiency of government departments. It became apparent that it would be some time before the Postal Censorship made up its mind about me, overwhelmed as it was with applicants, so in the meantime I looked round for something else.

The next thing I tried was the Fire Brigade as it seemed to me that if London was attacked fires would break out all over the city and that assisting with these would be a useful role. However, here I made a mistake: instead of opting to be a driver, as I did not feel I knew London well enough, I became a switchboard operator. Well, I had never liked telephones much since we had had a party line in Australia in the early days and everything I felt about the machine was confirmed here. I was posted to Basil Street, then the headquarters of the Knightsbridge area. Here the first thing I learnt was that there was no such thing as a fire engine – they were all appliances. This was reasonable considering that the term covered several kinds of machines including turntable ladders, mobile tanks, pumps and so on. Unfortunately some of these were without engines, particularly the pumps, so that a fleet of London taxis had been commandeered to deal with these and provide locomotion. The Fire Brigade had expanded terrifically in the last few days before the outbreak of war and only a skeleton force of the old uniformed Brigade remained. There were, in addition, the Auxiliary Fire Service who had received a modicum of training in peace time and had been issued with uniforms.

By this time the Germans had attacked Poland and were pushing on towards the Russian border, yet war was not yet declared. The living conditions in Basil Street left a certain amount to be desired, mainly because we were all sleeping on the floor; and the habits of the new intake who came from a wide stratum of the population, left a lot to be desired. However, after forty-eight hours I was sent to Down Street, one of the sub-stations situated off Piccadilly. It was a commercial garage and had been requisitioned by the Fire Brigade because it had sleeping quarters above that had been used by long-distance lorry drivers. Here the regular Fire Brigade was even thinner on the ground. At Down Street I met Anna de Wolkoff the daughter of a White Russian general who ran a small restaurant in South Kensington. She belonged to the British National Front, the party controlled by Sir Oswald Mosley, who supported Hitler. She tried to get me to attend various meetings with her and to join the party but without success.

It was while I was at Down Street that the uncertainties under which we had all been living were resolved and war was declared. We listened to Chamberlain's speech over the air and as it died away the sirens wailed out. This was only a mock attack, though we did not know it at the time. If the Germans had been able to attack it would have been a shambles as we were certainly not well prepared. Indeed we were all already exhausted having been on continuous standby for the previous seventy-two hours.

My recollection of my first day in the Fire Brigade is one of great exhaustion. Many of the women could not stand it: one developed diabetes due to this and another had a breakdown and had to be removed. The first night a crowd, hearing that Italy had joined the war against us, broke into and looted an Italian shop just down the road. This mob violence was an unpleasant aspect which I was surprised to see in an English crowd.

As I have said, Down Street was requisitioned because it had sleeping accommodation. What I do not think had been understood was that it had served as a brothel, and for the first few nights we had a certain amount of difficulty with the regular clientele. I had lived for some time in a flat in Curzon Street before going out to Sinai but that had been luxury in spite of its tiny size. Now I was seeing the seamy side of London life. However, once the war had started it was a great relief to us all as at last we thought we knew where we were going which gave a great sense of unity and purpose.

After a few days in Down Street I was sent off to another sub-station in one of the mews behind the King's Road, not far from Peter Jones. I found much the same state of affairs as at Down Street with only one or two trained personnel and the rest untried amateurs like myself. The woman in charge had been an actress in civilian life and was very highly strung and nervous. The garage was still piled high with the possessions of the previous owner and we had no proper messing arrangements, beds or bedding. I had quite a job to persuade her to let us go out in shifts to obtain food and bedding. After three or four days, I was sent back to Basil Street to deal with the vast influx of civilians wishing to join the Fire Brigade. After dealing with the rush I was sent to Knightsbridge Barracks for officer training. The first morning and, as it proved, my last, we were marched endlessly about the barrack square by the Guards NCOs, rather as if we had joined the army instead of a civilian service.

However, I was feeling very ill and after lunch, which I could not eat, I spent the afternoon being sick. I was stationed at Basil Street and Station Officer Hussey kindly sent for her own doctor who had a practice in South Kensington. It turned out that I had acute appendicitis and required an immediate operation. It was difficult at that time to get into any of the London hospitals as they were all being kept partially clear for the heavy casualties expected from air raids. Therefore I went into the Knaresborough Nursing Home, where the surgeon, Mr Abel, also operated. The operation went off all right but a clot from the wound moved first into the lungs, giving me pleurisy, and then into the left leg giving me thrombosis. I spent about six weeks in hospital. Before this I had never really known what pain was.

While I was still in the nursing home I was visited by Rik Wheeler who asked me to write up the Maiden Castle flints for him for the report that he was then preparing before he went off to the war, which he did not want to miss!

By the time I came out of hospital my mother had moved to Winchester Court, a large block of flats in Church Street, Kensington. The advantage of this was that it had a lift, as I was not very good on the stairs. The Fire Brigade had been very good to me and left me on their payroll for as long as possible, which was very necessary in view of the expenses I had incurred. They asked me to rejoin when I recovered but I decided that my leg incapacitated me to such an extent that this would be impossible.

In the spring the Censorship came up with an offer and I went to work in the Prudential building off Holborn, behind what was then Gamages. I began in the Irish mail like everyone else, amid the shower of holy wafers that fell out of every envelope. Other people's letters are incredibly boring so that I was greatly relieved after a month to be transferred to the Uncommon Language Department on account of my Greek. Here we got letters from all over the world. Identifying the language in which they were written was sometimes quite a problem; usually it was fairly easy to pick up the script but sometimes it was written in another language – rather like English being written in Greek letters. Once again I came across Anna de Wolkoff; she had been engaged in subversive activities in Mosley's National Socialist Party and, as she had written about them in letters, she fell foul of the Censorship and ended up in jail.

While I was working in the Prudential building, quite a number of my associates were killed or wounded by German planes flying low and machine-gunning the buses and streets when the rush-hour crowds were on their way to work. When I heard the machine-gun fire I took refuge in Gray's Inn and fortunately missed the worst of it. As the war went on with the nightly raids one got used to the smell of fallen buildings and the crunch of glass underfoot. What I remember most was the tiredness due to continual lack of sleep. One was also always having to find new ways to get to work as the usual routes were blocked by fallen debris.

About this time I decided I had better do something extra to help and became an air-raid warden doing two nights a week in a building in Church Street nearly opposite Winchester Court. In the autumn of 1940 I was going on duty one night when the Germans dropped a small bomb between

Syria, Cyprus, England and War 1939–1947

Winchester Court and the adjoining building. I saw it falling into the alley between the two buildings but failed to hear it explode, so close was I at the time. Winchester Court was a large multi-storeyed block built not long before the war, with steel framing and reinforced concrete, whereas the structure next door was an old three- to four-storeyed house built of brick and rubble. When we got downstairs the only thing standing of this building was the front wall and door which fell out when we opened it; and the only people who survived were those who had come downstairs to the front hall. Those in the rest of the building were buried under tons of rubble. After this bomb I lost any belief in personal immunity. My mother meanwhile was working for the WVS, which meant cooking for one day a week for the fire services on the river and making and sorting clothing the rest of the week.

After a year in the Postal Censorship Department, where I was not entirely happy, I managed to get a transfer to the Ministry of Information where Joan du Plat Taylor was already installed in the Book Censorship Department. Here I found myself in the Press Censorship which was under naval direction. This meant skimming through the daily Press looking for attempts to evade the regulations. This was the training period, as the Irish mail had been for the Postal Censorship. Fortunately I did not remain there as it was a soul-destroying job. From there I went to Travellers Censorship where we dealt with journalists, VIPs and others who were travelling on government business. In addition we coped with all the regimental journals, tide tables and nautical almanacks and odd periodicals of a vaguely subversive nature. I must say life in this section was never dull and we had to work extremely hard. It meant dealing with and meeting many of the leading journalists like John Gunther, a war correspondent, Mrs Roosevelt and many of the Arabian travellers like Freya Stark, Bertram Thomas and St John Philby before he was imprisoned.

In 1943 the British Council asked that I be transferred to them as they had just lost their Middle East officer who was drowned off South Africa when his ship was torpedoed. I was there for one year but I was not happy. I soon realized that I was not a born administrator and that I was much more suited to doing research. The British Council lacked the informality of the MOI, full as the latter was of temporary civil servants and where even the ministers were not above saying 'good morning' if they met you in the passage. By the beginning of 1944 I managed to get jaundice owing to overwork and my doctor advised me to give it up and try to get back to the Ministry.

What really depressed me at the British Council was that no-one really knew anything about the Middle East; they continually sent out unsuitable people with no training and then wondered why things went wrong. While I was there, someone thought it a good idea to make a present to Ibn Saud, the King of Saudi Arabia. The present was to be an illuminated copy of a Shia manuscript of a Sufi poet – a highly unsuitable gift as Ibn Saud was a strict Sunni – but I had great difficulty in explaining this to the higher officials who knew nothing of the different Islamic sects. Mercifully I cannot remember who the chairman of the British Council was at the time; however, I do remember that while I was there he went out to the Middle East. On his return he called a staff meeting of the higher grades. He had a message for us which he had learnt as a result of his trip, it was 'The Arabs do not like the Jews'. I was shattered, having had three years of the Arab Rebellion in Palestine, to realize how little people in responsible positions in Britain knew about events so near to them.

In due course I managed to get back to the Ministry of Information where, in the Reference Division, I wrote background papers for journalists and MPs and others sent abroad on foreign missions, or just for the British press. Starting with general subjects, I soon gravitated to the Middle East and the Balkans and spent most of my time writing papers on these subjects, some of which, like the Straits Question, the on-going problem of the rights of passage through the Bosphorus, involved considerable historical research. This brought me into close communication with Chatham House and I was able to feel that my early training on International Affairs when taking my degree had not been wasted. In fact, during this time in the Ministry, I really enjoyed myself as I was playing a positive role.

At the beginning of the war Joan and I, looking for something to fill our spare time and to get some activity in the open air, had bought a boat the *Ayios Philon* named after the site we had been digging in Cyprus. It was an ex-lifeboat, about twenty-six feet long, with a forward cabin and large open cockpit. On this we spent many happy and grubby hours at the weekends, cleaning and scraping and painting in the spring and enjoying the long lazy days in the summer. 1940 was one of the hottest summers I ever remember in England. Soon petrol rationing was introduced but before this happened, we had one of those nightmare short voyages one would like to forget about. Our immediate head in the Censorship Department of the MOI was a Commander Thompson who was a regular naval officer seconded to the Ministry out of the service because of his health. We had asked him and his secretary to lunch on the boat and we were surprised to see that two of my fellow air-raid wardens has also arrived – one a large Balt weighing about sixteen stone. When all these passengers were on board we sank well below our usual water line and, as she was clinker-built, she soon started taking in water. In preparation for the Commander's visit we had the previous day painted everything – including the seats. These had not dried completely, so that when he rose from his seat at the tiller his uniform trousers presented a speckled white appearance. The pump could not cope with the extra load and soon we were bailing with all available utensils including buckets and basins; we returned to our moorings in haste.

The river was never dull. There was always something to look at and an amazing amount of salvage to be picked up from the tide. I collected a splendid mahogany plank which the caretaker at the Institute of Archaeology made into a bookcase for me. There were other excitements, too, when boats caught fire on the same moorings, or when long boats came adrift and plunged down out of control on the tide. It was splendid listening to the V.1s passing overhead when the tide was out and we were sunk in a deep trough, but not so good when we rode high on the tide and felt completely exposed.

Meanwhile the war proceeded through its dark and gloomy days and splendid and exhilarating ones. First there were the incendiary bombs to cope with. I had remained at the ARP post in Church Street although we were now living in Elvaston Place in South Kensington, which was some fifteen minutes' walk away. My mother and I had been forced to move from Winchester Court as the bomb which had flattened the building next door had shattered all the mains to the flats which took a considerable time to repair.

The night the bombers raided London extensively with the idea of burning it down, I was on duty as usual. An incident was reported in a house off Church Street and, clasping a stirrup pump, Mary Peters, a fellow air-raid warden, and I set off. We found the place in confusion. It was a house, like so many in the area, in which rooms were let. Most of the tenants were in the front hall but someone was screaming from an upper floor and no-one had dared to go and see what was happening. An incendiary bomb had come through the roof and fallen on the bed of a man who was asleep. It broke his leg and set fire to the room. He had managed to jump out of bed and got as far as the first landing but there he had stuck and was lying across the stairs yelling blue murder. We only stopped long enough to see that he was not dangerously hurt and then pressed on to the bedroom which was by this time well alight. The smoke was so thick that we had to crawl on our hands and knees to get in. We then had to organize a bucket chain from down below to get sufficient water up to the fire; we managed to put it out though by now it had caught the curtains as well as the bed. Having sent for an ambulance and had the man removed to hospital, we were able to declare the incident closed. This kind of thing was typical of a night's work, after which one had to be at one's desk at 9.30 the next day.

We were now approaching the end of the war, with the Germans trying everything they could think of – first the V.1s and then the V.2s. One never knew where the latter were going to fall so one could do nothing about it. I hated the buzz bombs (V.1s) with their long slow approach, the engines cutting out and the silence, waiting for it to fall. The worst time I had in the Ministry was when one of these circled round the Senate House tower (where we were based) for some time before going off to explode elsewhere. One afternoon one of the V.1s exploded on Joan's flat at the corner of Queen's Gate and Cromwell Road. She went straight home to see what had happened and I followed her as soon as possible. All the doors and windows had been

The Road to El-Aguzein

blown out. We were busy moving the most valuable contents round to my flat when another bomb fell in almost the same place some two hours later. Rachel Wingate (the sister of Orde Wingate and a fellow air-raid warden) and I were halfway between the two places when the second fell. We took refuge in a porch of one of the houses and most of it fell on us, injuring Rachel's back. When we arrived back at Joan's flat we found that the remaining ceilings had been blown in and that she had quite a severe cut on her head, so that I had to take her to my flat and put her to bed. Just before this we had had to send to hospital their old maid who had been sitting in the kitchen when the original bomb fell, and who died more as a result of shock than of the injuries she received. Fortunately, Joan's mother had been out at the time of the incident.

I remained at the Ministry after the end of the war, even when it had moved from its original setting in the Senate House of the University of London to Montague Mansions behind Baker Street, and had changed its name from the Ministry of Information to the Central Office of Information. But it was no longer the same place; the wartime members were going back to their old jobs and we were surrounded by the incoming flood of demobilised soldiers. It also became much more like the rest of the Civil Service with a consequent tightening up of the regulations.

Then, in 1946, I was approached by Olga Tufnell, with whom I had worked in Palestine at Tell el-Duweir, to assist her with the publication of the Iron Age volume of Tell el-Duweir. Sir Henry Wellcome had since died but his Trustees were anxious that his work should be properly rounded off and the results published. At the same time I was approached by Professor Garstang to go back and dig with him at Mersin. This I had regretfully to decline as my mother was in no state to be left for any length of time because she was having more and more frequent heart attacks. In fact she died the following June of angina. In February 1948 I went out to Australia to try and settle up my affairs. But that is another story.

Chapter Ten
Round the World, Australia, Turkey 1948–1957

It seemed providential when my cousin, Arthur Price, told me he could arrange a round the world trip on a cargo boat calling at Australia and staying there about nine weeks, for the cut rate of £90. If I had known quite what it would involve I might not have been so eager to go. Arthur, who was a distant connection, had been married to Ursula, daughter of my cousin Fanny Bere. She had died some years before and Arthur, who had been severely wounded in the head in the First World War, had now been advised by his doctor to take a voyage round the world because he had not been at all well. Though I had known Arthur all my life I had never known him well, and only thought he wanted the sort of complete rest afforded by a long sea voyage. I did not know that the shrapnel in his head had progressively pressed on his brain and that a long sea voyage without a doctor on board was not the correct treatment. However, he obviously had some doubts about his health as he insisted on paying the passage of an Australian nursing sister to look after him, but she was far too young for this kind of thing and, again, did not know what she was in for.

Our ship, the *City of Capetown*, one of the Ellerman Line, was of about 10 000 tons burden and carried an Indian crew except for the officers. We sailed from Tilbury in the middle of February and, as soon as we cleared the Channel, fell in with the usual winter Atlantic gales. The nurse was seasick and within twenty-four hours Arthur had come to me to say that the crew were sawing the boat in half and we should all be drowned. The cold and the isolation of the *City of Capetown*, with accommodation for only four passengers, had been too much for him, and he really went quite mad. There followed a difficult crossing of twelve days instead of six to seven due to the weather. I also developed an abscess on a tooth, which the cold did not help. I had been going to stay with friends in Princeton and Harvard as, being a cargo boat, the ship stayed ten to twelve days at Brooklyn and nearly a week at Newport News, Virginia. However, as a result of this fracas I had to lug the nurse with me because Arthur blamed her as well as the crew and she could not be left alone. It was while we were in Virginia that I finished the last chapter of my first book *Britain and the Arab States*, and sent it back to Luzac for publication, and also an article on Palestinian temples for the journal *Iraq*. Working on these on board was very difficult because Arthur would hiss in my ear, at frequent intervals, 'It won't be long before the boat goes down.'

After nearly a month we sailed for Curaçao in the West Indies, a Dutch possession and at that time a miniature Holland. I had expected my first West Indian island to be lush and green but Curaçao was anything but that; in fact it resembled a Mediterranean island more than anything else and was dominated on the side that I saw by the huge oil tanks, at which we refuelled. I found the Panama Canal fascinating with its many locks and quite different from the Suez Canal, the only canal that I had previously seen. As the weather improved so Arthur seemed to get a little better, and he did not cause too much trouble during the long haul across the Pacific. This took twenty-one days from Panama to Brisbane through the trade winds. We saw land only twice – the Galapagos and Marquesas – for the rest it was water spouts and flying fish and the green blue of the Pacific, unlike any other ocean in the world, I would not have minded if it had gone on forever. The Captain was an old shellback who had served his apprenticeship under sail and who still delighted to talk of the relative merits of the *Cutty Sark*, the *Thermopylae*, *Ariel* or *Sir Lancelot*, or the Lock Line clippers trading to Australia.

We arrived at Brisbane on Anzac Day over two months out from Tilbury. I stayed on board to Sydney, where we arrived in dense fog, and then travelled on to Melbourne after a brief visit to the Nicholson Museum. I stayed with my mother's youngest sister, my aunt Dorothy Byron-Moore in Punt Road, and was maddened by my cousins' habit of introducing me as their 'English cousin'. I sorted out endless papers and books belonging to my mother, disposed of a good deal of stuff, and stayed with my other aunt, Marjory Palmer, at Dalvui near Terang in the Western District. I visited Eynesbury, where my mother had been born on the Weribee, and went back to my old home, The Uplands, at Vermont, still then in the hands of Dr Stevens to whom we had sold it twenty years before. It had scarcely changed and even some bits of our old furniture which we had sold them were still in the same places. It has since been destroyed by fire, and the whole area is now built over. I stayed nine weeks in Australia, I would have liked to stay six months, but I knew even after this short time that I could no longer go back there to live; I had been too long away and my interests were not those of my friends and relations. In truth, I was an expatriate.

In view of Arthur's uncertain health (poor Arthur, he died within three months of returning to England) I decided to return on another ship – the *City of Bristol*. She was slightly larger and newer and lacked the charm of the *City of Capetown*. Regrettably she also carried more passengers. It was August 1948 when I finally arrived back in London.

It was still the days of rationing and tight travel allowances. I had, of course, spent my £25 allowance so that when Margaret Munn-Rankin (whom I had met in the Ministry of Information) and I decided to go to stay with my cousin Dora at La Tourbie just above Monte Carlo, we had to do it on her £25. It was difficult for two people to live in Monte Carlo for even then £25 was a modest sum for such a place – although it helped that we were not paying for board and lodging. We went to the beach previously frequented by Sir Winston Churchill, but even a piece of bread and ham for lunch was expensive and, if Cousin Fanny Bere had not been staying in one of the better hotels and fed us from time to time, I do not know how we would have managed. We then went back to Paris for a few days and so back to London.

After the war it had been very difficult to get going again in Middle Eastern archaeology, there being no funds readily available. Margaret was trying to get her Diploma in Mesopotamian Archaeology and had given up her job in the Ministry six months earlier to enable her to do more intensive study. After my return from Australia I was no longer employed, except for a few months, by the Wellcome Trustees. But in 1949 things improved, John Waechter became the Student of the Institute of Anatolian Studies situated in Ankara and, with Professor Garstang's blessing, it was decided that Joan du Plat Taylor and I should go out and reinvestigate the lower levels of Sakce Gözü in southern Turkey. This was not quite what John wanted as he was more interested in earlier material, but he managed to examine several cave sites in the region as well. Our idea was to combine the Turkish excavations with a preliminary survey in Cyprus carried out on behalf of Sydney University and the Ashmolean Museum. In the winter of 1949 Joan and I examined a number of sites and finally decided on Myrtou-Pigades, a site where a bronze bull had been found in a well and where there were traces of a Mycenaean site.

We crossed over to Turkey from Cyprus and went up to Gaziaintab. When we were trying to buy baskets in the bazaar in Antakya (Antioch) we were approached by an Arab called Ganem who had worked with Woolley at Atchana. He came to work with us and became our foreman and general factotum. We were lucky in that we were able to borrow Sir Leonard Woolley's equipment from Atchana; Woolley was a charming and delightful man and an excellent lecturer and raconteur. Originally he had intended to go into the church, but while at Oxford changed his mind. He was sent for by the Warden, the famous Dr Spooner, who said 'I understand you have

The Road to El-Aguzein

given up the idea of taking Holy Orders, what do you want to do?' Woolley replied, 'A schoolmaster', having tried teaching during the vacation. To this Spooner said 'I have decided Mr Woolley, you will become an archaeologist.' He went on to dig in Italy, Egypt and Nubia, but it was his excavations at Ur of the Chaldees in Mesopotamia that made his name.

There was an amusing story of how he came to dig at Atchana. He was looking for a site in what was then northern Syria and is now in Turkey. He found Atchana, ancient Alalakh capital of the region in the second millennium BC, but always a punctilious man, he approached the Oriental Institute of Chicago who had been excavating in the area, and said he was interested in it. They raised no objection to his applying for Atchana as they considered it a site of no importance! Like Garstang, he also had a flair for finding prime sites.

We went down to Atchana and took what we needed and put it on a three-ton lorry to take to Sakce Gözü. Unfortunately we could not get the lorry down to the site as the country was traversed by irrigation channels and there were no roads. Everything had to be taken on horse-back and, as the site was four or five miles from the main road and across several water channels, this took quite a time. While we were here we were visited by Professor Garstang, and Seton Lloyd. Professor Garstang had just founded the British Institute of Archaeology at Ankara.

We camped just beside the mound of Coba Hüyük. Although it was April the snow still lay thick on the Kurdish hills, the Kurt Dağ, and when it rained, which it seemed to do quite a lot, it was almost impossible to get from one tent to another, so thick and clinging was the mud. The wolves were out too, and at night we used to see their eyes in a circle beyond the lights of the camp. We found that they had a fondness for toothpaste and soap, and if these were left out overnight they were always eaten by morning. Here we were adopted by a delightful little Turkish dog called Gumuş (silver) who acted as watch dog and greatly over-ate himself on the camp scraps. We tried to get a Turkish cook from Gaziaintab but the only man we could get was a pastry cook specialising in baklava for which the town was famous, sending its pastries all over Turkey. He knew nothing of everyday cookery and broke our one and only china teapot by trying to stew tea in it on top of a primus stove causing it to explode. He left that day.

We employed Kurds on the site, but they spoke very little Turkish between them, so that sometimes it was quite difficult to get our instructions across. On this site we had a Turkish woman commissar from the Antiquities Department at Gaziaintab, called Sabahat. She had been wounded in the French attack on Aintab in 1922, after which Ataturk changed the city's name to Gaziaintab to commemorate its brave resistance to the French. (Gazi means one who fights for Islam and was one of Ataturk's titles.)

We were very interested to find under the main tell, or *hüyük* as these mounds were called in Turkey, that the earliest settlers had lived in a kind of causewayed camp rather like those of the Neolithic inhabitants of Britain, for example, Maiden Castle and Whitehawk. Having dug out the ditches the inhabitants then proceeded to live in them judging by the debris and remains of hearths that we found. We were also able to identify and name the Coba bowls that occur here at the time of the Al'Ubaid occupation in the fourth millennium BC. At the same time we sent Sinclair Hood, the fourth member of the party and the most energetic, to tramp round the neighbouring mounds with a view to collecting sherds and dating them. He was a great walker and seemed to thoroughly enjoy going off all day with his rucksack and coming back with a great collection of sherds in the evening. He later became Director of the British School at Athens. We dug for about six weeks here and it remained very cold for most of the time, so much so that sorting the pottery became a very painful process and I lost all the skin off the ends of my fingers as a result. During this season I also had a terrible time with my leg; the weather was cold and wet and standing about in the cold for long hours did it no good, in fact at one time I wondered if I should ever be able to undertake excavations again it was so bad.

At the end of the season we gave the men a feast as we always did. A sheep was killed and cooked on the spot, but we were surprised to find that the right foreleg was cut off and ceremoniously buried. We were unable to find out whether this was a Kurdish or Turkish custom. We were also intrigued to see high on the mountainside lights moving at night. For these too, we could get no satisfactory explanation. When we asked the men the only reply was that they were the people of the mountain, but as there were no villages in the area I do not know who they were, unless they were hunters.

The journey back to Cyprus on one of the coal-burning Turkish Maritime Lines coasters was not uneventful. They went all round the coast from Istanbul to Iskanderun, and have long since disappeared. The ship had been coaling in Iskanderun and the decks had been washed, a not very frequent event on Turkish ships. The deck seams had opened up with the heat of the sun and all the coal dust and seawater had run into our second-class cabins which were situated aft just below the deck. It was in fact a kind of deck house with the saloon in the centre and cabins opening off. At dinner that night we were beset with cockroaches which even arrived clinging to the soup plates, while noises at night made Joan and me turn on our torches to find the cabin full of rats. I cannot say I regret the passing of the old Turkish coasters.

From Cyprus, after some preliminary excavations at Myrtou we flew to England. In those days it was a long flight; on the way out we had stopped at Athens for the night and then flown on. The return journey was dominated, as the outward one had been, by a glass fish that had been bought by my cousin Simon Staughton in Venice and which, for some reason, he had failed to take home with him. We collected the fish on the way out in Venice and it dogged my footsteps throughout the whole trip. It was packed in a very large box which, on the return journey faced with overweight luggage, I finally unravelled to find a very small fish inside layers and layers of packing and shavings. After I got the beastly thing back to England and gave it to Simon I was not pleased to hear that it had got broken after about six months. So much for glass fish.

On our return we had the report on Sakce Gözü to prepare, which took some time as Joan was now working as the Librarian at the Institute of Archaeology.

It was then, due to the kind offices of Sydney Smith, that I was offered the post of Secretary to the British School of Archaeology in Iraq. This I refused as I had no head for figures and also remembered what Gertrude Bell had said about life in Baghdad. The post was filled by my friend Barbara Parker.

The following year, 1950, we returned to Cyprus to start digging at Myrtou-Pigades. This turned out to be a Mycenaean temple site, very close to the surface of the ground — so close in fact that the surface of the pottery was affected. The first season we lived in a village house at Myrtou and had a large number of assistants, some lecturers and many students, a good many of whom have since done well in archaeology on their own account. Margaret Munn-Rankin, who had by this time been appointed Lecturer in Mesopotamian Archaeology and the History of Western Asia at Cambridge and had already dug with Max Mallowan at Nimrud; Mrs D. Gray, a lecturer in classics at Oxford; Diana Kirkbride, later Director of the British School of Archaeology in Iraq; Neville Chittick, who was to become Director of the African School of Archaeology; and Lord William Taylour, who was to make his name in Mycenaean archaeology with the British School in Athens, and Hector Catling, now Director of the School.

In 1951 I was appointed as Annual Student for the British Institute of Archaeology in Ankara. This entailed a survey of the pre-Classical sites in Cilicia, undertaken in the summer of that year. This was partly undertaken at the instigation of Professor Sydney Smith who was a museum man rather than a field archaeologist, and wished us to find one of the staging posts used by the Assyrian traders between Assyria and Kültepe in Turkey. He was using us in the same way that he had previously used Max Mallowan in his in his survey of the Ḫabur Valley.

I am unable to decide whether Cilicia is more unpleasant in the summer or in the winter: in the winter it is cold, wet and travel is difficult, in the summer it is hot, dusty, has constant thunderstorms and a high insect population, due to the cotton fields. We were camped at Sirkeli, where there was a spring of constant fresh water, near the railway line and just below the ancient hüyük in which I had dug a sounding on behalf of Professor Garstang fifteen years before. I still felt it was an important site, probably a provincial capital of Kizzawatna, a state in Anatolia in Hittite times.

Round the World, Australia, Turkey 1948–1957

While in Cilicia we were based at the Park Oteli in Adana. I have not the same happy memories of this place as the Goughs, whose paths we were continually crossing this season, and who mention it in their book *The Plain and the Rough Places*. They were surveying Anavaza and living for most of the time in a tent at the foot of the huge razor-backed hill rising from the plain, in what anyone else would have regarded as swamp. The Park Oteli had originally belonged to the French. It was E-shaped and situated on the original mound of the ancient site of Adana. It was full of doves and cats, the food was as bad as elsewhere in Turkey and the lavatories quite unspeakable. All Turkish hotel rooms seem to have a glass fan-light above the doors and as the unshaded lights in the corridors are never turned out at night it is difficult to get a good night's rest. The only good thing about the Park Oteli was that it had several double rooms in addition to the dormitories. By now I was quite used to travelling in Turkey, always carrying a small basin to wash in in the room, my own towel and tooth mug – otherwise there was only the communal basin on the landing.

John Waechter and I had gone ahead to collect the car and drive it over from Gaziaintab, where it had been since we had been at Sakce Gözü. There we were joined first by Joan and then Margaret and finally by James Mellaart, then just finishing his studies at London University. Our camp at Sirkeli was near the road, and anyway everyone always stopped at the spring for water. We lost many days this season waiting in Adana for permits to carry out our survey, sitting in the Museum with Naci Bey, the Director, and often we were confined to camp because of the constant storms.

John had to leave early, and after he had gone we suffered from thieves. In addition to ourselves we had Ganem, whom we had had at Sakce Gözü, and his wife Gevhah. They looked after the camp while we were out surveying. However, it was at night that we had most trouble. I was awakened one night in the tent to see a dark form removing my towel from the line on which it was hung over the bed. Without pausing to unwind the mosquito net in which I was enshrouded I leapt straight up with a furious yell, and he took to his heels. However, the thieves came back and each night used to sit smoking on the bank above us and waiting for us to go to sleep, after which they would descend and take anything that was lying about. After a few nights of this we started to feel the lack of sleep, even though remaining on guard in shifts, so we went to Ceyhan where the local *kaymakan*, the governor of a district of *kasa*, was based. He had gone to ground, so to speak, for the summer so that we had to communicate with him by notes put in a basket and pulled up to his bedroom window, where he was ensconced in his pyjamas. He saw our problem and supplied a posse of gendarmes who ousted the thieves from the bank above the camp where they then settled themselves. Here, again, the gendarmes kept themselves awake by smoking and coughing, and every now and then to show that they were awake, letting off a shot from their rifles. Our night's rest as a result was even more disturbed than before. So I went back to the kaymakan and begged him to take them away. They were replaced by the village watchman or *bekci*. One night while this worthy from the next village, which was by the way Bulgarian, was taking tea (or was it coffee?) with Ganem in his tent, the thieves decided to make a foray. They tried to break into the main tent where we had put James Mellaart, as the only male of the party, except Ganem, to guard our equipment. This tent was opposite the one I was sharing with Margaret, and I heard them when they fell over the guy ropes or tried to pull up the pegs holding down the tent skirt. Anyway, we all gave chase, or at least most of us did, the guard let off his blunderbuss with a great deal of noise and the thieves, like a herd of cattle, rushed off up the valley. The only person who never appeared was James, and when we came back and called to him he replied happily from within the tent, presumably still in bed, 'I am all right', which did not go down too well with the rest of us.

We also suffered badly from snakes and spiders, a kind of long-legged variety which hung on the tent walls looking horrible, although probably quite harmless. Margaret and I had what we thought were mice under the ground sheet spread on the floor of the tent. What was our disgust to find one day when Ganem was doing one of his spring cleans that we had been harbouring a particularly vicious-looking snake for at least a week.

I will always associate that summer in Cilicia with melons. Almost everyone, it seemed, who passed by left us huge water melons. They mounded up round us, but even in the heat we never had the capacity of the average Turk for consuming them.

The old Chrysler that we had was always breaking down, breaking its springs on the rough tracks, getting punctures or having some mechanical trouble, and because the petrol in Turkey was not clean, we used to strain it through a handkerchief as we poured it into the tank – collecting all kinds of interesting specimens in the process. Once we were arrested while taking a ferry across the Ceyhan. When the ferryman got us in mid-stream he decided that we were Russian spies come to destroy Adana. 'Bomba! Bomba, bombardiman Adana', he shouted. 'Casusluklar! birinci gizlice gozetlemek', 'Bombs, bombs to bombard Adana, spies to spy out the ground'. In vain we assured him we were not Russian but British. It was no good and he escorted us protesting to the next village where we had to show our permits to the headman before he would release us.

There were many mounds – they were everywhere but always difficult to approach. There was always an irrigation ditch or an impassable swamp or a river lying between us and the object of our desire. We climbed up them, but not always going the same way, so that we would avoid Agatha Christie's (later Lady Mallowan's) awful fate when she found she could not walk straight after going round mounds in Syria always in the same direction for some time. We collected sherds in bags, now kept in the Adana Museum, we photographed, we measured, we drew, we enquired after inscriptions and stones with drawings on them. We visited village headmen, we drank endless cups of sweet Turkish coffee and bottles and bottles of Turkish *gazoz*, a colourless sweet fizzy lemonade which failed to quench our thirst.

Finally the survey was over and Joan and James were going off to Cyprus to start the second season of the dig at Myrtou. Margaret and I were going to join them, but first we planned to spend a little time in Syria examining some material in the museums. Joan and James crossed to Cyprus on a Norwegian ship and Ganem, who helped to load the camping and surveying equipment, was horrified at the sight of the Norwegians sunbathing on the deck. He came back and assured me that they must all be very wicked people, and nothing we could say could convince him otherwise.

Before they left we had gone to Ganem's village near the mouth of the Orontes. Ganem and his wife were Alawis and so were probably descendants of the original inhabitants of the Jebel Ansariya north of the Lebanon who were bartered without their consent to Turkey at the time the Hatay was given over to that country by the French in the 1930s. Alawis are not Muslims but have a hidden religion controlled by their elders who wear white robes and meet in secret at night on the Ansariya mountain. They are mountaineers – fine looking people, proud and independent, whose ill luck it has been to settle on the border between two different cultures. They are certainly more Arab than Turk, and are not happy in their present position. We had a very interesting time when we were there sleeping on the floor of Ganem's house. It was some special festival, at the full moon, and all the men and women went down to the sea-shore and danced, separately of course, near the tomb of Sheikh Adi, a holy man.

After the others had left Margaret and I went first to Iskanderun where I had to pick up my new passport, having applied for a new one in Ankara, as these valuable documents tended to fill up rather rapidly in the Middle East, with the numerous stamps and visas required. The consul was on leave and only a local vice-consul was in charge and I found that my new passport did not include the British Empire, although I was going on to Cyprus, then a Crown Colony, and that I had been condemned to wander rather like the Flying Dutchman, forever round and round the Middle East. The vice-consul refused to stamp the passport valid for the British Empire – he probably had no power to do so anyway – and said I could have it fixed in Aleppo where there was at that time a consul-general. So we took a bus and went to Antakya (Antioch) where we stayed in what had been the Tourist Hotel under the French. I had stayed there before on my way to Aleppo with the Garstangs in 1936, but it bore little relation to the elegant hotel I remembered. Naked light bulbs dangled from torn sockets, the curtains hung askew from the valences, and the paint was peeling off the walls. For some reason the hotel was full and we had to spend the night in what had been a sitting-room, on extremely hard ex-French Empire-type sofas. The drains did not work and generations of Turks had used the basins as ashtrays. We tried to get some money from one of the few provincial Ottoman banks authorised to cash travellers' cheques in Turkey. But, though our cheques had been issued by the Ottoman Bank in London through Cooks and were stamped with the Ottoman Bank stamp, they were very reluctant to give us anything as, shortly before, a Cooks cheque had bounced on them. Finally we persuaded the manager to relent, and to seal the bargain he ordered a particularly repellent brand of green ice cream from a street vendor. Though I eat most things in the Middle East I have learnt by long experience that ice cream is better left alone. However, if we had refused he would have been mortally offended so, knowing the consequences, we ate it and got the money. Almost before we got back to the hotel we were starting to feel ill. This was awful for the chef who had been there since the days of the French Mandate and who was dying to try out some of his little-used dishes on us; but we were beyond caring and went to bed with a pot of yoghourt, and never went anywhere near the dining-room. Next day, still feeling dreadful, we took the bus to the frontier and at the Post of the Four Winds, that barren strip where Syria begins amid the limestone hills, got a taxi to Aleppo. I just managed to stagger as far as the British Consulate, where for once I met an understanding official, and then to the Claridge Palace Hotel where I took to my bed, not with gippy tummy but with an unidentified fever which lasted for the next few weeks. Perhaps the Claridge Palace Hotel in Aleppo is not the best place to have a severe fever in, but I know of few hotels that would not have turned a traveller away suffering as I was. We called in Dr Altounian who was still running his hospital there, but he could not identify the fever except to say it was not malaria, and he lost the specimens he took for identification. It may have been a form of relapsing fever, or even dengue fever: all I know is that it lasted for several weeks, my temperature went up to 105°, and I did not really care what happened to me. Poor Margaret sat in the window drawing the passers-by, with little chance to continue her studies.

After about a month I was able to move and my passport had been to Cairo and come back complete with the requisite 'Laissez-passer'. Margaret took me to Beirut where I boarded a ship for Cyprus, and as it was then late in the season she returned by bus to Turkey, and I agreed to meet her in Istanbul for the Orientalists' Conference that was to take place there in the autumn. I had by now missed most of the Myrtou season and, even when I got to Cyprus, was not in a very good state. So after about a fortnight I flew off to Istanbul for the conference.

The Turks were remarkably good hosts. They put us up in a girls' school and the conference was held in Istanbul University. It was like most of these conferences, being more important for the people you met than for the papers read. Claude Schaeffer who was always in a hurry was there with three briefcases, each representing a different excavation – Enkomi, Ugarit and

Round the World, Australia, Turkey 1948–1957

Marash. We had employed some of his workmen at Myrtou and when we asked them what Schaeffer said to them they replied that all he ever said was, 'Dig faster, faster'.

After the conference was over we went on several excursions from Ankara. Here again the Turks had made every effort to arrange matters; Boğazköy and Alaca were difficult of access in those days, and they put us up in local schools, at which some of the delegates complained bitterly. But when I thought of the local conditions they would have been subjected to if they had not been under the auspices of the Turkish Government, I had little sympathy with them. I stayed on in Ankara as I had to put in a certain amount of time in Turkey due to my scholarship with the Institute. I stayed till the end of November when winter had really set in on the Anatolian plateau. During this time I prepared the report on the Cilician Survey for publication in the *Journal for Anatolian Studies*.

After returning to London, I took a job for six months with the Institute of Archaeology reorganizing and re-labelling their slide collection. This took me through the summer of 1952, which meant that I did not go abroad for any length of time. By this time I was finding it difficult to keep on the flat at Elvaston Place without a more regular job, and was forced to take in French girls who were over here studying English. I got them from one of the technical colleges where they were studying, as I knew one of the staff teaching English. They were nearly all delightful.

By the following year (1953) Joan, Margaret and I had again collected sufficient money – I am not sure quite how – to get back to Turkey and do a small excavation. We also bought a second-hand Land-Rover for £350. This meant to a large extent the end of our troubles with unreliable cars not intended for the kind of rough work to which they were submitted. GAP 422 was a splendid vehicle, it could do everything but talk. Even so, we had our difficulties. The next time we went out to Turkey we drove down through Italy and shipped it from Naples by Turkish Maritime Lines, this time by their flagship the ss *Ankara*. As the Turks did not allow cars to go as deck cargo, which was the usual method of procedure on other lines, we had to get it into the hold via one of the loading bays. As the Land-Rover was higher than the opening in the ship's side she was suspended on planks over Naples harbour while six large Italian stevedores pulled and pushed, trying to get the canvas roof down low enough to get through. It was this difficult experience, with Joan at the wheel and only two planks between the car and the sea, that made us decide to avoid Naples in future as a port of departure. This was before the ss *Ankara* had been taken over by Swans for their Hellenic cruises, and it was both dirty and inefficient. All bills were different each day, and the stewards were so busy smuggling goods from Europe into Turkey, where there were always chronic shortages, that they had little time or inclination to attend to the wants of the passengers. When we crossed on the Bosphorus ferry to Asia we were accompanied by a dancing bear, one of

The Road to El-Aguzein

those itinerant entertainers whom one meets throughout Turkey, scraping a meagre living from the poor villagers.

During the Sakce Gözü season Sinclair Hood had collected some very interesting early sherds which he had told us came from a mound called Daghdaghli near the Gaziaintab road. On the basis of this material we applied for a permit to make a sounding in Daghdaghli. First we made a survey of sites near the Euphrates in the Gaziaintab Vilayet, and were surprised to find how many 'Ubaid sites there were – they must have been staging posts on the way to the copper mines in Anatolia. On this trip up the Euphrates we were extremely glad of the staying power of our Land-Rover which made its way up nearly impossible tracks and at one time over a large field full of basalt boulders which was so rough that only by using the hand throttle could we get through. The track was so bad by the river that Sabahat, our Turkish commissar, got out and walked. Ganem and Gevhah would have done so too had they not been so anxious to show Sabahat, who was a Turk, how much braver they were than she was.

Daghdaghli was not near anywhere in particular, and we had to get all our supplies from Gaziaintab. We were again fortunate in having Sabahat as our commissar, and Ganem and Gevhah to help us. Everything was fine except the site. When we arrived there was the mound but not a sherd of really early pottery, indeed all the top material appeared to be Islamic and then, nearby on a small neighbouring mound hardly visible in the corn, we found the early site – but it was called Erminoğlu and we had no permit to touch it. So we dug various trenches in Daghdaghli with differing results. We could not date the earlier material until fortunately we found a votive bowl with a bevelled rim and knew where we were in the fourth millennium BC.

We were camped on the edge of the mound under a tree and one night Margaret, who was sleeping outside the tent, observed a large land tortoise descending the hill after we had gone to bed. Now tortoises like to go on a certain line and this one found itself under my safari bed, which was fine till it met me. Then it pushed till I got up to see what it was. It was a case of one immovable object meeting another, and those large Turkish land tortoises cannot be deflected from their course. Another night I was also peacefully asleep in my bed when I felt a violent bump underneath, this was a mole who, coming down the mound, had chosen to surface under me. I seemed to be in the track of all the local animals on that site. Margaret, who could see all this from outside, though it a good deal funnier than I did at the time.

We were working here after the harvest when the villagers pay off all their debts for the year. Those who were owed anything came with their sacks and donkeys to the harvest fields and it was pathetic to see how little the family was often left with for the coming year when their debts were paid. This meant that almost immediately they had to begin borrowing again on next year's crop. We saw a lot of gipsies here too. They are in immense demand in Turkey as nearly all music is provided by them, and they were required to play at village weddings and festivals. They, too, were paid in kind at the end of the year, usually in grain. They came and played for us when we finished digging, I can still see the vivid yellow of the lutenist's shirt, and hear the deep notes of the zorna player. We meant to come back and dig properly at Erminoğlu but time overlook us and we never did.

In fact, delightful though it was excavating these smaller prehistoric sites, we realized that if we wanted to find anything really important we must tackle one of the larger town sites with all the financial and organizational problems that this involved. So, when we finished at Daghdaghli we reluctantly left Ganem and Gevhah behind and headed for Syria. We were exploring for sites north-west of Aleppo when we met a venerable *haj* (pilgrim) on the side of the road who took us to his village, Tell Rifa'at, some eighteen kilometres north-west of Aleppo. This was an historic site, the remains of the Aramaean city of Arpad, well known from the Assyrian records. It was a formidable mound over 80 feet in height, but was only the citadel set in the middle of a considerable town site, now largely covered by the modern village which had grown up in this century as a result of Bedu settling here due to drought years in the desert. We decided to excavate at Tell Rifa'at if possible but were faced, as usual, with the problems of raising money. Then I had an offer from Sydney University to become a lecturer in Archaeology under Jim Stewart who had been appointed Professor of their Department of Archaeology. I had known him in Cyprus before the war and although I was very tempted by the offer, I was unwilling to sever my connections with the Middle East, especially as we were hoping to start at Tell Rifa'at.

I also decided that if I was going to get anywhere in archaeology I must have a higher degree; Professor Sydney Smith, to whom I owe more than I can ever repay, had been trying to persuade me to do this for some time. However, he would not let me do the subject in which I was really interested, which was the development of Neolithic cultures in the Middle East. Instead he offered me a choice of an examination of Syrian sites in either the second or first millennium. I chose the earlier of the two, but though I knew the archaeological material I did not know the language and this proved a great handicap. Matters were not helped by the fact that the French had recorded their material so badly at Byblos, and to a certain extent at Ugarit, that it was impossible to make a proper appraisal of it. I was not the only archaeologist to break my head on this stuff. Bob Braidwood from the Oriental Institute, Chicago tried to sort out some of the Byblos levels also without too much success. The whole thing was a lesson to me never to ask someone to do something in which they are not intrinsically interested, because one will never get the same results as if they are really keen on a subject.

So for the next few years I settled down at the Institute of Archaeology and worked over the Syrian material and learnt a great deal. Max Mallowan who supervised my Ph.D. thesis was then Professor of Western Asiatic Archaeology at the Institute of Archaeology. Born in London of an Austrian father and a Parisian mother, he was short and chubby with a small moustache. I often thought that his wife, Agatha Christie, based her character Hercule Poirot upon him. He enjoyed good food and wine, and it was a great sorrow to him that in spite of all his efforts Agatha never enjoyed alcohol. Nevertheless she was a good trencherwoman and took to her husband's life with zest. Many of her books were written on his digs, including *Death on the Nile* and *Murder in Mesopotamia*. Her most amusing book, *Come Tell Me How You Live*, describes her experiences the first time she joined Max on an archaeological survey. She had a curious habit for such a large woman of preferring to sit on the floor rather than on a chair, which was somewhat disconcerting, especially as my flat in Elvaston Place was very draughty.

While I was working on the Syrian material I was sent for one day by Professor Gordon Childe, then Director of the Institute of Archaeology, which was still at its old site in the middle of Regent's Park. Childe was an Australian, born in Sydney, with a brilliant intellect but no aptitude for field work. His writings did a great deal to popularize archaeology, two of his best known works being, *The Dawn of European Civilization*, and *The Ancient Near East*. He was a poor lecturer and his extraordinary appearance masked an extremely kind heart and a very shy nature. To my surprise he said, 'I wish you to take up teaching the Extra Mural Diploma in Archaeology. Teaching and lecturing to adult students in the evenings.' I protested that I had never done this and had only spoken a few times in public when giving a lecture on one of the sites we had been excavating. However, he overruled my objections and I found myself going to Barnet to give a course on Egyptology, which at that time I was ill-fitted to give. I also embarked at the City Literary Institute on a course on 'Travellers in the Middle East', also at Childe's suggestion. But my big break came when Dr Margaret Murray sent for me to say that, as she was now well into her nineties, she had decided to give up lecturing and that as one of her old students and an archaeologist I was to take over her class in Egyptology at the City Literary Institute.

I cannot say how grateful I was to Mr White, then principal of the City Literary Institute, for his help and guidance, and encouragement to an inexperienced lecturer. Without his aid I might never have persisted, and with his help and at his insistence the Egyptology course I took over from Margaret Murray became upgraded to a University Tutorial Course, which it has remained for the last thirty years. I can truly say that my students have given me an immense amount of pleasure, and there is something infinitely rewarding in teaching people who wish to learn because they feel that they have somehow when younger missed out on educational opportunities which might have been theirs. The Diploma has brought satisfaction to so many since it was started in the 1950s. I began teaching the first year, but soon moved to the second, and then to the fourth, either Western Asia or Egypt.

In the early 1950s I did a great deal of work for the *Encyclopedia Britannica* which was then situated near Victoria Station. I wrote articles on Egypt, Jordan, Turkey, Syria and Palestine. In addition I acted as archaeological adviser for readers' queries. This entailed spending a lot of time in the Reading Room at the British Museum.

In 1956 Margaret, Joan and I managed to get back to Syria with the necessary concession to dig at Tell Rifa'at. And then, in 1957, I got my Ph.D.

Chapter Eleven
Syria, Egypt, Syria, 1956–1964

As usual there was great difficulty obtaining enough money to excavate at Tell Rifa'at; eventually we managed to get a grant from the American Wenner-Gren Foundation of $500. It does not sound very much but, combined with what else we had scraped together, we managed to get an expedition into the field in the spring of 1956. This consisted of Joan du Plat Taylor, Margaret Munn-Rankin, David Stronach, who had been a student of Margaret's at Cambridge and later became the Director of the British Institute of Persian Studies at Tehran and is now a professor in the USA; Carey Miller, who had been one of my students, as draughtswoman – she later joined the British Museum and became a senior illustrator; and Tony Peters as architect. After this excavation I often used my extra-mural students as supervisors at both Tell Rifa'at and Tell el-Fara'in.

By this time the Land-Rover was showing signs of wear and we sold it and bought a new one in Cambridge. This was a mistake as it was not properly serviced and tuned before we left, and it blew a gasket in France, not far from Dijon. Joan had to go back to Paris to collect another set of gaskets as there was no Land-Rover agent nearer than that. This delayed us by several days, so that when the spares were finally fitted we had to drive night and day to embark at Genoa. We had decided to go from there after our earlier experiences in Naples. As a result we did not finally arrive in Genoa until about 2.30 a.m. on the day that we were to sail, and rose rather jaded in the morning. When we got down to the docks, which are very considerable, the Land-Rover and I got separated from the others and, going all round the docks, I had to find my own way to the ship, one of the Adriatic Line. I did not know where the ship was, the bus bearing the others kept going in front of me, but I was constantly cut off by trains shunting, or heavy lorries blocking the way. This journey through Genoa docks bore all the elements of a nightmare – except that it was daytime and all too real. By the time the Land-Rover was in the slings on its way on board I was exhausted.

We had an uneventful voyage out, landing at Beirut and crossing the Lebanon to Damascus and then Aleppo. Here we met for the first time M. Soubi Souaf who was an assistant in the Aleppo Museum and who was to become both our mentor and our friend. He spoke French, having been educated partly at the Sorbonne and having previously worked with French expeditions; he was devoted to his subject. At the beginning of the season he came to me and said that he understood that the British got on very well with the Arabs and wondered why. I replied I hoped it was so but could give no reason. At the end of the season he came to me and said 'You wish to know why you get on with the Arabs? It is because you can make them laugh!'

We excavated for about six weeks that first season at Tell Rifa'at. It was very beautiful in the spring in Syria. The flowers were all out and the air was fresh and clean. We dug a trench down the outside of the large mound, finding the traces of the huge citadel wall which had kept out the Assyrians for so long in the eighth century BC. Margaret dug a trench down through the early layers coming at last to the Chalcolithic levels of the Tell Halaf period but as we were digging on the opposite side to the spring the mound may well have gone down to an earlier level on that side.

Tell Rifa'at was a large village, so large that it had been settled by different tribal groups, each of whom kept their own entity under a separate *mukhtar*, or head man, so that the village was divided into three almost equal parts. We tried to employ men from each, so as to cause no ill feeling, and quite a lot of our time was spent visiting the mukhtars, the station master who was an ardent Muslim Brother, the schoolmaster, and similar personages. The village houses were built largely of mud brick and many had those domed beehive roofs seen in so many pictures of villages in northern Syria. With its perpetual spring and rich fertile soil it grew roses for the manufacture of rose-petal jam in Aleppo; it was the centre of the local melon trade, and the gardens grew excellent lettuces, radishes, beans and apricots. All the fruit and vegetables were eaten by the local inhabitants a little before they were quite ripe, with the result that they all suffered from terrible sores on their mouths from eating unripe fruit. Otherwise the men were handsome and the girls were pretty. They had a tendency to dress in orange colours, with blues, purples and mauves, giving them a slightly mediaeval appearance. When we left the men came and gave an elaborate sword dance in the courtyard of the house we had rented and we were more than sorry to leave them.

Soubi was a great one for soirées, as he called them. On our part this meant an uneasy evening seated usually on hard chairs, or mud-brick benches, drinking tea or coffee and somehow eating quantities of sweet rice pudding. It did not matter much what time one went to see people, rice

The Road to El-Aguzein

always seemed to be offered; there is no doubt that a surfeit of this could be readily obtained.

In the first season we lived in a house rented from a local butcher. Our cook was a Kurd named Ahmed, obtained for us by Soubi. He was an expedition cook as he had already worked for the French at Cyrrhus, a site 23 kilometres north-west of Aleppo. He was quite a good cook when he wanted to be, but he was temperamental and drank heavily. His first language was Kurdish, his second Turkish and third Arabic, and in addition he had picked up a smattering of French. When his dishes were successful he remained in the kitchen, but when dicy or uncertain, he crouched by the dining table and sang in a sweet low voice, as if to compensate us for his mistakes. We had him for the full three seasons at Rifa'at and he waxed fat on the proceeds. He was not very religious and, as we lived in a highly religious village where there were more *hajjis* to the square metre than in most villages, he was not happy. The main cause of his misery came in the last season, when we were in a house situated uncomfortably near one of the mosques. It was the time of the celebrations of the birth of Mohommed and readings of the Quran and sermons were broadcast on loudspeakers to the faithful throughout the night. As a result we did not get very much sleep. However, as Christians, we would never have dared to complain. But Ahmed lost his sleep too and got up and disconnected the loudspeaker one day much to our relief.

We got involved in the life of the village in a remarkable way. We attended weddings, we assisted the sick and ill at our evening surgeries and in the second season we helped the village put out the Great Fire on one of the threshing floors. All the village threshing floors were on the edge of the village where the wind could blow freely upon them. Here for days on end the boys and girls, the men and old women sat on the heavy crude sledges dragged by oxen or donkeys over the heaped stalks. In the old days the sledges had flints inserted in the underside to cut up the grain and separate the grain from the chaff; but a later age had replaced the flints with iron or steel teeth, which were of devastating thoroughness, not only for the corn but for any unfortunate who fell off or was dragged under a sledge. This is what happened one day when a small boy fell off and was carried underneath. He was cut right through his back down to the bone, we could do little for him but clean him up, sticky with blood and chaff, and drive him into the nearest hospital in Aleppo, where he made a remarkable recovery. On the occasion of The Great Fire a heap of grain on one of the threshing floors caught fire. Officially no one was allowed to smoke while threshing as the fire risk was so high, but no Arab can be for long without a cigarette hanging out of his mouth, so that one unfortunate man dropped his in a pile of chaff and the whole thing went up like tinder. The holy men of the village did little to help. They regarded it as the will of God and, linking hands, went chanting round saying how wicked the village was and how they had brought it upon themselves. It was very serious as, in many cases, this grain was all that stood between a family and starvation for the following year. We were able to isolate some of the burning heaps by moving others, which the villagers were unable to do as they did not trust one another and, as a result of this and using the Land-Rover, we gained a lot of goodwill in the village.

This was in 1956 when Egypt and Syria were undergoing a kind of unwilling union and, as a result – or as they thought – Syria had been afflicted by God with a series of terrible droughts. The Bedu were forced to sell their animals and settle down penniless on the edge of the cultivation in exactly the same way as Tell Rifa'at had first been settled in the last century. One of the people in the village had been sous-officier in the French army and had retired back to his village after serving for over forty years. Another, now a poor man, had bankrupted himself in 1919 by feeding the whole of the French army for three days, the minimum required by Arab hospitality, when they were taking over Syria after ejecting King Feisal, who then went to Iraq.

At the end of the first season in 1958 we dumped our material in the British Consulate, but this caused difficulties later as, when I wished to return in 1960, Britain no longer had any relations with Syria which was coming under Egyptian control. This meant that before we could get our permits, or even a visa to enter the country, I had to go out to Turkey in 1959 with a friend, Elsa Coult, once a student of mine, to obtain a visa there and cross the border to Aleppo. Fortunately all our old friends were still in their former positions, including Dr Abdul Hak, the Director of Antiquities, to whom we owed many thanks. When I was in Aleppo this time an extraordinary thing happened to me. I was visiting the Madrassah Turuntaiyah in the Ali Bey quarter and was asked by the Muallim in charge if I would like to join the students and attend a course on Muslim theology there. To suggest this to a woman and a foreigner was quite remarkable, but it was one of those cases of sympathetic understanding which one gets in Arabic countries and nowhere else. Unfortunately I could not do this, but I have often regretted not having been able to take this unique opportunity, and think what a wonderful time I could have had sitting in the peace of the madrassah which had been a mosque and a teaching school for centuries. If one had only had the time to do this.

This journey to get permits and visas embroiled me in what I regard as one of the worst journeys that I have ever made. We were staying at the British Institute of Archaeology in Ankara having come out from England via Greece and Crete, before going on to Syria for our papers. We accomplished the outward journey with no trouble, but not so the return. Our troubles began almost as soon as we had crossed the Turkish frontier. We had taken a taxi from the frontier post to Antakya where we had to get the bus – but the taxi driver had to get shaved, so stopped on the way for several hours by a lake while he persuaded someone to do this for him. This

The Road to El-Aguzein

meant that we missed our connection to Adana and had to take a later bus, so that we arrived in Adana after the evening meal was over. Turks usually eat early and food is seldom obtainable on the spot in country hotels, we were too late that night for any and, as all the shops were shut, we went hungry to bed. Next day we had to catch the bus over the Taurus that was supposed to leave at 5.30 a.m. This was too early for breakfast but we obtained the usual glass of sweetened milkless tea from a man with a tray near the bus station. The bus failed to leave on time as the driver was suffering from a hangover, but we finally got off about one hour late, though still too early for most of the shops to be open. We had a breakdown on the way to Kayseri so that, beyond buying some apples en route while waiting for a tyre to be changed, we did not get any food that day either. We got in to Kayseri too late again for the evening meal.

Next day we managed a breakfast of cheese, tea and a piece of sesame seed bread. We also tried, without success, to change some money but the Ottoman Bank was not one authorized to change travellers cheques. We went to see the Özgüçs, the Turkish archaeologists who were working at Kültepe. Here we were fortunate enough to be offered lunch in the shape of an omelette. We had just enough money to buy bus tickets to Ankara and caught the 5 p.m. bus. By the time we reached the bus station nearly all the seats were full as I had tripped coming out of the hotel and sprained my ankle, so it took a long time to get to the bus station. We had a very uncomfortable ride and arrived in Ankara after midnight. We thought it was too late to go to the British Institute as everyone would have been in bed, so we decided on one of the hotels. We landed up in the Ankara Palas, then the best hotel. Turkey was having a drought so there was no water, and the hotel porter brought us half a tin of dark brown fluid to wash in.

Next morning we collected some money – always a lengthy affair in Turkey – fetched our cases from the British Institute and got on the bus for Konya. However, before we left we had some lunch. This was a mistake as by now our stomachs had contracted; the soup we had was bad and the results were disastrous. We had dinner in the Konya hotel where the manager had designs on my companion and tried to drink us under the table, a hopeless thing to do, but it meant we went to bed late, and the bus for Isparta left next morning, as usual at 5.30 a.m. Breakfastless we caught this and had the usual breakdown, so that we were late making the connection with the iron-ore lorries on which we should have made the next stage of the journey. Iron-ore as a seat leaves a certain amount to be desired and as a result we did not respond with our usual enthusiasm to the Turks' frequent exclamations of how beautiful the country was. Fortunately the lorries had waited for us, but the bus, on which we should have travelled on the next stage of the journey did not. We were therefore stranded in a town some distance away from Isparta and the railway line. The object of this exercise was to get to Izmir and catch a boat to Greece, so we were tied to a timetable.

Syria, Egypt, Syria, 1956–1964

Finally, after waiting several hours in a tea garden where only tea and coffee were obtainable, some of the Turks persuaded a lorry driver to take us to Isparta. We finally left about ten or eleven at night and arrived at Isparta at about midnight. We got a room in an hotel but no food, all they could offer was tea, sweet biscuits and apples and we ate the lot. The train was leaving next morning at 4.30 a.m. so we lay down fully dressed, asking to be called in good time. This the night porter failed to do, and we were awakened out of our exhausted sleep by the banshee wailing of the Posta as it hurtled through the outskirts of the town on the way to the station. Somehow we got an arabaci (a cab driver) and hurried at full trot to the station, the old araba (horse carriage) sliding and straining as we took the corners. We just had time to buy tickets, scoop up a water melon from a passer-by and leap on the train. It was a long hot day to Izmir. We stopped, but not at the sort of wayside stations that provided much refreshment, so that we were more than glad when we pulled into Izmir at about 8 p.m. We went to a second-class hotel on the sea front and asked for a room with a bath. We got one, but the shower it contained was right on the verandah under the street lamp and had no cover. We had to take turns holding up a towel while we washed. The meal in the hotel was long since over, but they consented to send out for something and we had our first meal since leaving Konya. In all a journey of six nights and five days with little food or sleep.

Next day we took the boat for the Piraeus. Here we decided to have a few days' rest before returning to England. To save money we usually stayed in a hotel on the waterfront. These hotels were not well thought of as they were the haunt of the prostitutes that hang around any large port, but the one we always stayed in was clean and cheap and, as long as the chambermaid Maria who kept it so stayed, so did we; when she left, we moved. We decided to go to Aegina and have several days in the first-class hotel there, for we had just enough to pay for bed and breakfast. We spent the days on the beach below the old temple eating a meagre lunch of bread and fruit we had bought on the way. In the evening we shared a plate of macaroni cheese or moussaka and half a carafe of retzina. Afrer doing this for several days we felt quite restored.

On the way out to Syria we had spent some time in Greece, going to Mycenae and Tiryns and taking photos for the second year Diploma Course in Archaeology which I was teaching at that time. At Mycenae we found the Belle Helene, the hotel where Schliemann stayed while digging there, too expensive so put up at a house in the village. As a rule Greek houses are extremely clean, but the washing facilities are usually nil, as are the lavatories, and this was no exception. The only place to wash was at the village trough so we had to wait till most people went to bed before starting to wash not only ourselves but our underwear.

We had then gone on to Crete to take slides and went round the island by bus. While in Heraklion we were eating our lunch on the sea wall one day

The Road to El-Aguzein

when we became aware of a crowd of people rushing past, all pointing out to sea. It was a fairly rough day but we could just make out a dark object near the edge of the rocks. Finally a boat was launched and they fished the object out of the water. It seemed to be the legs of a skin-diver's suit and all the Cretans surrounding us were most disappointed, and went away muttering, 'What a pity! No dead body!', which just shows how people enjoy themselves in different ways.

In 1960 we went back to Tell Rifa'at, this time with the support of grants from Cambridge University, Melbourne Institute of Archaeology and the Russell Trust. We did a two and a half months' season there in the summer, working mainly on the top of the mound, trying to sort out the stratification put forward by Hrożny (who was a Czech philologist) in 1924, and in M6, the East Gate, which Margaret cleared. We had Tony again and John McDougal, a young professional photographer. Peter Parr, the lecturer in Palestine Archaeology at the Institute of Archaeology, joined us for a short time, as did Allan Millard. Bill Leonard, one of my students, did the drawing and Elsa Coult did the recording. We were also greatly helped by our inspector, Adan Jundi, from Damascus, another French speaker who has since become director of part of the Damascus Museum.

Politically, working in the Middle East was much more difficult after Suez, with the distrust that the Arab governments felt towards the British. The British Consulate in Aleppo was closed, though it re-opened during the summer of 1960 when relations began to improve. It was annoying to see the British goods in the shops being replaced first by German, then by Japanese, and finally by Russian. All the villagers were very uneasy and I soon learnt that, fearing the worst, they all had arms stacked away under the floors of their houses. We rented a larger house in the village this time, next to one of the mukhtar's houses, and we were able to see him asleep on the roof of his house as we got up every day much earlier than he did. Being in the middle of the village instead of on the outskirts had several disadvantages; it was much noisier, but the house we had before was now too small as there were eight of us now instead of the previous six. As it was, we had one communal room for work and eating, and two large rooms where we all slept. A good deal of the work, including the photography, took place in the courtyard.

In 1960 we made three interesting discoveries in that season. In the Hellenistic level near the top of the Tell we came upon the remains of a dyeing plant with a large deposit of murex shells several metres deep nearby. (These molluscs produced the purple dye for which Syria was well-known in antiquity.) This showed that the dyeing was not only carried on in the coastal towns, as had been previously thought, but also that the shellfish were taken inland where dyeing also took place. Then we found remains of Aramaean houses with mud-brick upper structures and stone foundations. There was a whole series of these which Hrożny's excavations in 1924 had cut right through. In one we found the remains of a whole family, cut down presumably at the time of the Assyrian capture of the city in the eighth century BC and left lying on the floor. The city had been sacked and the remains that we found had been very much destroyed. In the East Gate there was evidence of a second storey to the mud-brick gate that had been burnt and had collapsed. In the ashes we found the burnt remains of a small ivory lion which would have been part of the furniture in the upper room, while in the main excavation we found a pair of bronze bulls' heads like those on Urartion cauldrons.

After taking the antiquities to Damascus we came back through Greece.

After we crossed the Greek frontier from Turkey we looked for a place to camp and found one in an olive grove. We were soon joined by the owner who asked us what nationality we were. We said English and showed him our GB plates, he appeared much relieved and told us that he had killed thirty-two Germans who had wished to camp there and buried them under the olive trees.

Following this encounter we went all round the northern Greek sites in Thessaly and Macedonia where John took some excellent photographs. The next year the preliminary report of our first two seasons at Tell Rifa'at was published in the journal *Iraq*.

In the early 1960s Max Mallowan decided to retire as Professor of Western Asiatic Archaeology at the Institute of Archaeology. To my surprise Professor Grimes, who had replaced Gordon Childe as Director, sent for me and asked me if I would put in for it, as he had heard favourable accounts of my teaching from the students. I did so, but when Seton Lloyd turned up as one of the candidates, it became apparent I had very little chance as he had more experience in Iraq than I. My sponsors were Dr Margaret Murray and Dr A. J. Arkell Assistant Professor at University College. Professor Emery (the Professor in charge of the Department of Egyptology at University College) who was one of the members of the Appointments Board, asked me if I ever had any difficulty controlling my men in the Middle East as surely they would never take orders from a woman. I was able to assure him I had never had any difficulty in that direction. I learnt later he never allowed women on his excavations.

The next year 1962, I decided to return to Egypt and see again some of the sites which I had not been to for some time, as well as spending some time in Luxor. So I went out in the summer after we had finished at Barkhale in Sussex where, since 1959, we had been digging at the causewayed campsite. Originally undertaken as a training dig for Extra-Mural students, it had been continued for a friend who wished to do this for a thesis on the British Neolithic, which came to nothing. At Luxor we decided to take a felucca and go up river towards Aswan as the best way of seeing the country; it was August and fairly hot. We got to Esna and then reached Edfu, but we never actually got as far as Aswan because it all took so long. The current

The Road to El-Aguzein

contrary winds, storms that prevented the small boat sailing, and delays in getting through the lock, which alone cost us the best part of two days, meant that we did not reach Aswan by boat. We had a good boatman and a bad one; the one who could sail smoked hashish and was impossible when he ran out of supplies. The boatmen were terrified of stopping anywhere, or of letting us get off. We were always wading ashore in unlikely looking places, anywhere where we could find a solitary spot. It was a great way of seeing the river, and the other riverine inhabitants. We lived on bread and lentil soup like the boatmen and felt far better than we ever had when staying in hotels. I still make this delicious soup.

It was then that I met for the first time Omm Seti, the Englishwoman who became a legend in her lifetime, living near the water tower in Abydos. She believed in reincarnation and thought she had been a serving girl in the temple at the time of Seti I. She had an intimate knowledge of the temple and long after she retired from the Egyptian Antiquities Service she continued to show interested visitors round, entertaining them with her anecdotes and keeping them up to date with the latest news from the BBC. Her faith was that of the Ancient Egyptians, she believed in Osiris and Isis, and Amenti the Egyptian Afterworld, so as a matter of course always removed her shoes when entering the temple precinct as it was holy ground. She was convinced that there were undiscovered rooms under the temple and claimed to have seen them once, but could never find the entrance again. It is more than likely they do exist as so many of the other temples have crypts.

Through Omm Seti I learnt that I was known in Egypt as Omm Tegir, Mother of Hats. This was because I have a large collection of skull caps called Tegirs, from all over the Middle East. Many have been given to me, the first one in 1937 when my photographic boy at Tell el-Duweir crocheted one for me. I now have well over a hundred, each one dissimilar and I try to wear a different one each day.

The next year, in April 1963, we came back with a group of students and took them over the ground we had covered the previous year at Luxor, Cairo and Aswan.

In the autumn of 1963, I had been asked by Rik Wheeler to fill in as one of Swan's lecturers on a Nile cruise because their lecturer had fallen ill. This took me down to Nubia and to all the Nubian temples, only some of which I had seen previously. It was a wonderful way of seeing Egypt, and the sites were all so large that there was always something fresh to see there. And that was the beginning of a long and happy association with Swan's.

Meanwhile we had been trying hard to get back to Tell Rifa'at and by the summer of 1964, four years after our last expedition, had managed with the help of friends to collect enough money to do so. However, in January, just before I was off on another Swan's cruise Peggy Drower, the Secretary of the Egypt Exploration Society, rang me up and asked if she could come and see me. I was not very anxious for this to happen as I was busy packing

Syria, Egypt, Syria, 1956–1964

before flying out that afternoon to Egypt; however, she insisted on coming. When she arrived she told me that the Society had received a fixed sum from a private donor, that they were anxious to dig a site in the Delta called Tell el-Fara'in (ancient Buto), the site of the predynastic capital of Lower Egypt and would I undertake it as their field director? I said I had never seen the site, and asked for time to consider the matter; I suggested I could perhaps go and see the site when I was in Egypt and then let her know. However, she replied that I must make up my mind on the spot or they would offer it to someone else. They wanted me because by this time I had become an expert on digging town sites, which is not a usual accomplishment for an Egyptologist. I had always wanted to dig in Egypt, I had been teaching Egyptology for the last ten years, I had started to visit the country regularly and had a good knowledge of the monuments and objects, so thinking that at last I had my heart's desire I said yes. But it was not enough to agree to go, the Society wanted an expedition mounted, if not right away, at least in the spring. In vain I pointed out that I was booked to go to Syria in the summer: 'You can fit in a survey first', I was told. Which I did not want to do, as I wished to go out on my own and look the site over first, but they would not agree to this either. So, unwittingly, I accepted. Before I left England I was sent for by the Treasurer of the EES. I was not used to people sending for me to go to their offices, and I went reluctantly. When I arrived, after a certain amount of beating about the bush, he said that he had heard that there was a wolf on the site and that he did not think it was a very safe place for a woman to go. I looked at him in amazement and said, 'Only one wolf?. When at Sakce Gözü we had been surrounded by wolves.' After this I heard no more objections about wolves. What I did not know was that I was being used as a catspaw by one of the warring factions of the EES committee.

The sponsor was supposed to supply two Land-Rovers as well as the money, but when pressed produced only one, and that had been so battered previously it only lasted one season. So in April and May I mounted an expedition to Tell el-Fara'in with five assistants; these were the architect Joan Martin, engineer, Reg Welch, photographer, David Syson and assistant field director Elsa Coult and site supervisor Michael Cane. Tell el-Fara'in was a series of long low sandy mounds in the Delta half way between Damanhur and Kafr es-Sheikh, and some 15 kilometres from the nearest town. It covered 177 acres, or rather feddans (an Egyptian land measure of approximately one acre) and consisted of the two main mounds covering the city sites of Pe and Dep and a huge temple enclosure with walls standing some 40 feet high. The mounds had been ravaged by the *sebakin* hunters who, in some cases, had left only the walls standing amid heaps of debris. It was now covered with low scrubby prickly thorn bushes, full of snakes and the haunt of jackals, foxes and the wolf.

On this delectable but damp spot we made our camp. It was wet and

The Road to El-Aguzein

cold and the mist sometimes did not clear till after midday. In the tents it was dank, and we had to sleep with all our clothes inside our sleeping bags to keep them dry. Fortunately we had an excellent *reis*, or foreman, called Ismaia who came from Giza and so was used to moving stones, and a very good inspector, Ahmed Nashati, from the Antiquities Department. He was of Turkish descent, coming from one of the Turkish administrative families settled in Egypt, although now he was an Alexandrene, and one of those Egyptians with whom it is very easy to get on. At the end of the season he asked me to wait over a few weeks and attend the ceremonies for the returning *hajjis*, as his brother had been to Mecca and was just on his way back. Unfortunately, I was unable to do so, as I had to hurry back to London to prepare to go out to Tell Rifa'at. Again this was a strange thing to ask a Christian, a Nazarene, to attend, and I took it as a mark of his esteem. Shortly afterwards he gave up archaeology for business, as he could not make much of a living at the former.

The site of Tell el-Fara'in was far too large for our limited resources. It was, as I said in my first report, an archaeologist's nightmare – too much of everything with a long way to go between sites. The water table was too high so that to get down below the level of the later periods would entail pumping. The first season I set out to make a survey of the site, and to make a sounding in depth on the smaller of the two mounds. This revealed that there was a very heavy top hamper of Roman and Ptolemaic material overlying the earlier periods. Also, as we investigated the site, it became apparent that in its last stages it had been a vast industrial area with smoking kilns all over the place. However, this was not all apparent in the first few weeks. A further complication was that we had great difficulty getting the men to work for more than one day without receiving their pay, but we gradually got them used to us and the idea of working for a week at a time and getting paid at the end of it.

After the preliminary survey I went back to England, and then on to Syria to do what was to be the final season at Tell Rifa'at. This year 1960 we went via Turkey and had a somewhat larger party than usual, nearly all my Extra-Mural students. The 1964 season at Tell Rifa'at was a difficult one. We had too many people for the accommodation and the Inspector was a Druze who was disliked by the village; he tried to get the men to ask for more money than I could pay them, but they refused. He left us half way through the season and was replaced by Soubi. Several of the students got sick and we were close enough to Aleppo for others to go out at night, so that they could not work by day. The photographer turned out to be useless without his wife and had to be sent home when she left, and one of the two architects was equally useless.

The most interesting find that season was the evidence of how early the Aramaeans had been on the site; they had settled there while they were still in a nomadic state, even before they had started building houses.

Syria, Egypt, Syria, 1956–1964

Just before the end of the dig, I hurt my leg and had to send the rest of the group off without me while I waited till I could drive the Land Rover again. This also messed up my plans for acting as lecturer on a Swan's Hellenic Cruise to Egypt in September and I had to send them a cable to say I could not go. Soubi helped me in every way and came out two or three times a week to see how I was getting on. After a week or so I recovered enough to be able to drive the Land Rover to Beirut and so take ship to Marseilles.

The next year 1965 I went back to Tell el-Fara'in in the summer. The village where the track to Ibtu, the village nearest the site, branched off the main road was called el-Aguzein and for the next few years I was constantly on the road to el-Aguzein. When I first took this road, I was probably happier than I had ever been in my life. After thirty years I had achieved my life's ambition: to become a Field Director of an excavation in Egypt. If I had known that I was just being used as a pawn by others for their own ends, who cared nothing for the work, I should never have undertaken it. When I left the site five years later, my archaeological career broken by the faceless men who had not even the courage to confront me, I knew that the road to el-Aguzein had for me been the most disastrous one I had ever taken.

Chapter Twelve
Balsham and Egypt 1957–1968

In September 1957 Margaret Munn-Rankin and I bought a cottage at Balsham which lay within the ten mile limit, beyond which at that time lecturers at Cambridge were not permitted to reside. She had been living in a University flat at Causewayside but, though convenient, it was very noisy and there was no room for books or expansion. My flat in Elvaston Place had also come to the end of its lease and the renewal price was greatly increased. So we decided to try and find a cottage in the country not too far away from Cambridge.

After looking round for some time we found one which, with about an acre of land, suited us very well. It had been the stables of the house next door which in its turn had originally been a coaching inn on the main road to Newmarket, now only a cul-de-sac. The cottage was very nice and faced south, with a long garden of mixed flowers and fruit trees. We later bought two other parcels of land: a building plot opposite, where we put a garage, needed for our two cars; the original garage was in the house under my bedroom, which consequently always smelt of petrol fumes. The other piece was a long slice beside the garden, at a slightly higher level, which we hoped would prevent us being overlooked. Margaret was the gardener and laid out a very attractive one. I just cut the hedges but we gradually eliminated these as they caused so much work and replaced them as we could by brick walls which looked better and did not take the goodness from the soil, as well as affording us some protection from the prevailing strong westerly winds. I still had my job lecturing at London University, so used to commute to London from Tuesdays to Fridays each week during the winter months. In 1963 Margaret took a sabbatical to go to Iran and I took over her classes on the Archaeology of Mesopotamia and the History of Western Asia at Cambridge, which I managed to combine with my job lecturing for London

University, which meant I taught at Cambridge on Mondays and Fridays and the other days in London.

Meanwhile I was spending every summer excavating in Egypt. Tell el-Fara'in was such a large site that when we first examined it it was difficult to know where to begin. I set out with two objectives: to try to establish with certainty whether the site was Buto – the ancient Pe and Dep – and to establish the age of the mounds. To do this was quite difficult as the *sabakhin* whom I have mentioned previously had left very little standing except the walls. We dug a trench some 7 metres deep on Site C, which I decided must be Pe as previously a cache of metal objects, including several figurines of Horus, had been found by accident near one end of Mound C, at the farm of el-Baz (this was also one of the many words for 'hawk').

The villagers of Ibtu, the nearest large village, were, with a very few exceptions, all called El-Sekhemawy – the name of a Second Dynasty king. They also all wore brown woollen belts which were tied round their waists and fell in two strands with several knots almost to their feet at the back. It took me a couple of years to pluck up courage to ask them why they wore these, as they always had to be switched out of the way when they sat down. When I finally did ask, they replied, 'We have always worn these since we were kings of Egypt'. I had another curious experience when talking about ants here. These were soldier ants and, though I knew the Arabic for ant, I did not know the Arabic for this variety, so I asked one of the locals and he replied. 'We call them Persis.' So I said 'Persians?' and he said 'Yes, because they walk just like the Persian army'. The Persian army came into Egypt in 525 BC. Is this an example of folk memory?

Tell el-Fara'in was in a remote area, and many of the people had never seen anyone white before. They came for miles just to stand on the sides of the trenches and stare at us. For the first two years we lived in tents but it was not very comfortable because of the humidity both at night and up till about midday. We could seldom photograph before about noon as a Scotch mist often hung over the site. Using mud bricks I started building a kitchen, a lavatory, a shower and a hut for the *reis*. These were all domed as it saved wood, all of which had to be imported and was therefore expensive. It was also not well seasoned and tended to warp badly after a season or two. However, we were better off than the American Expedition at Mendes which built their expedition house of pressed sugar cane which warped so much that they had to take it down after one season and rebuild at very considerable expense.

After the second season, in 1966 I managed to save enough to build a baked brick house. This had one large room with two wings stretching off it in which were the bedrooms, stores and darkroom, the large room had lots of windows facing north, from which direction came the sweet north wind. The pottery shed, built of mud brick, was in the courtyard outside. Here I obtained many insights into Egyptian building methods. I learnt that a mud-brick wall could not be more than 5 feet high without being buttressed, and that if one wished to increase the height of the wall one had to take the whole thing down and begin again. I learnt that rice straw was the best to place in the mud plaster with which every wall had to be coated to keep out the rain. One day I had a deputation from the village complaining that we had paid the mud-brick man and the mud-brick horse too much money – which enabled him to go to the next village and buy another wife. My village was outraged that one should be obtained from 'outside'.

I found that the builder of mud brick had nothing to do with the builders of baked brick. We bought our baked bricks by the thousand, and I also found that you had to test these. If you could break these with your hands, you rejected the lot and started again. I had an inspector who said that he would help me count the bricks I bought if he could have two men to help him. I asked why these were required and he replied, 'If each man picks up two bricks and carries them several paces and puts them down I will count how many times he does this and we will know the number of bricks.' He had never heard of the normal way of counting a stack.

I had the same trouble with the village carpenter. He said, 'I must have a table.' Well, I quite understood this, any carpenter had to have a bench. But not this one – what he wanted was a table to stand on, just like the ancient Egyptians. I was reminded of Meket Re's models of the XIth Dynasty (2123–1991 BC) from Thebes when I saw our carpenter standing on the table and sawing through planks upright from one end to the other not, as one would normally do, placing the plank on the bench side ways on. He also made the house fit his doors and windows. If these did not fit, he just cut away the bricks of the doorways and window openings till a rough match was achieved. This caused a lot of damage to the house and I began to understand why none of the village houses had well fitting doors: the origin of the story of the Scorpions of Isis, when the scorpions got under the door, became all too obvious. We also had scorpions and had to remember to shake out our shoes every morning. Also fleas. I was so used to the presence of these in the Near East that I had forgotten they were a hazard to our staff who were quite unused to dealing with them. In addition there were a large number of snakes on the site some of which, apart from the cobras which were quite common, I caught and took back to the Natural History Museum. These were listed as partially venomous, a definition which left something to be desired.

A leading Sekhemawy, who was an agricultural engineer, more or less controlled the village. He lived in feudal splendour with his mother, and had six armed guards who accompanied him everywhere. When he came to see us he always had them with him, and when we went there to dinner they stood along the walls of the dining-room behind our chairs. His house was built largely of spoils from the site, and was entered through two pillars and up a series of steps – rather like the model of the house of Meket Re'.

Balsham and Egypt 1957–1968

Our excavation house was built at some distance from the village so that we would not be disturbed by the dogs and a constant stream of visitors. Even so, we had rather more than I liked. We took on our men by looking at them as Petrie always did – that way we got the best of the bunch. We had, of course, to take on the poor of the village as our workmen and I soon found out why they were so called – they were unemployable.

I used one local girl to cook and two to bring water from the stand pipe in the village, to where the sweet water was piped. This task used to fill most of their day. We used to supply ourselves with hot water for washing and the shower by leaving the tins in which we kept the water outside our doors in the sun; this meant that we could always have a hot wash. We also laid in some large metal washing pans to bath in; they were used by Egyptians to wash their clothes and were easily available from itinerant salesmen.

The legend about Pe begins: 'Very old and grey is the city of Pe' and this is perfectly true even today. The top soil was a kind of grey sand, not very pleasant to work as it was very saline. It was also difficult to grow any vegetables because of the salt, for though we could get some to grow in the first years, the soil got steadily more saline as the new Aswan High Dam took over and the water table rose. This was also the story of the wells at Ibtu and el-Baz; these had once been sweet water but were now brackish.

The Six-Day War in the summer of 1967 occurred while I was working at Tell el-Fara'in. We were quite all right during the war because although our men brought their transistors to work from which came a flow of propaganda about British and American imperialists, they fortunately did not connect us with the imperialists. At the beginning of the war I was sent for, together with the whole expedition, by the Governor of Kafr es-Sheikh, within whose area we were working. After a long conversation and several glasses of tea, he decided not to intern us, as had been his first intention. We therefore worked throughout the Six-Day War without too much inconvenience except for the cables that the EES kept sending me, asking me what I was going to do next. As I did not want to draw attention to myself I was not very keen on them doing this.

All went well till the war was over. Then, when Nasser resigned everything came unstuck. Crowds of people from Dissûq, our nearest town, came milling about our camp at night, causing our trigger happy guards to let off their guns, which I had to implore them not to do as we would have had short shrift if anyone had been shot. After this the local policeman, a very nice lieutenant who had been part of Farouq's personal guard and who had been exiled here from Alexandria as a result, came and told us that he could no longer be responsible for our safety and that we must leave for Alexandria forthwith. I had heard on our transistor through the overseas service of the BBC that a Greek cargo ship had been chartered by the British Government to take off 'distressed British subjects' from Egypt and that it would be

The Road to El-Aguzein

arriving in Alexandria in a couple of days, so I was not as reluctant to move as I might have been. What I had discovered when I went to see the Governor was that my own Land Rover, which had already done several seasons, was starting to seize up. Although no water ran out when it was stationary, when it got hot with running, the water poured out through pin-prick holes in the radiator and, what was worse, the horn started to blow. The police had advised us to go at 3 o'clock in the morning, and not to tell anyone that we were leaving. This is very difficult to do when one's horn is blowing all the time. In addition I had to carry jerry cans of water to pour into the radiator as it emptied so rapidly. We also had to take a fully armed soldier with us in the front seat, and his rifle took up a lot of room. I took enough food for several days and plenty of water because I did not know what conditions would be like in Alexandria. There had already been riots there, and the British Consulate had been burnt and British cars destroyed.

When we arrived in Alexandria we went straight to the secret police and the colonel in charge was very helpful. He asked where we usually stayed and I said the Hotel Cecil, but of course I had not been able to make any contact with them. He then rang them up and, to my great surprise, they immediately agreed to take us. After that he offered to place our two Land-Rovers in the garages belonging to the secret police because, as he said, 'If these are seen in the street with GB plates they will be destroyed.' He sent us with an escort to the Cecil, having told us not to go out in any circumstances, and said he would let me know when the ship came in and we could join it.

He did let me know about three days later, again at 3 o'clock in the morning, that we must rise, go to the headquarters of the secret police and collect our Land-Rovers and then go to the docks. The driver of the other Land-Rover left his car keys in the hotel and we had to do the whole journey twice over before we could begin our trek to the docks, guarded in front and behind by truck loads of armed Egyptian sailors. When we arrived at the docks we were not welcomed by the British contingent from the Embassy in Cairo. They wanted to know how we had got there and when they discovered that we had come out under Egyptian auspices they wished to have nothing to do with us. When I asked what we should do about loading our Land-Rovers they suggested that we should leave them with all our equipment on the docks. I was not prepared to do this and finally arranged with the Greek first officer that we should load the Land-Rovers on the deck. However, the ship had no car loading equipment. Fortunately I saw my friend, the colonel in charge of the secret police, on the dock and he arranged for slings to be made available, if I could manoeuvre the laden Land Rovers on to them. This is not as easy as it looks and is usually the work of specially trained crews. I had to do it all with the help of one Egyptian soldier, who had not the faintest idea of what I was trying to do. I must say that I had nothing but the greatest assistance from all the Egyptians in the port at Alexandria.

They could not imagine why I was going. 'What are you leaving for?', they kept asking. By the end I rather wondered myself.

When we got on board I was not surprised to see that the Embassy staff had taken all the cabins, leaving the British women and children lying on the deck. We could get water on board but no food, so it was fortunate that we had plenty of bread and bully beef. Some of us slept in the Land-Rovers to prevent anything being stolen, and others managed to get makeshift accommodation on deck. We passed an uneasy night on the way to Cyprus where we were unloaded. As I had two fully laden Land-Rovers I shipped three members of my eight-member team back by air from Cyprus. I would not have done it if I had known we were to be charged first-class fares for travelling in the bomb bay of a service aircraft from Cyprus. The rates for the overnight cargo ship were excessive, too. It is not a good thing to be a 'distressed British subject' unless you belong to the Establishment.

In Cyprus we had to wait several days for a Cypriot ship bound for Greece, where we were hoping to pick up the Hellenic Mediterranean Lines on which we had already got tickets. When we got to Athens we stayed at the British School who gave us every facility, and I was deeply indebted to Professor A. W. Lawrence, the Greek classical scholar who was staying there doing some research and whom I knew, for lending me enough money to get the expedition home, as it had, of course, been impossible to obtain money in Alexandria. Anyway, we were so short of cash that year that if the war had not come I doubt if we would have been able to complete the season.

In France, once we had landed at Marseilles, we proceeded to our usual garage for a check up and overhaul. The French mechanics were not able to deal with the horn or the radiator, so I travelled the 800 miles through France with a water can ready in one hand, and the horn blowing intermittently. It was not a pleasant journey.

As soon as I crossed the Channel (we used to fly from Southend to Calais and vice versa) I had the horn disconnected and had a quiet if not a very safe journey home to Balsham. In the wake of the 1967 war things were difficult in Egypt. The defeat of their army had made the Egyptians very anti-foreign and they were not anxious to have us working in the Delta. However, we were able to complete another season in 1968, with funds supplied partly by the Metropolitan Museum of New York but, again, there was not sufficient money available to enable a really full-scale operation to be carried out.

In 1967 we had discovered an inscription to the goddess Wadjet on a statue of one of her priests, so it was almost certain that the temple site we were excavating was that of the Cobra Goddess of Lower Egypt.

The last season that I excavated at Tell el Fara'in was 1968. There were dissensions on the EES Committee, of which I knew nothing, the arrangement being that the field directors were not, as they should have been, automatically members of the Committee. I had not discovered anything very much because a town site needs years of careful excavating on a large scale, a fact that the Committee was unable to understand. They had also not got the funds to do it properly. Again, in 1968 I was surprised to find that Dr Edwards, Keeper of the Egyptian Department at the British Museum, instead of supporting the application for a grant that I had asked for, was supporting my second-in-command, Dorothy Charlesworth, to obtain a separate grant from the British Academy; naturally she got it and conducted what was to all intents and purposes a separate excavation. I had originally asked her to come only because I thought that we might find glass and she was an expert on the subject – rare among British archaeologists. She refused to do any report on the glass we had found and in 1968 I left the excavation in a very low frame of mind. The next season the work was carried on under her direction and in 1970 the Egyptian Government shut down all work in the Delta for the next few years. I have never seen Tell el-Fara'in since. Eighteen years later a friend of mine visited the site and was warmly greeted by the villagers at Pe when they found she was English.

More than ten years later Peggy Drower the ex-secretary and Robert Anderson the then secretary of the Egypt Exploration Society came to see me in Cairo where I was lecturing on a Nile cruise. They asked me if I would like to do another season at Tell el Fara'in as they had heard the Germans wished to take over the concession. I was more than a little surprised after all that had happened and I could not see that anything would be achieved by doing this as most of the season would have had to be spent clearing out the trenches and repairing the house after such a long time. I refused as I knew that they still had not realised what a very large amount of money was needed to properly excavate a site of this size and complexity, where at least three electric water pumps were needed before one could even start digging. I feel that before any excavating on archaeological sites is undertaken they should be carefully examined, not only by the appointed Field Director but also by a special sub-committee to see if the work is feasible.

Perhaps I never should have accepted the field directorship, but it is easy to be wise after the event. And I cannot help thinking, with Margaret Murray, that it is better to have dug in Egypt than not at all. Nothing else has its splendour or perhaps its disappointments.

Chapter Thirteen
Swan Song

I have already mentioned how I was asked to lecture for Swan Hellenic on their Nile cruises in 1963. I had never thought of doing anything like that but I had spent a good deal of time in Egypt during the last few years, visiting many out of the way places, and had already taken several parties of students out to visit Cairo, Aswan and Luxor. So I felt that I might be able to do such a thing, and agreed.

My first trip was on the old paddle steamer *Sudan* for the Egyptian part of the tour and on the Sudan Railways steamer for the Nubian portion. In those days we had about seventy-five passengers and two tour managers. I loved the *Sudan*, she was so quiet, the only sound was the noise of the water as her paddles turned, she was very manoeuvrable and could turn on that vanished coin, a sixpence. I had been to all the Egyptian sites that we visited, but some of the Nubian temples were new to me. It was a magical experience arriving in the dawn at some half-ruined sandstone temple on the edge of the desert, with an avenue of sphinxes leading up to it, or to see a temple cut into the Nubian sandstone. Sometimes these temples were quite hard to locate and our tour managers had to go looking for them in the dark with torches. During these explorations they found many snakes of all sizes on their way down to the river to drink. I have always thought since that the ancient Egyptian idea of the Afterworld must have been based on accounts of Egyptians who had been to Nubia and seen the same thing.

The Sudan Railways steamers were a special breed of their own. They consisted of a central portion with an engine and dining saloon, and cabins of course, with two barges attached on either side with more sleeping accommodation. Most cabins had no washing facilities, or if they did it was only a hand basin.

All went well until we reached the village of 'Aneiba. This lay on the

The Road to El-Aguzein

Nile's west bank opposite Kasr Ibrim and at that time was a pleasant village shaded by palm trees – it is now under Lake Nasser. It was the site of ancient Ma'in, which had once been the Nubian capital and the seat of the viceroy under the New Kingdom. About 2 kilometres from the village was a single tomb, that of an official called Pennut, who had held a post under Ramesses VI. It was reached by a narrow causeway and the tomb was cut into the rock at some distance from ground level. It was in a somewhat dilapidated condition and had a large tomb shaft going down about 6 metres just inside the door. One tour manager stood on each side of the shaft telling the passengers to step either to the right or the left. However, one little Englishman, who had taken the cruise on his retirement, slipped through their hands and fell down the shaft, narrowly missing a large boulder which lay on the sand at the bottom, and landing with only a scratched elbow. The difficulty was to get him up again. In those days Swan's carried a doctor and, for the only time in my experience, this one was young and active having just completed his training. He went down the shaft using the hand holds cut by the ancient Egyptians for their tomb workers. We had come out to see the tomb on a variety of animals, donkeys and camels, and by tying their headropes together we were able to pull out the passenger with no ill effects. This was the only time on a cruise that I nearly lost a passenger down a tomb.

However, I had many adventures on these trips, one of them being the time I nearly ended up in jail. We were on the West Bank visiting the Tomb of Nakht when I was approached by a small boy whom I knew, to ask me when a certain tour manager was coming back. The tourist policeman thought that he was bothering me and hit out at him, the boy saw the blow coming and ducked, so the blow hit me. Without pausing for thought I hit the policeman, giving him a good upper cut which knocked him over. This took him by surprise, but was very popular with the locals. He threatened to take me to prison and had to be placated with some backshish. It turned out that he came from Damanhur in the Delta which is very close to Tell el-Fara'in, and when he discovered I had dug at Fara'in he claimed me as a neighbour. Ever since I have received a friendly welcome from him on the West Bank, rushing up and embracing me warmly. To this day the villagers remember the incident.

I found going back again and again to the Egyptian and Nubian sites very rewarding, as they are all so large that it takes many visits to become well acquainted with them. I particularly liked Nubia, and the early carvings on rocks beside the later temples. But even more than the temples I enjoyed the Egyptian fortresses. These were built of mud brick, and were elaborately designed with land and river gates, well built barracks, drawbridges, ramps for the soldiers to gain quicker access to the ramparts, and beautifully constructed towers and moats. Many of these had been trading posts and had obtained Nubian rarities, like bows, stools, hides, spices, gum arabic, ivory and ebony, along with Nubian boys in return for Egyptian manufactured goods. They had been garrisoned by recruits with a small band of seasoned soldiers in overall charge. These reminded me of the one we dug at Sheikh Zuweyed.

The temple and the commander's house were the most imposing buildings on each site, and the burials were always in extra-mural cemeteries. By the time I got to Nubia, the whole world of the Nubian people was already threatened by the building of the new High Dam and the creation of what was to be Lake Nasser – an immense artificial lake, 10 kilometres across and 500 kilometres long would stretch from Aswan, south to Wadi Halfa. All the pretty little clean Nubian villages nestling along the side of the river, their charming whitewashed houses decorated with plates from the hotels in Egypt where their owners had once worked as waiters and cooks, were to be flooded. When I knew them there were no able-bodied men to be seen in the villages, only old men, women and children, all the adult men were away working. They had little land to cultivate and supported themselves largely by fishing and hunting. The Nubians did not appreciate the idea of their land being flooded to make a large artificial lake, and when we passed through the gap in the dam they used to stand on the deck and chant, 'May God destroy the dam.'

The Nile

O great river rising from your caverns
Below the cataracts
Ruled by Khnum, the ram-headed god
Who made men on his potter's wheel.
The two Hapis with their fish and fowl
The reeds and grasses are your soul
Satet and Anuket attendant goddesses
Control your inundation
You spread throughout the land bringing
. fruitfulness
To the Black Land – and now controlled and
  fettered
After all these years – Egypt,
'Gift of the Nile' – now knows the Nile
No more – The Nubians pray
'May God destroy the dam
And give us back our land'.
How long the crops by salt denied
Will grow in strength beside the tide.
The upper palm trees droop and sway
Their roots denied the water way
All this for some electric light

The Road to El-Aguzein

> Or to show off the Soviet's might
> There's many in the land today
> Would wish the dam a world away.
> (From *Egyptian Poems*, M.V. S-W, 1987)

The most impressive of the temples was that of Abu Simbel, 'the finest bit of rock work in Nubia', as Petrie used to say. It was lovely arriving overnight and rising before the dawn to see the sun strike on the statues in the sanctuary. Most Egyptian temples and sacred buildings still have a strong feeling, which many people are conscious of, but since Abu Simbel was raised to prevent it, too, being lost beneath Lake Nasser's waters it has somehow lost its soul, remarkable though this achievement was as a feat of engineering. I liked Gerf Hussein almost as much, and the little temple of the XVIIIth Dynasty at Amada. This last was built, not cut into the rock, as are so many of the Nubian temples. It was successfully moved by the French to a position on the side of the new lake. Several years later the guard was killed by what the local inhabitants said was a wolf. He was found with his gun by the temple door and had been eaten, all but his boots. Technically speaking, naturalists say that there are no wolves in Egypt and Nubia, but the Egyptians and Nubians maintain that there is one, and there is certainly a large wolf-like animal, as I know because we had one when I was at Tell el-Fara'in.

In Nubia it used to be extremely cold when visiting the temples early in the morning. One of the tour managers, Brian Wright, and I both got a curious disease which lasted for about a year. We used to sneeze three times and then be sick – which could be very awkward. Fortunately whatever it was slowly passed off.

On one occasion when we were going up the Nile to Nubia before the dam was finally closed we had the economic geographer Professor Dudley Stamp from London University as one of the passengers. He said he thought that the new High Dam would be a disaster because adequate surveys had not been made; he believed that the Nubian sandstone was badly fissured and that water would seep out beyond the lake edge and form malarial swamps. Time has proved him right. Before the drought in Ethiopia, which has prevented the lake filling for the last eight years, the water level was much higher and some years ago an earthquake was caused by the weight of water over a line of weakness in the earth running up from the Great Rift Valley to the south. The fish in the lake have not so far been exploited as much as they might have been, and the vast expanse of water has led to much evaporation which in turn has caused considerable cloud cover over Aswan and the neighbouring area and northward as far as Luxor. It has probably been partly the cause of the violent electrical storms with torrential rain that have swept the Lower Nile Valley of recent years. The salt content of the water has also greatly increased, because of evaporation in shallow Lake Nasser.

In 1965 I returned to the Nile with Swans and have lectured there every year since. After a few seasons it became impossible to use the old *Sudan*, because the planks of the bottom had become rotten, and instead we used the MS *Delta*, a boat which had been entirely rebuilt, as it had caught fire on the slips during a refit and was, except for the metal base, an entirely new vessel. This was chartered by Swan Hellenic in 1971. It took fewer passengers than the *Sudan* – only fifty-six. It had been designed by one of the engineering professors at Alexandria University and was a very heavy boat. All the fittings and beds were very solid. It belonged to the Egyptian Government and was chartered by Eastmar for Swan's exclusive use. The difficulty with this was that the deck crew was rather aged, and we seldom had a good boat manager after the first one. On several occasions the *Delta* caught fire – a common occurrence on Nile boats. In our case it was the funnel that was the cause. In May 1979, however, the *Delta* sank, not from burning but as the result of a freak storm. We sank opposite the village of Ramada about 15 kilometres south of Edfu. It was the first day of the cruise and we were coming north from Aswan. It was the time of the Khamseen, which blows the 50-day wind from the south, and is very hot, with a temperature of about 107 degrees Fahrenheit.

After lunch on 5 May, at about 2.15 p.m., the sky turned a yellow/brown and the wind veered to the north and a black cloud appeared with yellow streaks running from it. The *Delta* was proceeding down the east side of the river. The bank rises quite steeply at this point and has a few rocky patches. The head *reis* informed the boat manager, Mr Fawzi, that he wished to cross the river and moor on the other side, which was shallow and reed covered, but before the boat could reach the other side there was a sharp squall which hit the *Delta* broadside on and, as she had not much freeboard, the water started coming over the starboard side, partly flooding the lower deck, the dining saloon, and the forward part of the ship. Even so, the *Delta* reached the west bank of the river and an attempt was made to moor her by launching the ship's felucca (dinghy). At this point the vessel lay parallel to the bank, but some way out, and the wind dropped for a moment. Somehow the rope was not attached to the anchor, which was thrown overboard with nothing to secure it to the vessel. The wind then rose again and a heavy shower of hail fell, soaking all who were standing on the upper deck trying to counterbalance the list that the ship had taken to starboard. The *Delta* then swung across the river with her bow pointing to the east bank. She shipped further water and the engine room became flooded, the steering ceased to work, and the electric lights went out. Fortunately, she then drifted onto a sandbank in the middle of the river before starting to sink. The wind veered again to the south. The occupants of the felucca, three able-bodied sailors and one of the assistant reises, were too afraid to return to the ship because they had failed to make a proper mooring, and our only means of communication with the shore was cut off. The point where the *Delta* stuck was opposite the Gebel Seray, where the road and railway from Aswan to Luxor came close to the shore, and the mountain rises straight up behind.

When the hail stopped Geoffrey Howard, the tour manager and a former Lieutenant-Colonel in the Second World War, put a notice on the board that all passengers should pack their suitcases and overnight bags with all that they immediately required, and take a bottle of mineral water as it was still very hot. The boat manager tried to prevent some of the passengers doing this by telling them they must leave at once, though they could not because the felucca had not returned. As a result some people did not get back to their cabins and these soon went under water. By this time some small fishing boats had come out from the east bank and had begun evacuating the crew and passengers. These boats were very small, being made out of paraffin tins, and only just held two people and an overnight bag – we had to leave our suitcases behind. To reach the boats the passengers had to go down the companionway and through the water on the lower deck, which was now over a metre deep. Murad Gaddes, the son of one of the Luxor shopkeepers, who was in charge of the shop on board, was very helpful, he stood up to his waist in water helping the passengers to embark on these very flimsy craft; another who was very helpful was Muhammad Suliman, the chief sailor.

I went to my cabin which was on the top deck, packed my two suitcases and my overnight bag and put my soaking clothes into a plastic bag; this I thought would at least give me a change of clothes. I lost only my laundry and the gifts that I had brought for Omm Sety that I had placed on one of the upper shelves of the wardrobe and forgot.

It took about half an hour to ferry all the passengers ashore. I went in the second to last boat and Geoffrey followed in the last one. I decided not to wade through the water as I saw no point in getting wet, so I climbed down the outside of the ship with, I must admit, a certain amount of difficulty owing to my bottle of water and overnight bag. By 3.30 p.m. all the passengers and crew were ashore. The crew had lost nearly all their possessions as the water had penetrated the lower deck, where their cabins were, first.

Tala'at al-Kholy, the accountant, had been sent to Edfu to inform the police and to organize some kind of transport. He had taken with him the keys of the safe on board, so that we were unable to obtain our passports. At this stage we did not know that Edfu too was a disaster area as a result of the series of storms which had cut off the electricity and water supplies as well as the road and rail links with the rest of Egypt. Many of the mud-brick houses had collapsed, animals had been washed into the river, children drowned, and many trees had been blown down.

After waiting by the side of the road for some time, several police trucks came from Edfu and took us to the police station. We spent some hours waiting on the verandah of this building; it was very hot and the mosquitoes were out in force. Geoffrey had fortunately brought some whisky and our maitre d'hotel, Karim, got some biscuits and oranges for the passengers. At about 10 p.m. we were told by the police we could go to an hotel, from which they must have ejected the Egyptians. Then the problem arose as to what to do with the crew; I did not see why they should be left sitting up all night on the verandah and suggested that they came with us. After all, I had been working with them for eight years and, as the boat manager and reis had both taken off, I thought someone should do something for them. The police could not see why I was bothering about them and threatened to put me in jail if I made any more problems, but after driving me around Edfu for about twenty minutes the lieutenant of police agreed that they could come with us. All Edfu was in darkness as the lights had failed but some of us had torches. Most provincial Egyptian hotels are quite high with a few rooms on each floor, and of course no lift. We struggled up the stairs in the dark and found beds. There was of course no water either to wash in or to flush the lavatories. We spent a slightly uncomfortable night with bedbugs below and mosquitoes above.

Next morning after some tea, I thought that we had better go to see the temple of Edfu so we took horse carriages and went round there. It too had suffered and the walls were running with water. While we were inside two tourist buses arrived from Aswan (the road having been repaired) sent by our Eastmar agent who had heard of our plight. These took us to the New Cataract Hotel where, as it was the end of the high season, we were lucky enough to find rooms for all of us. This enabled me to wash my shirt and trousers which had got soaked on the *Delta*, and be ready for a fresh start. However, everyone was not so lucky. One passenger had packed about six blouses and nothing else, some had left behind their sunglasses, or their hats or, worse still, their vital medicines. We spent one night in Aswan and next day took the road to Luxor where the *Lotus*, which had been sailing empty to Cairo, was recalled for us by Eastmar. Not surprisingly some of the passengers were unwilling to get on to another boat. However, I pointed out to them that we would be moored for several days at Luxor and if they did not want to proceed with the tour they could fly home from Luxor. Only those who had lost all their luggage opted to do this, and that was, in fact, very few of the party.

We had arrived in Luxor 48 hours late but we missed none of the sites on the schedule. A few months later, one of the American passengers, Joan Chilton Daly, a former journalist and now a lawyer, published an article in the *New York Times* on Sunday, 12 August 1979, called 'Sinking slowly in the Nile'. As she said, the sinking in the Nile produced a camaraderie that nothing else could have achieved. Geoffrey Howard appeared in a scarlet T-shirt marked Open University and we all mixed in happily together. Efforts were made to raise the *Delta*, but too late, she was a very heavy vessel and, though two barges were placed alongside and frogmen ran wires underneath the hull, it was not possible to pump her out and lift her clear of the Nile mud. Some years later her superstructure, which had remained obstinately clear of the surface, was dynamited away as she was a danger to shipping. Poor old *Delta*, I had enjoyed being on her and we had an efficient crew in most cases, if not in an emergency.

It took a year for a new boat to be obtained and in the meantime we had to make do with the *Memphis*, a very much smaller affair and, again, an old boat which had originally been a paddle steamer. Her disadvantage from my point of view was that her lounge bar, where I had to give my talks, was fitted up with seats with high backs so that I could not see the audience that I was talking to. There was also an infernal ice-making machine in the bar, which went off at about five-minute intervals all the time I was talking. Then in 1981 we went onto the new *Nile Star*. I did not like this nearly as much as it is totally enclosed, not like the *Sudan* and the *Delta* which had cabins opening onto the open deck. I now had a cabin down on the lower deck and for the first few voyages suffered from the most fearful nightmares in which the *Delta* sank over and over again. I was not alone, Tala'at al-Kholy, the accountant from *Delta* who was then the *Nile Star*'s Assistant Manager and is now the Manager suffered in the same way. I was rather annoyed as I did not see why it should have affected me, but who would expect to be shipwrecked in the Nile? It is an experience one could do without. During this time I was also editing the *Nile Handbook*, for Swans, an account of the main sites that we visited. This took a great deal of time.

I also did a certain amount of travelling in Turkey, as I refused to lecture except where I had previously worked. These Anatolian trips were most interesting and I was able to see Turkey gradually developing. When I first went to the south coast no attempt had been made to cultivate the rich valleys that had been exploited by the Greeks, and all one saw were decaying villages and rotting orchards. Now it is a very different story and at last the Turks seem to have taken to agriculture, with miles of irrigation channels and acres of tomatoes under plastic greenhouses. The hotels, too, have improved out of all recognition.

But it is Syria and Egypt that I prefer above all. I did two Syrian trips for Swan Hellenic before they decided that Syria was too difficult. I was saddened by the decline of Aleppo; when I first knew it, it had been the entrepôt of Syria but, cut off from its natural port of Iskanderun, it has greatly declined and most of its trade has gone to Damascus. Still, there is nothing quite to compare with the old city of Aleppo, its honey-coloured stone and beautiful houses, crowned by the citadel. Somehow, of all the places in the world that I have seen, Aleppo remains for me the most beautiful – perhaps because there in one of its mosques I was offered the way of peace – even though I could not take it.

Swan Song

Then, there is Egypt; if one has drunk the waters of the Nile one is said to always come back. I must have visited Egypt over a hundred times but for me there is always something new. Each trip offers me the chance of seeing something I have never seen before. Its sites are so vast, the material so great, all other civilizations are finite – in Egypt alone, the depths cannot be plumbed. I have been so often on the *Nile Star* that it has become a kind of second home to me. I enjoyed excellent relations with the staff who looked after me very well; in fact my real trouble was to prevent the boat manager, Nabil Riad (who sadly died in 1987), ordering special dishes for me, and the chef Ahmed from preparing them, and I have made many friends. I even had two Setons from New York who claimed me as a kinswoman and with whom I corresponded for many years.

The call of the *mu'adhdhin* from the *jami* (mosque), the call of the birds on the river, and the churning paddle wheels, the silent screw; the greatest river in the world has been my home for so long I can hardly remember when I did not know it. The fishermen casting their nets, the passenger who asked 'What fish is that?' when there is only a hole in the water where it has been. The Great Desert that comes right to the edge of the river – and which, after Sinai, means for me more than all the cultivation of the valley. But Egypt is changing so fast, the old water wheels and *shadufs* are disappearing to be replaced by diesel engines. The old cultivation with the hoe is being replaced by tractors, factories are gradually increasing, all the villages now have water and electric light. Soon the old, ageless, Egypt that has persisted for centuries will disappear altogether. I am glad that I was privileged to see it.

But it is not only the country that is changing, it is the tourists and the monuments. When I began there were six boats on the Nile, now there are 100 boats. When I first went to Egypt one could swim in the Nile; now it is more a drain than a river, with untold rubbish cast into it in spite of a law forbidding one to throw anything in the Nile. And the monuments – the rise in the water table due to the new High Dam has caused salt infiltration and rising damp, for which so far no cure has been found, and the endless thousands of people tramping through the monuments wear away the stone underfoot, while their camera bags and sticks damage the walls of the tombs against which they lean in the confined space. Sometimes I think that we shall be the last generation to see these wonderful treasures, which seem to have been preserved for us, only so that we shall destroy them.

Nature, however, may do the job for us. We are now beginning to see the results of the protracted drought in Ethiopia, the drying up of Lake Nasser, a shrinking Nile, the river virtually unnavigable and vital crops such as rice and wheat already being affected. The mighty Nile has ceased to be the highway of Egypt. I can only look to the future of Egypt with foreboding unless the rain belt returns.

In 1977 I gave up University teaching, having taught for twenty-five years. To my surprise and pleasure Professor Harry Smith arranged for me to become an Honorary Research Fellow of University College, where I had originally been trained nearly fifty years before.

When the Tutankhamun Exhibition was on at the British Museum in 1971 I had given a short course of talks on the subject. One of my students, who was the English agent for Hasso Ebling, a firm of German publishers, asked me to write an English text for an art book on Tutankhamun which was to be published in four languages, German, French, Dutch and Sweden, to cover another Tutankhamun exhibition that was travelling round Europe. The photographs taken by Khodansha, a Japanese publishing company, were very good, far the best I have ever seen. The book won the award of the year at the Frankfurt Book Fair, which pleased me very much. This led to a further art book in 1981 on the art treasures of the Iraq Museum, published under the title *Les Trésors de Babylone* a title I did not think suitable. For this, too, the photos were taken by Khodansha and were works of art in themselves.

In 1979 I had been asked by Benn to write their new Blue Guide to Egypt (now published by A & C Black) which I did in collaboration with Peter Stocks from the British Library, he writing the Islamic section and Cairo, and I that on Ancient Egypt. This took four and a half years to do and entailed many journeys for me and my ex-students to the more remote parts of Egypt like the Khargah Oasis, the Bahariyah Oasis and the Fayum, where we spent a week checking the Ptolemaic and Middle Kingdom sites. Since then we have been trying to arrange a trip to Siwa, but this presents problems.

In the summer of 1981 Margaret died of a brain tumour and two years later Joan du Plat Taylor died of a tumour on the liver. Joan was an archaeologist who was not well known outside professional circles. She was trained by the Wheelers at Verulamium and Maiden Castle and became Assistant Keeper of the Cyprus Museum in Nicosia in 1932, a post she held until the outbreak of the Second World War. In 1945 she was appointed Librarian at the Institute of Archaeology in London. As well as our digs in Cyprus, she excavated in Sicily at Motya, and did several excavations in southern Italy for the British School of Archaeology in Rome. After working on a Bronze Age wreck off Cape Gelidonya near Bodrum in Turkey, she became interested in nautical archaeology, a subject then in its infancy. It is mainly due to her work that good relations were established between the diving fraternity and archaeologists, in pursuance of this she lectured all over Britain. She also edited the *International Journal for Nautical Archaeology*, a science whose implications are only now being fully realised.

So, in 1983, I was left, the last of the four friends who had settled in Balsham to be near one another, my cousin, Betty Farran, having been the first to go in 1976. Margaret's death presented me with a difficult problem. She had always done the garden, which was her creation and about which I knew very little. Also we had gradually increased our land till we had $2\frac{1}{2}$

acres. This was a formidable task for one who knew little about the subject, even if a lot was down to grass. However, with the help of Colin Jacobs whom I had known since he was a butcher's boy in the local shop, though he has now turned to full-time gardening, I am managing to make some sort of show.

In 1963 we had bought a dog and a cat – Brock, a Jack Russell terrier, and Aswad, a half Persian black and white cat – from Five Mile Bottom a village nearby. Of course we became devoted to these animals and after their deaths in 1979 one of my tour managers on the Nile, Stella Stupples, who was then breeding Siamese cats, gave me a seal-point Siamese to replace them. I myself knew nothing about Siamese, and not much about cats, but Bastet, called after the Egyptian cat goddess, taught me a lot. On her untimely death in 1982 I got two further Siamese; Satet and Anuket. Satet died in 1984 as a result of a virus caught in kennels, owing to my frequent absences during the summer as I had done five Swan Hellenic cruises. So I replaced her with another seal-point, this time a male, Horus, who has put Anuket's nose out of joint!

I hope I have not given the wrong impression, that I am sitting back in the sun (if it ever shines in this country) with my two cats, or alternatively I am crouched over my fire trying to keep warm. Well it is not quite like that. I realized when I was teaching that one could not teach, or at least I could not, and do the requisite research for writing, therefore I deliberately left most of the writing I intended to do until I had retired from teaching. In addition to the books already mentioned, I have had two short books on Egypt published: *Ptolemaic Temples* and *el-Amarna* and a book of Egyptian poems, and there are others in the pipeline. I am still lecturing, I am still travelling and still working.

El-Aguzein – in a way my whole life till then had been travelling towards it – well, things never work out as you expect. This was my Ithaca, it gave me the journey, it is but a symbol.

An Unfound Site
(with apologies to Rupert Brooke)

If I should die think only this
   of me
There is a mound I have not
   seen
There is a hill I never climbed
There is a site I have not found.

Regret not now the long delays
The wasted hours by war and
   strife

The Road to El-Aguzein

Know only here there was a life
That still enjoyed its many days.

Remember still the early hours
Before the dawn and swung the mists
From Delta fields or Turkish hills
Ere the dark sun had shown his powers.

When I shall die lay me to rest
On some high hill where I may see
If not the desert's changing face
At least the sky at least the sea.

Other Publications

Britain and the Arab States, Luzac, 1948
Ptolemaic Temples, Waterloo Printing Co., 1977
Les Trésors de Tutankhamon, Hasso Ebling, 1980
Les Trésors de Babylone, Hasso Ebling, 1981
Blue Guide to Egypt, with Peter Stocks, Benn, 1983, 2 ed. A & C Black 1988
El-Amarna, Waterloo Printing Co., 1984
Egyptian Poems, Merlin Books, 1987
Egyptian Stories and Legends, The Rubicon Press, 1988
Greek Poems (in preparation)
Short History of Egypt (in preparation)

Select Bibliography

Christie Mallowan, Agatha *Come Tell Me How You Live*, Collins, 1946
Drower, Margaret S. *Flinders Petrie*, Gollancz, 1985
Gough, Mary *The Plain and the Rough Places*, Chatto and Windus, 1954
Hawkes, Jacquetta *Mortimer Wheeler*
Mallowan, Max *Mallowan's Memoirs*, Weidenfeld and Nicolson, 1982
Murray, Margaret A. *My First One Hundred Years*, William Kimber, 1963
Petrie, Flinders *Seventy Years in Archaeology*, Sampson Low, 1931
Scott, Ernest *Life of Matthew Flinders*, Angus & Robertson, 1914
Seton-Williams, Margaret and Stocks, Peter *Blue Guide to Egypt*, Benn, 1983; A. & C. Black, 2 ed. 1988
Wheeler, R. E. M. *Maiden Castle Dorset*, Society of Antiquaries London Research Committee Report, 1943
Woolley, Sir Leonard *Dead Towns and Living Men*, Lutterworth Press, 1954

Glossary

Adits – Horizontal entrance. (Mining term)
Afrit – Arabic, one of the five species of Jin or Genii, traditionally defined by Mohammed.
Aid, Idu – Arabic, the three day feast which follows the end of Ramadan, often called the Idu al-Fitr or al-Aidu al-Saghir.
Amorine – Arabic, tribesman of Southern Palestine.
Batter – (Archaeological term). The slope on the sides of walls or cuttings when the angle is changed.
Beni Sakr – Arabic, one of the largest Arabian tribes in Jordan.
Blue clay – Impermeable clay layer sealing in the water table.
Casemates – Boxes made of stone filled with earth usually found in the interior of rampart or glacis construction.
Cattle Duffers – Cattle rustlers.
Causewayed Camp – The type of Neolithic camps when the ditches were interrupted by causeways.
Circassians – Groups of Caucasians settled by Abdul Hamid on the eastern borders of Syria and Jordan.
Crannog – Artificial island made of alternating layers of peat and brushwood surrounded by a stockade and set in a bog or swamp, occuring in Ireland and Scotland.
Drang Nach Sudosten – The German push towards the east to reach Baghdad before the First World War.
Druze – A Lebanese sect with a secret religion, not strictly Muslim.
Engaged Columns – When two columns are keyed together to give greater support.
Farwah – Arabic, a sheepskin coat.
Feddan – Egyptian land measure, approx. one acre.
Felucca – Small sailing boat or dinghy with lateen sail.
Fellahin – Arab or Egyptian peasant, usually a farmer.

The Road to El-Aguzein

Firman – Permits issued by the Ottoman Government before the First World War to enable archaeologists to excavate.
Fosse – Ditch or trench to do with fortifications.
Glacis – Sloping earth rampart covered by white plaster, usually Hyksos in date in the Middle East.
Habara – Arabic, a type of bustard.
Hajj – Arabic, literally 'the setting out' referring to the pilgrimage to Mecca made in the twelfth month of the Muslim year. Extended by popular usage to all those who have made the pilgrimage.
Hatay, The – The Sanjaq of Alexandretta, ceded by the French Mandatory power to Turkey in 1939. It was previously a part of Syria and has been a point of contention ever since.
Helawi – Arabic name for Halva, a sweetmeat made from honey and sesame seeds.
Hill Fort – Iron Age camp defended by multiple banks and ditches occurring mainly in Southern England.
Howeitat – Arabic, a tribe in Southern Jordan.
Jarrah – Australian hard wood from Eucalyptus Marginata.
Jar Stamps – Stamped jar handles of Hellenistic date with the names of their places of origin, mainly the Greek Islands, indicating where the wine came from.
Kavas – Uniformed employees of Consulates in Turkey.
Kuftis – Inhabitants of Kuft (Coptos) Egypt, trained by Petrie and now acting as foreman on nearly all Egyptian excavations.
Marl – Soil consisting of clay and carbonate of lime.
Megaron – Open porch with two columns leading to two or more rooms, basis of Greek temples.
Mu'allin – Arabic, a teacher in a school or mosque.
Mu'azzin – Arabic, the caller of the Azan or summons to prayer, originally done by calling from the minarets of the mosque, now largely replaced by a tape recording.
Mudd – Arabic, container in which coffee is ground.
Mudir – Arabic, a headman or director.
Picnic Races – Country race meetings to which one took picnics.
Plano-Convex bricks – Bricks shaped in an elongated oval, the base flat and the upper surface curved or hog-backed.
Posta – Local Turkish train.
Ramadan – Arabic, the ninth month of the Muslim year in which a fast is observed during the hours of daylight.
Reis – A foreman or a captain of a boat.
Saddle quern – Convex stone on which grain was placed for grinding.
Shaduf – Arabic, a device for raising water, consisting of a bucket or skin on a long pole counterbalanced by a lump of mud.
Shellback – Old sailor who had begun his career in the days of sail.

Glossary

Slant – The path taken by sailing ships across the ocean.
Sondage – A test trench.
Straights Question – The straights near Istanbul between Europe and Asia. Under the Montreux Convention of 1922 the day to day control was vested in Turkey but at the same time they were declared an international waterway.
Wadi Ghuzzeh – Dry wadi bed south of Gaza.
Wakil – Arabic, another name for headman.
Warral – Arabic, large lizard.

Index

al, el and es have been ignored in alphabetization

Abdeah (Ebod'a) 43
Abdul Hak, Dr 117
Abdul Hamid, Sultan 53, 71
Abdulla (guard at Sheikh Zuweyed) 38
Abel, Mr (surgeon) 94
Abraham 88
Abu Kemal 89
Abu Sefah *see* Tell Abu Sefah
Abu Selymeh *see* Sheikh Zuweyed
Abu Simbel 136
Abu Tawil (Arab at Tell el-Duweir) 76
Abydos 122
Adana 59, 60, 61, 65, 66, 67, 105, 118
Adana Museum 62, 106
Aden 20
Adi, Sheikh 107
Adriaticà Line 57, 84, 114
Aegina 119
Agar, Elizabeth 25
Agora (Athens) 72
el-Aguzein 125
Ahmed (chef on *Nile Star*) 141
Ahmed (Kurdish cook) 116
Ahmed Nashati 124
Ahmet I, Sultan 58
Aintab *see* Gaziaintab
air raid warden 94–5, 97–8
Akaba 82
Akshehir 64
Alaca 109
Alalakh *see* Atchana
Alawis 107

Albright, Professor WF 35
Aleppo 54, 55, 87–9, 108, 111, 115, 117, 140
Alexandria 34, 129–30
Ali (cook in Trans-Jordan) 80
Ali Bey Yalgan 62
Alishar Hüyük excavations 53
Allen, Dereck 55
Altounian, Dr 87–8, 108
Altounian, Mrs 87
Al'Ubaid occupation 103
Amada 136
Amanus mountains 59
el-Amarna (Seton-Williams) 143
Ambelikou 91
Amenti 122
America *see* United States *and individual cities*
American Mining Corporation 91
American School (Athens) 72
American School (Jerusalem) 35
Amman 79, 80, 81, 82
Amorine Sheikhs 75
Anastasi I papyrus 42
Anatolia *see* Turkey *and individual sites*
Anatolian Studies, Journal for 109
Anavaza 67, 105
Anazabus 67, 105
Ancient Near East, The (Childe) 112
Anderson, Robert 132
'Aneiba 133
Anglo-Egyptian Treaty 35
Angora *see* Ankara

Index

Ankara 54, 57, 58–9, 107, 118
Ankara, SS 109
Ankara Palas Oteli 118
Ansariya mountains 107
Antakya (Antioch) 101, 107, 117
Anthedon 42; *see also* Sheikh Zuweyed
Anti-Taurus mountains 59
Antioch *see* Antakya (Antioch)
Apliki 91
Aquitania, SS 84
Arabia Deserta (Doughty) 64, 81
Aramaeans 120, 124
Arinna, Sun Goddess of 58
el-Arish 42, 43, 46, 47
Arkell, Dr AJ 121
Arpad *see* Tell Rifa'at
Arrian 59
Ashmolean Museum 89, 101
Assiut 35
Assyria/Assyrians 71, 78, 104, 121
Aswan 121, 133, 135, 136, 139
Aswan High Dam 129, 135, 136, 141
Ataturk, Kamal 53, 54, 60, 92, 102
Atchana 101, 102
Athens 72, 103
August (driver) 86, 90
Auj'a el-Hafir (Nessana) 43
Austen, Miss (later Mrs Bulleid) 22
Auxiliary Fire Service 92
Ayia Sofia 58
Ayios Philon (boat) 96–7

Babylon 89
Baghdad 59, 89–90, 104
Bahariyah Oasis 142
Bainsfather, Bruce 11
Balikh, river 71
Balkans 96
Balsham 126–7, 131, 142–3
Baltic States 27, 29
Barkhale (Sussex) 121
Basil Street 92, 93
Basra 89
Bassul, Madame 87
Bayyadin Bedu 45
el-Baz 129
Bedu 43, 45, 46, 75, 82, 88, 90, 117
Béguin, Comte de 26
Beirut 54, 87, 90, 108, 115
Beisan (Beth-Shan) 35, 49
Belgae 31
Belgrade 72
Bell, Gertrude 89, 104

Belle Helene hotel (Mycenae) 119
Ben-Dor, Dr Immanuel 49
Benaki Museum (Athens) 72
Beni Sakr 80–1
Benoit, Mademoiselle 12
Benton, Theodora 72
Bere, Fanny 99, 101
Berlin 29, 71–2
Beske mound 89
Beth-Shan (Beisan) 35, 49
Blue Guide to Egypt 142
Bodrum 142
Boğazköy (Hattušaš) 53, 56, 109
Bonney, Holbrook 74, 77
book censorship 95
Boston 83, 84
Botos (Arab surveyor) 49, 51
Box, Judge 10
Boyd, Gwenda 18
Boyd, Mary 18
Bradford, Gus 55
Braidwood, Bob 84, 111
Brighton and Hove Archaeological Club 32
Brisbane 100
Britain and the Arab States (Seton-Williams) 100
British Academy 132
British Council 95–6
British Institute of Archaeology in Ankara 102, 104, 117
British Institute of Persian Studies (Tehran) 114
British Museum 76, 142
British School of Archaeology (Athens) 72, 103, 104, 131
British School of Archaeology (Egypt) 34
British School of Archaeology (Iraq) 104
British School of Archaeology (Jerusalem) 52, 86
British School of Archaeology (Rome) 142
Bronze Age 30, 49, 50, 51, 76, 78, 91
Brunton, Guy 77
Buda-Pest 72
Bulleid, Dr Arthur 22
Burns, JD 11
bushrangers 9
Buto *see* Tell el-Fara'in
Buxton, John 49
Byblos 54, 111

Index

Byron-Moore, Dorothy 100
Bystander 11

Caesarea by Anavazus 67
Cairo 34–5, 72, 77, 133
Cairo Museum 35
Calstock (Tasmania) 3
Cambridge University 120, 126–7
Cane, Michael 123
Carchemish 53
casemates 56
Castle of the Stars *see* Qalat el Nedjem
Catling, Hector 104
Causewayed campsite (Sussex) 121
Cecil Hotel (Alexandria) 130
censorship 92, 94–5
Central Office of Information *see* Ministry of Information
Ceyhan (river) 60, 65, 106
Ceyhan (town) 60–1, 65, 66, 105
Chalcolithic levels 75–6, 88, 115
Chamberlain, Neville 92, 93
Champollion, SS 34
Charlesworth, Dorothy 132
Chatham House 96
Chaushli site 60
Checkens (Circassians) 71
Chicago 84
Chicago Oriental Institute 53, 83, 102, 111
Childe, Professor Gordon 112, 121
Chilton Daly, Joan 139
Chittick, Neville 104
Christie, Agatha 106, 112
Chukur Ova 58–67
Church Mission Society 41
Church Street, Kensington 94–5, 97
Cilicia 104–5
Cilician plain *see* Chukur Ova
Circassians *see* Checkens
City Literary Institute 112–13
City of Bristol, SS 101
City of Capetown, SS 99
'City of Delight, The' 42
Claridge Palace Hotel (Aleppo) 108
Clay, Rachel (later Maxwell-Hyslop) 21, 31, 55
Clyde Girls Grammer School 14–15, 16
Coade, Mr (teacher) 15
Coba Hüyük 102
Cobra Goddess of Lower Egypt 131
Codrington, Dr K de B 24
Cohen, Barbara 21

Cold Water Mound *see* Souk Su Hüyük site
Collingwood, Kim (later Lady Wheeler) 55
Collingwood, RG 87
Colombo 19–20
Colt expedition 43
Colt, H. Dunscombe 43
Connemara 70
Contzen (German engineer) 53
Cooks camp 82
copper 91
Corinth 72
Cotton, Molly 25, 55
Coult, Elsa 117, 120, 123
Crawford, OGS 30, 73
Crespigny, Nancy de *see* de Crespigny, Nancy
Crete 117, 119–20
Cromwell, Oliver 4, 5
Crowfoot, Joan 49
Crown Film Unit 29
Crusader Castles (Fedden and Thompson) 66
Ctesiphon 89
Curaçao 100
Curwen, Dr Cecil 32
Curzon Street 33, 93
Cyprus 64, 67–8, 72, 73, 74, 82, 84, 86, 90–1, 101, 103, 104, 108, 131
Cyprus Museum 86, 91
Cyrrhus 116

Daghdaghli 110–11
Dalvui sheep station 8
Daly, Joan Chilton *see* Chilton Daly, Joan
Damanhur 123, 134
Damascus 90, 115, 121, 140
Damascus Museum 120
Dandenongs 9, 14
Daniels, Pete 72
Davies, Barbara 14–15
Dawn of European Civilization, The (Childe) 112
de Crespigny, Nancy 18, 19, 21, 26, 31, 70, 83
de Wolkoff, Anna 93, 94
Dead Towns and Living Men (Woolley) 54
Decauvilles 32
Delphi 72
Delta, MV 136–40

Index

Dep 123, 127
Diab (Arab at Tel el-Duweir) 76
Dijon 114
Dikaios, Porphyrios 68, 86, 91
Disraeli, Benjamin 68
Dissûq 129
'Distressed British subject' 129, 131
Dorchester 31, 32
Dorset Natural History and Field Club 22
Doughty, Charles 64, 81
Down Street 92–3
Drew, Lieutenant-Colonel CD 22
Drogheda 4
Drower, Peggy 122–3, 132
Druze 51, 124
du Plat Taylor, Joan *see* Taylor, Joan du Plat
Dublin Museum 70
Dunard, René 54
Dunbabbin, Tom 72
Dunn, Alison 57, 65, 66, 67
Dunsany, Lord 70
Dunscombe Colt, H *see* Colt, H Dunscombe
Dura Europos 89
Duweir *see* Tell el-Duweir
'Dwelling of Sese, The' 42
Dyson, David 123

Eastmar 136, 139
Ebod'a *see* Abdeah (Ebod'a)
Edfu 121, 136, 138–9
Edward I 4
Edward III 5
Edwards, Dr (of British Museum) 132
Egypt 77, 121–3, 129, 131–2
Egypt Exploration Society 122–3, 129, 131–2
Egyptian Antiquaries Service 122
Elijah bus 86, 88, 90
Elisha's Fountain 49
Elizabeth I 4
Ellerman Lines 99, 101
Ellis, Jack 37, 38
Elusa *see* Khalasah (Elusa)
Elvaston Place 109, 112, 126
Emery, Professor 121
Encyclopedia Britannica 113
Engelbach, Rex 77
Enkomi 108
Erimi 68, 86
Erminoğlu 110–11

Eski Membridge site 88
Esna 121
Essex, 2nd Earl 4
Ethiopian drought 136, 141
Euphrates 88, 89, 110
Evans, Sir Arthur 17
Extra Mural Diploma teaching 112
Eynesbury 5, 100
Ezion Geber 82

Fascism 26
Fara'in *see* Tell el-Fara'in
Farmer, Frances 27, 28
Farran, Betty 142
Fayum 77, 142
Fedden, Robin 66
Feisal, King 117
Fire Brigade 92–4
fires 14, 15–16, 116–17
firman 53, 71
Fischer, Dr Clarence 35
Fitzgerald, GM (Fitz) 49
Fitzgerald, James Fitzmaurice 4
Flinders, Captain Matthew 17, 43
Fosdyke, John 72
Fox, Sir Cyril 30

Galapagos 100
Galle Face Hotel (Colombo) 20
Ganem (Arab foreman) 101, 105, 106, 107, 110, 111
Garden mound *see* Tell el-Jenayn (Tell of the Garden)
Garrod, Professor Dorothy 26
Garstang, Professor John 41, 48–54, 57, 60, 62, 63, 64, 65, 67, 70–1, 98, 101, 102
Garstang, Madame 49, 55, 57, 60, 63, 67
Garstang, Meroe 49
Gaza 35, 37, 39, 41, 44, 48
Gaziaintab (Aintab) 101, 102, 105, 110
Gebel Seray 138
Geddye, Ione 24
Genoa 114–15
geology 24
Georgic, SS 83, 84
Gerf Hussein 136
German language 19
Gevhah (wife of Ganem) 105, 107, 110
Giza 35, 77
Glanville, Professor 23, 24
Glastonbury 22

Index

Glenmore sheep station 18
Golden Horn 58
Gough, Mary 67, 105
Gough, Michael 67, 105
Gozan *see* Tell Halaf
Grace Virginia 72
Grand Hotel Bassul (Beirut) 87, 90
Gray, Mrs D 104
Great Syrian Desert 90
Great War *see* World War I
Greece 72–3, 117, 118, 121
Grimes, Professor 121
Guido, Margaret *see* Preston, Peggy
Gunther, John 95
Gurney, Robert 62

Habur river 71, 104
Haidar Pasha 54, 55
Haifa 84
Hail 80
Halep *see* Aleppo
Hamidiye regiment 71
Hammada 79
Hanging Rock 14
Harding, Gerald 77, 79
Hardy, Thomas 21
Hare, Superintendent 9
Hargreaves, Dr 41, 46
Harvard 100
Harvard Mission to Ireland 68, 69–70
Hasso Ebling 142
Hastings, Warren 74
Hawara 77
Hebron 78
Heidelberg jaw 25
helawi (halva) 41
Hellenic Mediterranean Lines 131
Hellenistic period 42, 51, 120
Hembury 30
Hencken, Hugh 69, 83
Hencken, Thalassa (Cruso) 83
Henderson, Miss (Clyde School) 14
Heraklion 119
Herodotus 89
hieroglyphs 24
Highmoor 9–10
Hill, Dr (American) 72
Himalaya, SS 5
Hit 89
Hittites 53
Hoare, Sir Samuel 34–5
Hoca, Nasreddin 64
Hogarth, David 89

Honorary Research fellow 142
Hood, Sinclair 103, 110
Hopkins, Elizabeth 5–6
Horemhab 42
Hortu 64
Hotel Baron (Aleppo) 88
Hotel Cecil (Alexandria) 130
Hotel Claridge Palace (Aleppo) 87, 88
'House of the Four Winds, The' 51, 54
Howard, Geoffrey 138, 139
Howeitat Bedu 82
Hrozny (Czech philologist) 120–1
Hussey, Station Officer 93
Hyksos 75–6

Ibn Jubyr 54
Ibn Saud, King 95–6
Ibrahim Pasha 71
Ibtu 125, 127, 129
Icel *see* Mersin
illhealth 41, 44, 49, 70–1, 91, 93–4, 108
Imperial Airways 89
Inge, Charles 74, 79
Institute of Anatolian Studies (Ankara) 101
Institute of Archaeology (London) 21, 23, 37, 97, 104, 109, 111
International Journal for Nautical Archaeology 142
Iran *see* individual sites
Iraq 100, 121
Ireland 3–5, 68, 69–70
Iron Age 30–1, 75–6; *see also* Maiden Castle (Dorset)
Isis 122, 128
Iskanderun 65, 103, 107, 140
Ismail (Egyptian foreman) 124
Isparta 118–19
Istanbul 55, 58, 59, 71, 72, 103, 108
Istanbul Museum 58
Istanbul University 108–9
Italian-Abyssinian war 34, 45
Italy 109
Ithaca 72
IYU sheep station 9
Izmir 118, 119

Jabbul, Plain of 86–8
Jacobs, Colin 143
Jaffa 74
Jarvis, Major 37, 45, 77–8
Jericho 41, 49–51

Index

Jerusalem 35, 36, 37, 41, 49, 74, 76, 80, 82
Jerusalem Museum 78
Journal for Anatolian Studies 109
judo 15, 18
Jundi, Adan 120

Kafr es-Sheikh 123, 129
el-Kantarah (Kantara) 35, 42
Karaoğlan 64
Karim (maitre d'hotel) 139
Karnak 42
Kasr Ibrim 134
Katrina (cook) 86
kaymakam 105–6
Kayseri 59, 118
'Kazanli' (poem) 65
Kazanli site 60, 64–5
Keith-Roach, Edward 80
Kelly, Dan 9
Kelly, James 9
Kelly, Kate 9
Kelly, Ned 9
Kenyon, Kathleen 50, 51
Keayang sheep station 8
Khalasah (Elusa) 43
Khamseen 136
Khargah Oasis 142
Khirokitia 68, 86
Khodansha 142
al-Kholy, Tala'at *see* Tala'at al-Kholy
Kilmorie 13
King, Professor 24
King's Domain 7
King's Road 93
Kirkbride, Diana 104
Kirkman, James 74, 77
Kirk's Bazaar 2
Kizil Irmak 58
Kizzawatna 104
Knaresborough Nursing Home 94
Knightsbridge Barracks 93
Konya 118, 119
Kuftis 51
Kültepe 104, 118
Kurt Dăg 59, 102

Lachish *see* Tell el-Duweir
Lachish Letters 76
Lahun 77
Lake Nasser *see* Nasser, lake
Larsen House (Jerusalem) 74, 80

Larsen, Mr and Mrs 35, 74
Latakia 54
Lawrence, Professor AW 131
Lawrence, TE 54, 82
Lebanon 115
Leningrad 27, 28
Leonard, Bill 120
Letters from Syria (Stark) 88
Levant Company 88
light railways (Decauvilles) 32
Liverpool University 49, 52, 70
Lloyd, Seton 89, 102, 121
Lloyd Tristino steamer 57
Lod (Lydda) 35
London 20–1
London Museum 23, 24, 83
London School of Economics 21
London University: lecturing at 126–7
Londra Palas Oteli (Istanbul) 58
Lorraine, Sir Percy 54
Lotus (Nile steamer) 139
Luxor 121, 133, 136, 139
Lydda (Lod) 35

el-Ma'alla 20
McDougal, John 120, 121
Macedonia 121
Mackay, Donald 78
McNair Scott, Lesley *see* Scott, Lesley McNair
Macrae, Don 13, 14
Macrae, Ethel 14
Macrae, Finlay 13
Macrae, Ian 13
Macrae, Joan 13
Macrae, Stanley (Bill) 13
McVicar, Pat 15
Madrassah Turuntaiyah 117
Maiden Castle (Dorset) 21–3, 24, 30–2, 55–6, 94
Ma'in 134
Mallowan, Lady (1st) *see* Christie, Agatha
Mallowan, Lady (2nd) *see* Parker, Barbara
Mallowan, Max 71, 104, 111–12, 121
Malta fever 70–1
Manifold, Mrs Jane *see* Synnots, Jane (Mrs Thomas Manifold)
Manifold, Thomas 3
Marash 109
Marquesas 100
marriage proposal 84–5

Index

Marseilles 34, 84, 131
Marshall, Dorothy 25, 70
Marston, Sir Charles 49
Martin, Joan 123
Matthews (English consul at Mersin) 63–4
Maude, General 89
Maxwell-Hyslop, Rachel *see* Clay, Rachel
Meath 69
Mein, Adrian 7, 8, 9, 17
Mein, Patricia 7, 8
Mein, Pultney Walford (Uncle Pultney) 7, 9
Mein, Tasmania (Aunt Tassie) 7, 9, 17, 86
Meket Re 128
Melbourne 5, 7, 11–12, 100
Melbourne Institute of Archaeology 120
Melbourne University 17, 26; Science Club 19
Mellaart, James 105, 106, 107
Memphis (Nile steamer) 140
Mendes 127
Mere Lake Village 22
Mersin (Icel) 60, 61, 63, 64, 98
Merun, Sheikh 66
Mesolithic occupation 50
Mesopotamia 88, 102
Mesorea 68
Methods and Aims of Archaeology (Petrie) 36
Metropolitan Museum of New York 83, 131
Milan 55
Millar, Carey 114
Millard, Allan 120
Ministry of Information 95, 96, 98
Missis 66–7
Mitla Pass 77
Montague Mansions 98
Monte Carlo 101
Morphou 91
Moscow 28
Moseley, Sir Oswald 93
Mosul 89
Mother of Hats 122
Motya 142
Movius, Hallam L Junior 69, 70, 83
Muhammad Suliman 138
Munn-Rankin, Margaret 101, 104–6, 107–15, 120, 126, 142

Murad Gaddes 138
murex shells 120
Murray, Dr Margaret 24, 34, 78, 112, 121, 132
museums *see individual museums eg* British Museum
Muwatalis (1296–72 BC) 60
Mycenae 72, 119
Myrtou 103, 104, 107, 108, 109
Myrtou-Pigades 101, 104

Nabil Riad 141
Naci Bey 105
Nafud Desert 80
Nairn Transport 89, 90
Nakht, Tomb of 134
Naples 109, 114
Nasreddin Hoca 64
Nasser, lake 134, 135, 136–7, 141
National Front 93, 94
Navarro, Toti 32
Nazism, rise of 25–6
Nebuchadnezzar 76
Negeb 43
Neilson Expedition 70
Neklawi Bedu 46
Nelson, Francis 57
Neo-Babylonians 76
Neolithic levels 30, 32, 49, 50
Nessana *see* Auj'a el-Hafir (Nessana)
New Cataract Hotel (Aswan) 139
New York 83; *see also* Metropolitan Museum of New York
Newport News 100
Nicholson Museum 100
Nicosia 86, 91
Nile cruises 133–40, 141
Nile Handbook 140
Nile Star (Nile steamer) 140, 141
Nile, The (poem) 135–6
Nimrud 71, 76, 104
Nixon, Bishop 3
Nubia 122, 133–6

Observer 11
Olympia 72
Omm Seti 122, 138
Omm Tegir 122
Oppenheim, Baron von 71–2
Orient Express 54–5, 57, 88
Oriental Institute *see* Chicago Oriental Institute

156

Index

Orientalists' Conference, Istanbul 108–9
O'Riordain, Sean 70
Ormonde, RMS 18, 19–20
Orontes river 107
Osiris 122
Osten, Von der 53
Özgüçs 118

Pacific Ocean 100
Palestine 35, 52, 73, 74; *see also individual sites eg* Tell Duweir
Palmer, Claude 8
Palmer, Claudia 9
Palmer, Marjory (Aunt Marjory) 8, 100
Palmer, Neville 8
Palmer, Valerie (Bobby) 8
Panama Canal 100
Pape, Carl 37, 38, 47
Paris 55, 84, 91, 101, 114
Park Oteli (Adana) 105
Parker, Barbara 55, 83–4, 104
Parker, Delia 24
Parr, Peter 120
Payne, Joan Crowfoot *see* Crowfoot, Joan
Pe 123, 127, 129, 132
Peabody Collection 83
Pelusium 42
Pennsylvania Museum 83
Pennut 134
Pera 58
Persian period 76
Peters, Mary 97
Peters, Tony 114, 120
Petra 82
Petrie, Lady 35, 37, 38, 39–40, 41, 44, 45, 48, 74, 86
Petrie, Sir Flinders 32, 34, 35–6, 38, 42, 43, 45, 48, 51, 74, 75, 78
Philadelphia Hotel (Amman) 82
Philadelphia (USA) *see* Pennsylvania Museum
Philby, St John 95
photography 36, 47, 60, 62, 74, 76, 119
Piggott, Mrs Peggy *see* Preston, Peggy
Piggott, Stuart 25
Piraeus 72–3, 119
Plain and the Rough Places, The (M and M Gough) 105
Plain of Jabbul 86–8
Polish Corridor 29
Port Said 20
Post of the Four Winds 108

Posta 59, 119
postal censorship 92, 94–5
prehistory 23, 24
preservation 69
press censorship 95
Preston, Pamela 25
Preston, Peggy 25, 32
Price, Arthur 99, 100, 101
Princeton 100
Prudential Building 94
Ptolemaic Temples (Seton-Williams) 143
Puente Viasgo caves 26

Qalat el Nedjem 88
Qasr Azraq 79

Rafah 42, 44, 45, 47
railways (Decauvilles) 32
Ramadi 89, 90
Ramesses II 42, 43
Ramesses VI 134
Rameta 6, 7
Raphia *see* Rafah
Ras el-Ain 71
Red River (Kizil Irmak) 58
Red Sea 20
Reisner, George 49
Revere, Paul 84
Rifa'at *see* Tell Rifa'at
Riga 29
Romanians 90
Romano-British temple 31
Romeli Hisar 58
Roosevelt, Mrs 95
Ross, Rosemary 22, 25
Rowe, Alan 49, 50, 51, 52
Royal Archaeological Institute 21, 24
Royal Geographical Society 25
Royal Institution 25
Russell Pasha 46
Russell Trust 120
Russia: trip to 26–9
Rutbah fort 90
Rutherford, Ernest 25
Ryland, G 27, 29

Saar (Germany) 25
Sabahat (Turkish inspector) 102, 110
St David's Cathedral (Hobart) 3
St Exupéry 45
St Kilda (Melbourne) 5, 14
Sakce Gözü (Sakce Geuzi) 52, 101, 102–3, 104, 110

Index

salination 136–7, 141
Salonika 55
sandstorms 43–4, 81
Saqqara 35, 77
Sawarka Bedu 45
Sbeitah (Subeta) 43
Schaeffer, Claude 54, 108–9
Schliemann, Heinrich 119
Schmidt, Dr Aage 49
Schmidt, E 53
Scorpions of Isis 128
Scott, Professor Ernest 17, 43
Scott, Lesley McNair 21, 32, 34, 35, 55
El-Sekhemawy 127
Senate House (London University) 97, 98
Sennacherib of Assyria 76
Seti I 42, 122
Seton, Elizabeth 5
Seton, James 5
Seton, Jane 5
Seton, John 5
Seton, Monsignor 3
Seton, Mother (of New York) 3
Seton-Williams, Ellie (Mrs) 6, 31–2, 33
Seton-Williams, Gordon 2, 2–3, 3, 6, 16
Seton-Williams, MV: ancestors 2–6; Australia visit 100–1; Balsham 126–7, 131, 142–3; childhood 7–18; Chukur Ova 57–68; Clyde School 14–15, 16; Cyprus (1939) 86, 90–1; education 12, 14–17, 23–4, 29–30, 111–13; Egypt 121–3, 129–32; England 19–33, 55–6; Greece (1937) 72–3; Harvard Mission to Ireland (1937) 69–70; higher degree 111–13; Honary Research Fellow at UC 142; illhealth 41, 49, 70–1, 91, 93–4, 108; introduction to Egyptology 13; Jericho 41, 49–51; Maiden Castle see Maiden Castle; marriage proposal 84–5; Omm Tegir 122; round the world 99–101; Russia 26–9; Sheikh Zuweyed 34–48; Six Day War 129–31; Swan Hellenic cruises 133–41; Syria (1939) 86–90; teaching 112–13, 141–2; Tell el-Duweir 74–9; Tell Halaf material in Berlin 71–2; Tell Keisan 51–2; Trans-Jordan 79–82; University College 23–4, 29–30, 142; US 83–4; World War II 91–8
Seventy Years of Archaeology (Petrie) 35

Shammar Bedu 90
Shehab, Emir Maurice 87
Sheikh Zuweyed 34–48, 75
Shenbarrow 32
Shinnie, Peter 55
Sik 82
Simon Artz (shop in Port Said) 20
Sinai 32, 77; Sheikh Zuweyed 34–48, 75
Sirkeli 60–1, 104, 105
Sis 66, 67
Siwa 142
Six Day War 129–31
Smith, Professor Harry 141–2
Smith, Professor Sydney 83, 104, 111
smuggling 46
Snake Castle see Yilan Kalisi (Snake Castle)
Society of Antiquaries 22, 24, 25
Sofia 55, 72
Solomon 82
Sons of Sinbad (Villiers) 20
Souaf, Soubi 115, 116, 124, 125
Souk Su Hüyük site 60, 61–2, 65
Spensley, Howard 25
Spooner, Dr 101–2
Stamp, Professor Dudley 136
Stark, Freya 88, 95
Starkey, John 32, 74, 77, 78
Staughton, Arthur (Uncle Arthur) 8, 11
Staughton, Dora 21, 101
Staughton, Eliza Mary (Ellie) see Seton-Williams, Ellie (Mrs)
Staughton, Elizabeth 8
Staughton, Elsie 8
Staughton, Lory 8
Staughton, Mary 5
Staughton, Mrs Samuel see Hopkins, Elizabeth
Staughton, Samuel Thomas 5–6
Staughton, Simon 5, 21, 103–4
Staughton, Steven 5
Staughton, Tasmania see Mein, Tasmania
Staughton, Tom 25
Stewart, Jim 111
Stocks, Peter 142
stratification 43, 53, 55, 69, 120
Stronach, David 114
Stupples, Stella 143
Sturdy, Bernard 32, 55
Subeta see Sbeitah (Subeta)

158

Index

Sudan (paddle steamer) 13, 136
Sudan Railways steamers 133–4
Suez 20
Suez Canal 20, 45–6, 100
Suleymeneye 58
Sun Goddess of Arinna 58
Sussex Archaeological Society 32
Swans Hellenic cruises 122, 125, 133–41
Swan Hellenic 109
Sydney 100
Sydney University 101, 111
Synagh, David 4
Synagh, Nicholas 4–5
Synagh *see also* Synnots
Synnots, Captain Walter 3
Synnots, Colonel David 4
Synnots, Jane (Mrs Thomas Manifold) 3
Synnots, Marianne (Maria) 3, 5
Synnots, Nugent 3
Synnots, Sir Walter 5
Synnots, Timothy 5
Synnots, William 3
Synnots *see also* Synagh
Syria 86–90, 111; *see also* Tell Rifa'at

Tala'at al-Kholy 138, 140
Tanta: riots 34–5
Tarsus 59, 60, 66
Tasmania 3
Taurus Express 54, 59, 60, 66, 67, 89
Taurus mountains 59, 62, 118
Taylor, Joan du Plat 55, 64, 67–8, 72–3, 86–91, 95, 96, 97–8, 101, 104, 105, 107, 109, 113, 114, 142
Taylour, Lord William 104
Teasdale, Drs 41
Tell Abu Sefah 42
Tell Abu Selymeh *see* Sheikh Zuweyed
Tell el-Ajjul 38, 39, 74, 78
Tell el-Duweir 32, 37, 56, 73, 74–9
Tell el-Fara'in 114, 123–4, 125, 127–9, 131–2, 132, 134
Tell Halaf 71–2
Tell el-Jenayn (Tell of the Garden) 42
Tell Keisan 48, 51–2
Tell Rifa'at 111, 113, 114–17, 120–1, 122, 124–5
Tell Sheikh Zuweyed 34–48, 75
Temple of the Tooth (Colombo) 19

Terang 100
Terrabin Bedu 45, 48, 75
Thebes 128
Thessaly 121
Thomas, Bertram 95
Thompson, Commander 96
Thompson, Dorothy 72
Thompson, Homer 72
Thompson, John 66
Tigris Palace Hotel (Bagdad) 89–90
Tiryns 72, 119
'To Charles Doughty' (poem) 81
Toorak 7, 13, 17
Toprakkale 67
Toros Expressi *see* Taurus Express
Toros Oteli (Mersin) 61, 62
Trabazon *see* Trebizond
Trans-Jordan 79–82
travellers censorship 95
Travels in Arabia Deserta (Doughty) 64, 81
'Travellers in the Middle East' course 112
Treaty of Berlin 68
Trebizond 63–4
Trésers du Babylone, Les 142
Trieste 55
Trois Frères cave 26
Tucker, Miss (headmistress) 15
Tudor period 4
Tufnell, Olga 74, 77, 98
Turkey 52–5, 57–68, 70–1, 101–3, 109–11; *see also* individual sites
Turkish Maritime Lines 103, 109
Tutankhamun Exhibition 142

Ugarit 54, 108
Ummayad caliphs 79
undulant fever 70–1
'Unfound Site, An' (Seton-Williams) 143–4
United States 83–4, 100
universities *see individual places eg* Melbourne University
University College, London 21, 23, 29–30; Honorary Research Fellow 142; Petrie Collection 34
Uplands, The 10, 16, 17, 100
Ur 102

V-1s, (Bombs) 96–7
Varna 72

159

Index

Veniti 31
Vermont (near Melbourne) 10, 100
Verulamium 142
Vespasian 31
Vienna 72
Villiers, Alan 20
volcanic eruptions 61

Wace, Alan 72
Wadi Araba 82
Wadi Dhobai 79
Wadi Ghuzzeh 45, 75
Wadi Halfa 135
Wadi Nakhabir 78
Wadjet (goddess) 131
Waechter, John 35, 37, 38, 41, 48, 57, 58, 59, 60, 62, 64, 65, 66, 78, 79–82, 86–90, 101, 105
Walford Mein, *see* Mein, Pultney Walford
War in Pictures 11
Waratah, SS 8
wasm 45, 80
Wassukanni 71
water 45
'Way to the Land of the Philistines' 42
'Ways of Horus, The' 42
Webb, Jessie 17
Wedlake, Bill 22, 30, 55
Weinberg, Saul 72
Welch, Reg 123
welfare *see* illhealth
Wellcome, Sir Henry 74, 98
Wellcome Expedition 74–9
Wellcome Trustees 101
'Well of Menma're, The' 42
Wenner-Gren Foundation 114
Wexford 4
Wheeler, Kim (3rd wife) 55
Wheeler, Mavis (2nd wife) 88–9

Wheeler, RE Mortimer (Rik) 18, 21, 22, 23, 24, 30, 32, 36, 54, 55–6, 88–9, 94, 122
Wheeler, Tessa (1st wife) 21, 22, 23, 30, 34, 54
White, Mr (of City Literary Institute) 112
Whitehawk Camp 32
Wilhelm II, Kaiser 53, 87
Williams, Montague 2–3
Williams, Seton Gordon Nixon *see* Seton-Williams, Gordon
Williams, Walter Synnot 3
Williamson, RP Ross 32
Williamstown 2, 19
Winchester Court 94–5, 97
Wind, Sand and Stars (St Exupéry) 45
Wingate, Rachel 98
Winkler, Hugo 53
Witch of Endor 15
Wolkoff, Anna de *see* de Wolkoff, Anna
Woolley, Sir Leonard 53–4, 101, 102
World War I 10–11
World War II 91–8
Wright, Brian 136
WVS 95

Xenophon 59

Yalgan, Ali Bey *see* Ali Bey Yalgan
Yamkhad 88
Yarmuk Tepe *see* Souk Su Hüyük site
Yates Classical Library 23
Yemen 75
Yeni Palas Oteli (Adana) 60
Yenice 60
Yilan Kalisi (Snake Castle) 65–7
YWCA 83

Zionism 52
Zuweyed *see* Sheikh Zuweyed

For Product Safety Concerns and Information please contact our EU representative GPSR@taylorandfrancis.com
Taylor & Francis Verlag GmbH, Kaufingerstraße 24, 80331 München, Germany

www.ingramcontent.com/pod-product-compliance
Lightning Source LLC
Chambersburg PA
CBHW051646230426
43669CB00013B/2460